WHAT TO LISTEN FOR IN

WHAT TO LISTEN FOR IN

r O
c k

*A
Stylistic
Analysis*

KEN STEPHENSON

YALE UNIVERSITY PRESS / NEW HAVEN AND LONDON

Designed by Mary Valencia
Set in Janson and Big House types by The Composing Room of Michigan, Inc.
Printed in the United States of America by Sheridan Books.

Library of Congress Cataloging-in-Publication Data

Stephenson, Ken, 1959–
    What to listen for in rock : a stylistic analysis / Ken Stephenson.
        p.   cm.
Includes bibliographical references (p.), discography (p.), and index.
    ISBN 0-300-09239-3 (alk. paper)
    1. Rock music—Analysis, appreciation.   I. Title.
    MT146 .S74   2002
    781.66'117—dc21

                                                        2001006564

A catalogue record for this book is available from the British Library.

The paper in this book meets the guidelines for permanence and durability
of the Committee on Production Guidelines for Book Longevity of the Council
on Library Resources.

10 9 8 7 6 5 4 3 2 1

Contents

acknowledgments

As I write these acknowledgments, I am amazed at the number of people to whom I am indebted. First, I wish to thank my mentor, Gordon McQuere, who told me in 1984 that I would write this book someday and who has continued to give me professional encouragement and advice over the years.

I gratefully acknowledge the help of Harry Haskell at Yale University Press, who has guided me through the publishing process, and of Karen Gangel, whose careful editing has made every page of the book better.

Many students have given me ideas and help with particular songs over the years, but I must not neglect to mention Scott Newman, who faithfully tracked down information on several songs for me. I also extend my thanks to Julie Haydon, a student of Professor Kevin Holm-Hudson, at Northwestern University, whose Internet conversation with me helped shape the section on "Does Anybody Really Know What Time It Is?"

I could not have written the book without a good used-record store, so I extend my hearty gratitude to Ruth Fillmore of Shadowplay, here in Norman, Oklahoma, for all her help. And although I haven't met him, I must thank Joel Whitburn, whose reference book on Top 40 music was indispensable to me.

The University of Oklahoma has provided a beautiful office, computers, postage, long-distance privileges, a sabbatical, money to help pay copyright clearances, and opportunities to teach this material and refine the ideas in discussions with students. Sincere thanks go to my administrators and to the tax-payers of Oklahoma for supporting the institution.

The most pleasant surprise during the process was the unexpected phone call I received one morning from John Waite. Mr. Waite, thanks for the de-lightful and inspiring conversation. I'm so sorry the lawyers and publishers didn't support you in your willingness to let me quote your beautiful song.

The most difficult task in assembling this book was the acquisition of per-mission to quote copyrighted material. I'm grateful to Professor Joe Steussy at the University of Texas at El Paso for his advice and encouragement at the be-ginning of the road. My thanks go out to all the representatives, managers, and lawyers who spoke with me during the process. Blessings to Sally Warkaske at Hal Leonard for her patience and understanding and to David Olsen at War-ner Brothers for finally making things happen there. If my reader ever con-templates pursuing a project such as this, remember those names. And special thanks to John Baruck, manager for Kevin Cronin, for responding first and positively after I sent out requests for copyright permission. Would that the whole process had gone as smoothly! REO Speedwagon is now my second fa-vorite group.

Deepest thanks also to Lisa Thomas, legal representative for Chicago, and to Malinda Ramirez of HK Management for all their help in making my ado-lescent dream come true. To Mr. Jimmy Pankow and Mr. Robert Lamm, thank you for creating the music that led me home, for the conversations, and for be-ing gracious hosts to my wife and me. Many of my teachers influenced me sig-nificantly, but especially Mrs. Buenger the Singer, who got me interested in music theory in the sixth grade. In high school my friends John Thomas, Greg Moore, and Steve Erickson and I shared many hours at the church or in the basement listening to records and learning how to play what we heard. Thanks to my mother and father for the lessons and instruments and for putting up with that dreadful basement band. I am grateful to several friends and col-leagues: Carl Rath, for helping me track down details for many songs, and Michael Lee and Roger Rideout, for their valued advice and encouragement. Thanks to my children, Brad and Anna, for their patience and for watching Gilligan with me when I couldn't think. And to my wife, Nancy, for all the en-couragement and help and for listening to all my stories.

Finally, to quote John of Salisbury (N.B. Roger), "I earnestly beseech my reader . . . to remember me in his prayers to the Most High, and to petition God to grant me . . . knowledge of the truth, love of what is good, and devotion to Himself, as well as that we may accomplish, in thought, word, and action, what is pleasing to His divine will."

introduction

In the 1980s and 1990s, after two and a half decades of resistance, American colleges and universities at last moved toward accepting rock as a legitimate subject of study. As late as 1976, Robert Pielke, author of *You Say You Want a Revolution*, requested permission from George Mason University to teach a multidisciplinary course in rock and was turned down. In just a few years, however, Pielke began seeing attitudes and policies change. Of rock's eventual recognition, he explains: "The significance of rock music as a cultural phenomenon has long been recognized even by its most ardent detractors. Thus the scholarly community has been unable to avoid its impact."[1]

Yet the significance of rock, not just as a generic cultural phenomenon but as music, has not been universally recognized; Pielke's proposed class was to have emphasized only its history, social impact, and meaning. Academic music circles have been much slower to acknowledge rock. As Andrew Chester wrote: "The acceptance of a cultural definition of the object of criticism [rock] leads inevitably to a cultural as opposed to an aesthetic criticism. Musical form and musical practice are studied as an aspect of social relations, and significance is determined by social, not musical, criteria."[2]

This exclusion of rock from music curriculums is changing, albeit slowly. The *NASM Handbook* states that all students in professional baccalaureate degrees in music "should have experience with . . . contemporary 'pop' music."[3]

Many college music educators, however, assume that its inclusion is merely to provide accessible examples of traditional structures, a result of a second assumption: that rock stubbornly adheres in the most unsophisticated way to the simplest principles of the common practice. Christopher Gordon's *Form and Content in Commercial Music*, for instance, teaches standard common-practice chord progressions and claims that they are valid for popular music, his list of which explicitly includes rock.[4] Stefan Kostka expresses the belief clearly: "Perhaps the healthiest and most vital continuation of traditional harmony was in the 'popular' music of the twentieth century, which includes everything from Broadway musicals to folk music to jazz to rock music."[5]

The assumption that rock is simply a crude extension of common-practice music is false. Rock, in fact, exhibits melodic, rhythmic, and harmonic characteristics that are not found in any other musical style. This is not to say that rock was created in a musical vacuum; no musical style ever is. The stylistic norms of rock depend on ideas from the common practice, but differ from common-practice norms in crucial ways. An understanding of the typical patterns peculiar to rock is essential to the analysis of individual rock pieces, and vital to the explanation of this music's power as a vehicle of expression for the culture that claims it as its own.

Few have attempted to establish the stylistic norms of rock. As mentioned before, most of the academics interested in rock have taken a sociological approach, whereas music scholars have, in general, not been forced until recently to accept its legitimacy. Even within the circle of scholars who deal with the musical aspects of the genre, however, a further factor has limited work on defining normal structures: the rise of the notion that traditional theoretical models, because of inherent biases, cannot accommodate or are inappropriate for dealing with the music. For instance, Robert Walser, in his *Running with the Devil*, states the deconstructionist view that traditional, formalist analysis of any music, including heavy metal, the subject of the book, is worthless unless it is used to reveal the political message inherent in the act of composition. In his words, structural analysis is "useful only if it is grounded culturally and historically and if it acknowledges its interests forthrightly."[6] Charles Keil, speaking of unnotated music in general, gives a nodding acknowledgment to the value of musical analysis but says that it "will not go far in accounting for expression."[7]

Approaches like Walser's arbitrarily deny the possibility of value in purely musical analysis, while those like Keil's simply bypass aspects of form, harmony, and the like in their concentration on other, less formal aspects. As Richard Middleton, author of *Studying Popular Music*, puts it: "There is in fact a common tendency for the 'critique of musicology' to go too far. . . . By associating musicology *as such* with classical music and completely separating that sphere from the sphere of popular music, [the critic of traditional musicology] throws away any chance for musical analysis."[8] Chester's lament that the prevailingly "patronizing" attitude that "precludes the possibility of an aesthetic based on the specificity of rock as a musical genre" leaves us with little in the way of musical analysis of rock is as true today as it was in 1970, when he expressed it.[9]

Perhaps the clearest summary of the arguments against a musicological approach to the analysis of rock is offered by Roy Shuker, in his *Understanding Popular Music*. Shuker points out that few musicological, structural analyses of rock have been published; he lists only three works.[10] Although he acknowledges the need for more research in this area, he feels that it should be subject to severe limitations because of certain flaws in such an approach:

1) The musicological approach excludes the sociological approach.
2) No one but musicologists would understand these analyses.
3) Structural analyses of rock pieces do not align with the way listeners and composers of rock talk about the music.

Each of these criticisms deserves a response.

As to the first, Shuker says, "The obvious difficulty with the musicological approach is that the preoccupation with the [musical] text in and of itself omits any consideration of music as a social phenomenon."[11] Using that kind of argument, we could simply turn the tables and say that the obvious difficulty with the sociological approach is that its preoccupation with the social context omits any consideration of music as music. I agree, however, with Shuker's observations that "what is needed . . . is an approach which embraces both traditional musicology and [the] affective aspects of music."[12] Yet in an age of specialization, the only way of preparing for this multifaceted approach is to have musicologists and sociologists continue their respective work while learning from one another in a spirit of mutual deference.

As to the second, the "pretentious" language of the musicologist's analyses, Shuker contends that the overspecialized terminology "erects barriers to the musically nonliterate" and that "there is much to be said for utilizing musicology, provided that such analysis is kept easily accessible to those who have never encountered music theory."[13] Such a limitation is unacceptable if knowledge and discourse are to advance. If medical research, for instance, were limited to works easily accessible to those unfamiliar with chemistry and biology, we would see fewer advances in that field. And if sociological analyses of rock were limited to works easily accessible to those who have never studied sociology, academic treatments of rock would be scarce indeed. The reader must bear some of the burden for the resolution of the disparity between the sophistication of the written argument and the ability of the reader to understand it. If the author must always descend to the reader's level, the reader's level, and the state of public knowledge, will never rise.

As to the third, the disparity between the concerns theorists have about this music and the way players and listeners think about it, Shuker says, "Traditional musicology neglects the social context, emphasises the transcription of the music (the score), and elevates harmonic and rhythmic structure to pride of place as an evaluative criterion. Rock, on the other hand, emphasises interpretation through performance, and is received primarily in terms of the body and emotions rather than as pure text."[14] The reasons for raising this critique, which is not unique to Shuker, are puzzling. In other fields, this disparity seems to be taken for granted as normal. In fact, this disparity might be said to define what most research is all about. Five-year-olds cannot express a set of grammatical rules consistently, but this does not stop Noam Chomsky from seeking the rules that children as well as adults seem to follow. That the producers and receivers of language do not normally think in terms of grammar does not invalidate the research. Most people do not know why eggs are nutritious, and chickens know even less about the matter, but the ignorance of producer and consumer does not invalidate research in biochemistry. I would be no less likely to float if I knew the mathematics of relativity, but the disparity between the way I experience gravity and the way Einstein understood it does not invalidate his research. Research means attempting to discover new knowledge, and if the object of some particular research project is an aspect of human activity, then by definition a disparity will arise between the way the average human agent understands her activity and the way the researcher understands it. Whether the subjects of the research adopt the researcher's mode of understanding is irrelevant because although that mode may not benefit some people (e.g., some pitchers think about physiology whereas others think only about focus or the batter), improvement of skills is usually not the purpose of research. Shuker is not trying to make pop musicians better; neither am I. Therefore, whether they agree with my way of thinking does not matter.

But in fact harmonies and scales are not as irrelevant to rock composers as Shuker assumes. Listening to many of the songs by such composers as Buddy Holly, Brian Wilson, George Harrison, Carly Simon, Billy Joel, and Sting makes it clear that they are indeed interested in harmony. Concerning harmonic invention and exploration in some of the Beatles' compositions, Paul McCartney explains: "We were just trying to improve all the time, and we'd listen to something that somebody else had done, and we'd just try and beat it a bit. We'd try and beat what we were doing. And, I mean, by the time we got to something like 'From Me to You,' it was nice 'cause the—I remember being very pleased with the chord in the middle, which was different from what— [demonstrates at piano]. Going to that minor chord there was like, 'Ooh, you know this is something we haven't done before.'"[15] I can also vouch for many guitarists, bassists, keyboardists, and vocalists I have worked with in saying that they pay careful attention to the structural aspects of the songs they compose, arrange, and perform. As for casual listeners, most may not think of such things as important; but anyone who can hum the tune of a favorite song or detect a wrong note in a dance band's rendition of a rock standard (even without being able to explain that ability) merely lacks terminology and trained discernment.

Some writers concentrate on other matters vital to this body of music, whose importance I do not wish to deny. But I do wish to argue that inherent political messages, for instance, do not constitute everything in this music. In fact, it seems reasonable to suppose that without a clear understanding of the normal structural features of rock, the determination of meaning—conveyed, intended, or assumed—in a given piece of rock will be prone to error. In Nattiez's terminology, if we wish "to show how poietic and esthetic interpretants are linked with the work's material presence, we must first have a *description* of that material's constituents."[16] Middleton agrees; concerning the antiformalist approach of Antoine Hennion, he says, "By *sticking* at the level of ethnographic description, Hennion cannot get any deeper analytically than this; he cannot . . . link the terms and criteria of musicians and audience with an independent account of what actually happens in the music, so he is not able to *explain* how the music works and has its effects."[17] In other words, we have many monographs about rock that purport to tell what it means without attempting to define what it is.

Despite all the hindrances, a small body of work analyzing rock has been published. Notable contributions include Wilfred Mellers' *Twilight of the Gods: The Music of the Beatles*; Philip Tagg's hermeneutic study of Abba's "Fernando" and the theme from *Kojak*; pertinent passages in Middleton's *Studying Popular Music*; Joe Steussy's end-of-chapter analyses in his *Rock and Roll: Its History and Stylistic Development*; and a collection of essays by several authors entitled *Understanding Rock*.[18] Most of this literature concentrates on analyses of individual works; Middleton and Steussy contribute toward establishing stylistic norms, but in each case the treatment is sporadic and forms only part of a work with a broader or different overall topic.

What is needed then is a foundation of ideas about stylistic norms, something akin to what the typical undergraduate textbook does for earlier tonal music. Perhaps others can build onto or add detail work to certain corners of the foundation. Perhaps a Schenkeresque figure (perhaps indeed a Schenkerian) can tear out portions of the foundation and suggest a new shape for the edifice. But a starting point is needed, and I offer this work.

The book is primarily intended as a mid-level undergraduate text. But because many of the issues have not been dealt with before in either academic or nonacademic publications, I have attempted to address two audiences: academics who wish to know more about the structure of rock, and rock musicians who wish to know more of the theory and history of their music (and of other historic styles that influenced rock music). The book will require that professors and students be familiar with or have access to some of the standard pieces of the repertoire. For them, I provide in the back of the book a short list of albums (or CDs, for those who insist on that term) that will get the reader through most of the examples in the book and provide many of the classic pieces of the genre. Nonacademics should be able to read music and understand how to build scales and chords by note name (not just finger position). For them, I provide a glossary of basic theoretical terms and concepts. If further information is needed, I recommend picking up one of the standard beginning texts, such as Kostka and Payne's *Tonal Harmony* or Turek's *Elements of Music*.[19]

Of each group I ask indulgence when they reach passages primarily intended for another audience. I suggest, however, that members of each group, whether using the book as a classroom text or studying it privately, read through and attempt some of the exercises in each chapter. The distinctive material in this book may at times seem simple, but rock has a way of deceiving its listeners into thinking it is what it isn't. Even the simplest material found here may not be grasped unless the reader engages it through fingers on an instrument, through pencil on paper, and—most important of all—by listening.

Before proceeding with the theory of rock, we must deal with the thorny problem of the its definition. In this book, the term *rock* refers to the mainstreams of popular music since 1954, whether they be classified as rock 'n' roll, rhythm and blues (R&B), soul, country rock, folk rock, hard rock, and so on. Other writers, such as Steussy, have similar views of the term. In fact, a list of the styles, movements, and performers treated in Steussy's book forms an excellent denotative definition of the body of music treated here. I argue that a number of systems, structures, and relationships in the realms of pitch and rhythm both tie the members of this body together and distinguish it from other bodies of music. If my argument is successful, *rock* could then be defined as the body of music that does what is described here.

I must not overstate the case, however. Not all rock reflects every point I discuss in this book. (Neither does every piece by Brahms include every harmonic combination known to common-practice theory.) But almost every rock piece includes at least some of the features outlined here. When I refer to a structure as "normal," I uses the word in the statistical sense; use of the word in no way indicates a deficiency or lack of quality in alternate structures. Because experience has taught me to anticipate skepticism about what is normal in rock, each chapter contains many titles and examples of rock songs with structures that contradict the norms of the common practice. I will readily admit that these choices were not randomly compiled and that some rock songs do follow the standards of, for instance, common-practice harmonic progression. The author of stylistic analysis runs the danger of being accused of missing all the anomalous trees in the attempt to see the forest; music would be uninteresting if it were otherwise. Of course stylistic analysis simplifies complexities and ignores exceptions; it is the nature of generalizations to do so. But generalizations are nonetheless useful. Without an established understanding of the stylistic norms of rock, we run the risk of two weightier errors: first, of underappreciating the genre because of a mistaken belief in its adherence to centuries-old standards; the second, of being surprised by structures common in the genre and of reading too much into their local significance (under the mistaken assumption that these standard structures are moments of creative transcendence), while missing other, truly significant structures or events.

A note on the source of examples: in the case of practically every piece of rock music, if a composer's score exists (and in many cases no scores ever existed), it is unavailable to the general public. The commercial piano-vocal arrangements available through publishing houses are usually derived from attempted transcriptions of recordings. Such arrangements therefore have no direct connection to any score or instructions given by the composer to the performers. And in fact, because such arrangements are targeted to consumers of a particular level of ability and because of the difficulties of notating the often intricate melodies of the music, published versions often differ substantially from the recorded song. Because of these facts, this book treats the best-known recording of a song as the definitive artifact, despite the ontological problems involved in the position. All examples are my own transcriptions from recordings, though any transcription is an abstraction and necessarily alters rhythms and pitches by forcing them to conform to accepted categories of

notation. I recognize the problem but remain comfortable with using transcriptions. Abstraction and generalization are facts of life; to avoid them entirely would necessitate the end of communication. Therefore I freely accept
the responsibility for any differences between the original recording and my
transcriptions. Unless the difference involves an outright mistake (I won't
deny the possibility!), I do not believe that such differences compromise the
points made in the book. Many argue that the intricacies of a rock song not
amenable to Western notation are precisely the most interesting features. My
response, echoing sentiments expressed above, is simply that the rhythmic patterns, harmonies, scales, and the like that are amenable to Western notation
also interest many people.

Whenever I discuss the theory of rock with a class, someone asks whether
rock composers, who as a rule are musically illiterate, are conscious of the musical patterns I have described. I am always excited by this question; it usually
does not occur to students that the question of whether Bach knew about harmonic functions or Beethoven about form theory might also be an interesting
one. My hunch is that most rock musicians learned and continue their craft au-
rally and are no more aware of the theory behind what they do than the five-
year-old is about Chomskian grammar. Whether they are aware of their ac-
complishment or not, however, does not alter the fact that rock musicians,
while having played an important role in a cultural revolution, have at the same
time established a stylistically distinct musical language.

Recently some students told me that the analysis of music was a purely mental exercise that somehow missed its meaning, which they assured me was an
expression of the soul. One went so far as to say that studying music diminished
the joy she experienced as a listener. Although I tried to explain that the mind
was part of the soul and that mental exercise can bring joy (and though I suggested that if studying music ruined it for them, they should perhaps not spend
so much time and money studying the subject), they pointed out to me that I
could get away with my analytical habit because it was clear to them that I bal-
anced it with an approach that they saw as more valuable. Taking that remark
as a compliment, I wish to close this introduction with a couple of words about
what the music means.

Many authors have attempted to tell us what rock means. I have already indicated that I tend to disagree with these assessments. As an example, Edward
Macan, in his book on English progressive rock, says that various aspects of the
music "mean" various aspects of the hippie culture of the late 1960s and early
1970s—that, for instance, an improvisatory solo over an ostinato, by inducing
a sense of timelessness, means an acid trip.[20] I can only respond by saying that

it doesn't mean that to me. When I first learned this music, my friends and I didn't get high; we just listened over and over and tried to play what we heard. We trained ourselves to hear the harmonies, we tried to coordinate our rhythms, and we learned which scales to use to improvise solos. Something has to mean something else *to* someone. To a person in America, *biscuit* probably signifies a type of breakfast bread. To a person in England the same word probably means a sweet, crispy snack cake. To the authors who say that rock means acid trips and political revolution, I say that rock from the 1960s and 1970s is now played on commercial oldies stations and listened to by (among others) office workers, thereby increasing the productivity of the capitalistic institutions whose downfall it was supposed to have called for. Because meaning can never be absolute or eternal, other interpretive schemes must be possible.

I remember distinctly the moment I fell in love with rock: it was the first time I heard Chicago's "Make Me Smile." It is hard to describe my sense of wonder and excitement—as if I had found my way back to a home I never knew I had. To borrow David Copperfield's words upon first seeing Dora Spenlow, it was "anything that no one ever saw, and everything that everybody ever wanted. I was swallowed up in an abyss of love in an instant." I could say that all of my professional life has ultimately been a search for the explanation of that moment. I now know that the beauty I heard in the VI-III succession in the verse has partly to do with descending-4th root movement and the presence of the root of the second chord in the first, a pattern which seems to me to strike a chord with my English heritage, since, as I explain in chapter 3, I find a similar pattern in English folk melody. And I now know that the antiperiodic structure of the song suggests a timelessness that, striking a chord with my Christian beliefs, offers a glimpse of heaven.

The study of this music has certainly not reduced my joy. On the contrary, my study of this music, besides increasing my passion for it, has heightened my sense of wonder toward other things—toward music theory, the miracle of hearing, history and heritage, and the truths that rock reveals for me. It is my hope that this book will also increase my readers' enjoyment.

Students, I hope you keep reading.

1

phrase rhythm

Because musical pitches function in time, it is difficult to discuss the function of tones or harmonies without an understanding of the temporal framework of a style. So we begin this study of rock by establishing some stylistic norms of its phrase rhythm. This chapter answers the following questions: (1) Typically, how long is the shortest formal unit larger than a measure (i.e., how many measures usually group together) and (2) how do vocal phrases lie within these formal units?

Rock borrows standard structures from earlier song styles, although it often alters and combines them in new ways. The purpose of this book is not only to set out the stylistic standards of rock but to eliminate common misconceptions

1

by distinguishing rock's standards from those of earlier styles. As a result, we first need to look briefly at phrase rhythm as it applies to both repertoires, beginning with the issue of phrase length.

Defining normal lengths in terms of measures can be problematic in either of these bodies of music. Because performers and listeners of both rock and earlier folk music depend so much more on aural tradition than on scores, in many pieces it is impossible to determine objectively how long a measure is or how many beats a measure contains. One listener might count "1-2-1-2" where another would count "1-2-3-4." Or one might count 1-and-2-and" where another counts "1-2-1-2." This problem is not insurmountable, however. In much traditional music, for instance, we could simply stipulate that a measure is the amount of time between the last strong beat of one phrase and the first strong beat of the next. Therefore, in "Betsy From Pike," while a transcriber might use either a moderately paced compound meter or a fast triple meter, the stipulated method would favor the triple meter. (See example 1.1.) In rock, steady backbeats (beats 2 and 4) on the snare drum usually help make the length of a measure clear.

1.1. Determination of the length of a measure in primarily nonnotated music by examination of cadence.

Sometimes, however, we may find it more useful to avoid the term *measure* altogether and simply talk in terms of relative length of time, referring to the ratio of the lengths of the spans of melodic motion and of melodic rest. The term *melodic motion* refers to the period of rhythmic activity within a given phrase; it lasts from the beginning of a phrase to the attack time of its last (metrically accented) note. The term *melodic rest* refers to the period of rhythmic inactivity normally associated with cadences; it lasts from the attack time of the last note of one phrase to the beginning of the next phrase. Therefore, the melodic rest at the end of a phrase normally incorporates a long note as well as a literal rest. According to these definitions, in the case of a four-measure unit with the melodic cadence on the fourth downbeat, such as in "Betsy From Pike" or "Daisy," the span of melodic motion is three times as long as the span of melodic rest. (See example 1.2.) When speaking of ratios in this way, listeners may disagree on what span of time to call a beat or on how many beats make up a measure while still agreeing on the basic temporal recipe of the phrase, which in each of the examples above is three parts melodic motion followed by one part melodic rest.

1.2. Different metrical interpretations of "Daisy." The ratio of melodic motion to melodic rest remains constant: 3:1.

The pattern found in "Betsy From Pike" and "Daisy" is typical of traditional tonal song. Folk songs, nursery songs, nineteenth- and early twentieth-century popular songs, and the like normally exhibit a regular unit length of four measures. (See example 1.3.) The division of these units is normally marked by a cadence—in the literal sense of that word: a falling off of melodic motion or of rhythmic energy, or in simpler terms, a long last note. (See Chapter 3.) This clear delineation of phrases by means of a melodic rest comes as no surprise; this kind of music is primarily vocal, and the tunes simply need to provide the singer with some breathing time at regular intervals. In a four-measure phrase, the cadence, or long note, normally comes on the downbeat of the fourth measure. Placement of the cadential note on the fourth downbeat creates a motion-to-rest ratio of 3:1. Again, quite naturally, the pattern perfectly suits the nature of the music: because the music is primarily vocal music, to preserve continuity the melody needs to be active as long as possible, given the singer's need to breathe.

1.3. Elements of standard phrase rhythm in folk and popular song before the rock era: (a) "Cindy," (b) "Oh, Susanna!" (c) "Tenting To-night," and (d) "Over The Rainbow."

1.3 a.

1.3 b.

1.3 c.

1.3 d.

When music moves in a regular series of four-bar units, many listeners perceive a phenomenon known as *hypermeter*—that is, the a regular pattern of accents in the downbeats of successive measures. Theorists have long debated how downbeat accents are arranged in these typical four-measure groups: do they alternate strong-weak-strong-weak as the accents do in a four-beat measure, or does the importance of the cadence result in a weak-strong-weak-strong pattern—or even a more subtle pattern such as strong-weak-weak-strong? Lerdahl and Jackendoff, who summarize this debate well, point out (correctly, I believe) that writers such as Meyer and Cooper err by confusing metrical accent and harmonic or melodic resolution, and that, as a result, these four-measure units normally correspond to beginning-accented hypermeasures.[1] William Rothstein agrees:

> Because of the difference between phrase structure and hypermeter, phrases—especially the simpler ones—can end very comfortably in relatively weak metrical positions, for example in the last bar of a four-bar hypermeasure. When a phrase ends in this way, there is no contradiction between the weak metrical position and the arrival of an important tonal goal (presumably a cadence). This is because the experience of "accent" —of heightened importance—that is involved in reaching a tonal goal is not the same as the experience of a metrical accent—the impulse felt upon reaching a metrical downbeat. . . . Rhythmic theorists of our time have often found themselves unable to follow hypermeter even in simple instances because they have been paralyzed by their confusion of categories.[2]

When a piece consists mostly of four-bar groups, then, each of those forms a hypermeasure. The downbeats of the four measures relate to one another in the same way the four beats in a regular measure do: strong-weak-strong-weak. As a result, the odd-numbered measures in a four-bar hypermeasure can be called strong measures, and the downbeats of these measures strong downbeats. In the same way, the even-numbered measures are weak measures, and their downbeats weak downbeats.

Rock normally proceeds in four-bar units just as traditional songs do. In most rock songs, the rigid adherence to this standard encourages the perception of hypermeter and contributes to the widely acknowledged perception of a natural, steady—even driving—beat.

Rock and traditional song, therefore, share the prevalence of the four-bar unit. But the similarity ends there. Melodic cadences in rock do not contribute as regularly to the delineation of these units as they do in traditional music. Instead, the perception of these units normally arises as a result of repetitive patterns in the instrumental accompaniment, for instance, the regular recurrence of tonic harmony or of an instrumental hook every four (or two or eight) measures. (See example 1.4.) Because rock depends less on the vocal phrase than on harmony for continuity and formal delineation, the vocal phrase is free to line up within these units in a variety of ways. Generally speaking, where a melodic

1.4. Length of morphological unit as defined by regular repetition of (a) the harmonic pattern in the Bee Gees' "I Started A Joke" and (b) the instrumental hook in Chicago's "25 Or 6 To 4."

1.4 a.

I Started A Joke. Words and Music by Barry Gibb, Maurice Gibb and Robin Gibb. Copyright © 1968 by Gibb Brothers Music. Copyright Renewed. All Rights Administered by Careers-BMG Music Publishing, Inc. International Copyright Secured All Rights Reserved

1.4 b.

"25 Or 6 To 4". Written by Robert Lamm. © 1970 Lamminations Music/ Aurelius Music (ASCAP). All Rights Reserved. Used By Permission.

cadence in traditional music normally occurs on a weak downbeat, namely the downbeat of the fourth measure, a melodic cadence in rock normally occurs on a strong downbeat.

This norm is not as prevalent in rock as the traditional norm is in traditional music; in rock traditional cadence placement often exists side-by-side with the newer pattern (the contrast sometimes contributing to the delineation of form;

see Chapter 6, "Form"). In addition, the rhythmic models involving a cadence on a strong downbeat are numerous enough that no particular one can be called a new standard. But much rock employs hypermetrically strong cadences exclusively—or almost so—and most of the rest of the repertoire makes frequent use of the newer pattern. Even in pieces where the newer pattern is infrequent, it lends, because of its lack of association with any other style, a distinctive quality to the phrase structure.

Because vocal phrases do not normally line up with hypermeasures in a single, traditional way, the term *phrase* cannot be used as it commonly is in theoretical literature to refer indiscriminately to both the melodic line and the morphological unit. We need to distinguish between the word *phrase*, which refers only to a vocal phrase (i.e., a melodic passage that might be notated under a single phrase marking), and the terms *unit* and *hypermeasure*, which refer to the smallest morphological (i.e., formal) division larger than a measure. Although any given beat is part of a morphological unit, not every beat is part of a phrase. Where phrase lengths are measured, pickups and syncopations are treated as rhythmic embellishments; lengths are calculated by counting downbeats.

Now let's define some of these standard phrase rhythms and look at some examples.

2 + 2 MODEL

Within the general category of cadences on hypermetrically strong downbeats, several patterns are found. The most common we will call the 2 + 2 model. In this most frequent pattern, the vocal cadence comes on the third downbeat of the four; two measures of melodic activity are followed by two measures of melodic rest, creating a motion-to-rest ratio of 1:1, as in Chuck Berry's "Roll Over Beethoven." (See example 1.5.)

1.5. Motion-to-rest ratio of 1:1 in first hypermeasure of Chuck Berry's "Roll Over, Beethoven," as indicated in (a) transcription and (b) a metrical chart.

1.5 a.

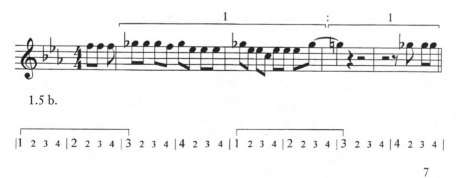

1.5 b.

|1 2 3 4 |2 2 3 4 |3 2 3 4 |4 2 3 4 |1 2 3 4 |2 2 3 4 |3 2 3 4 |4 2 3 4 |

The 2 + 2 model is a salient characteristic of much blues music and, therefore, pervades the early blues-based rock repertoire, which played an important role in the further development of the style. Among other features (see esp. Chapter 5, "Harmonic Succession"), the 2 + 2 model plays a part in many later rock pieces that otherwise bear few resemblances to the blues. Thirty-seven years after "Roll Over Beethoven," for instance, one finds it in Sting's "If I Ever Lose My Faith In You." (See example 1.6.) In fact, the 2 + 2 model forms the basis for the phrase structure of hundreds of rock songs, including Chicago's "25 Or 6 To 4"; the Beach Boys' "Help Me, Rhonda"; Steely Dan's "Rikki, Don't Lose That Number"; Credence Clearwater Revival's "Bad Moon Rising"; the Eagles' "Already Gone"; Toto's "I Won't Hold You Back"; Billy Joel's "Summer, Highland Falls"; Elton John's "Love Lies Bleeding"; Christine McVie's "Got A Hold On Me"; Supertramp's "Give A Little Bit"; Electric Light Orchestra's "Turn To Stone"; Tom Petty's "Refugee"; Tina Turner's "The Best"; the Beatles' "No Reply" (1964), "She's A Woman" (1964), and "Being For The Benefit Of Mr. Kite"; the Rolling Stones' "Jumping Jack Flash"; and Lindsey Buckingham's "Don't Look Down." Many songs not employing the 2 + 2 model throughout use it as the basic phrase structure of one section. The multitude of songs featuring the 2 + 2 model and its resulting 1:1 motion-to-rest ratio only in the chorus or the refrain includes Aretha Franklin's "Do Right Woman," the Eagles' "Heartache Tonight," and Emerson, Lake & Palmer's "Still . . . You Turn Me On."

1.6. 2 + 2 model in Sting's "If I Ever Lose My Faith In You."

If I Ever Lose My Faith In You. Written and Composed by Sting. © 1992 G.M. SUMNER. Published by MAGNETIC PUBLISHING LTD. and Administered by EMI BLACKWOOD. MUSIC INC. in the USA and Canada. All Rights Reserved International Copyright Secured Used by Permission

As noted above, traditional music such as folk song is primarily vocal, and the 3:1 ratio found in most phrases of that music suits the partially conflicting needs of having the voice carry the continuity of the piece and allowing the singer to breathe. Rock, however, is widely acknowledged as primarily rhythmic; the voice need not carry the burden of establishing continuity as it does in earlier popular styles. Instead, the hypermeter (frequently strengthened, after all, by the melody's agogic accents on the strong downbeats, as indicated above) keeps the piece moving, especially between vocal phrases; nothing but a continuation of the beat by instrumentalists is required in the period of melodic rest between phrases of the 2 + 2 model. However, unwilling to settle for the bare minimum required to preserve continuity, musicians sometimes fill the primary melody's period of rest with background-vocal motives or instrumental hooks, thereby creating a call-and-response pattern, as in the verse to the Beach Boys' "Help Me, Rhonda," the Beatles' "The Night Before," the first verses in Emerson, Lake & Palmer's "Karn Evil 9," and the first line of James Taylor's "Your Smiling Face." (See example 1.7.)

1.7. A period of melodic rest in a vocal line filled by an instrumental line in the Beach Boys' "Help Me, Rhonda."

HELP ME RHONDA, by Brian Wilson and Mike Love. © 1965 (Renewed) Irving Music, Inc. All Rights Reserved. Used by Permission. WARNER BROS. PUBLICATIONS U.S. INC., Miami, FL 33014

EXTENSION-OVERLAP MODEL

In the most usual scenario, the 2 + 2 model, the melodic phrase in rock comes to a cadence sooner than its traditional counterpart, on the third downbeat rather than the fourth. In many other instances, the melodic phrase lasts longer than the traditional norm; it is not uncommon in rock for a melodic phrase beginning near the first downbeat of a four-measure unit to delay coming to a cadence until the fifth downbeat—that is, the first downbeat of a new four-measure (sometimes two-measure) unit. In this way, the closure of one gesture, a melodic phrase, happens at the same time as the beginning of another gesture, a hypermeasure, but with no disruption of the regular four-bar

9

hypermeter. Following William Rothstein's lead, we shall call this combination an overlap.[3]

The extension-overlap model is rarely used as the consistent phrase structure for an entire song, or even an entire section, because of the logistical problems inherent in the use of melodic overlap: if one phrase ends on the first downbeat of a hypermeasure, how can the singer perform the beginning of the following phrase? One solution would be simply to wait another four measures before the beginning of the second phrase; the resulting combination of four measures of melodic motion and four measures of melodic rest creates a 1:1 ratio one morphological level higher than that of the common 2 + 2 model. Through this method, Neil Young's "Harvest Moon" proceeds exclusively by extended, five-measure phrases while maintaining a consistent four-measure hypermeter. A listener counting in double-length measures, however, would say the song simply uses the 2 + 2 model. It is clear, then, that consistent use of the extension-overlap model is hard to distinguish and need not be looked for as a common occurrence.

More often the extension-overlap model is used at one or two key points in a song's form. The verse of the Eagles' "Take It To The Limit," for instance, consists of two 2 + 2 units and one extended phrase whose cadence overlaps with the inception of four bars of melodic rest. Example 1.8 includes several rock songs that demonstrate overlap, that is, vocal phrases that come to rest on (or very near) the first downbeat of a new four-bar hypermeasure. Some instances precede four measures of melodic rest; in others the hypermeasure after the extended phrase contains its own short vocal phrase. Additional examples are found in Michael Jackson's "Billie Jean," Simon and Garfunkel's "Mrs. Robinson," the chorus of Heart's "Magic Man," the chorus of Don Henley's "The Heart Of The Matter," "Up On The Roof" (recorded by the Drifters in 1963 and James Taylor in 1979), Paul McCartney's "Jet," the chorus of Billy Joel's "Rosalinda's Eyes," and the chorus of "Because Of You" by 98°.

In numerous rock songs, an overlap occurs at the end of a refrain or chorus. In some cases (e.g., "Born To Run," shown as example 1.8c), the vocal cadence coincides with the beginning of the return of an introductory hook. The overlap, as noted above, normally forces the delay of the ensuing verse, and a repetition of the introductory material provides a natural way of leading back into the verse. Even when an overlap is involved, however, many songs are able to have one chorus (or verse) immediately follow another by having one of two configurations at the beginning of the section, or through electronic techniques. Both of the compositional configurations are found frequently even when no overlap is involved.

1.8. Vocal phrases with cadences on a fifth downbeat, i.e., the first downbeat of a subsequent hypermeter, in (a) a generic metrical chart, (b) the Beatles' "If I Fell," and (c) Bruce Springsteen's "Born To Run."

1.8 a.

|1 2 3 4 |2 2 3 4 |3 2 3 4 |4 2 3 4 |1 2 3 4 | etc.

1.8 b.

If I Fell. from A HARD DAY'S NIGHT. Words and Music by John Lennon and Paul McCartney. Copyright © 1964 Sony/ATV Songs LLC. Copyright Renewed. All Rights Administered by Sony/ATV Music Publishing, 8 Music Square West, Nashville, TN. 37203. International Copyright Secured All Rights Reserved

1.8 c.

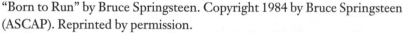

"Born to Run" by Bruce Springsteen. Copyright 1984 by Bruce Springsteen (ASCAP). Reprinted by permission.

In the first of these patterns, the first vocal phrase of the section begins on the second or third beat of the first measure of the four-measure unit. (See example 1.9.) When combined with a last phrase extended to a cadence on the fifth downbeat in the manner described above, the delayed beginning allows the immediate repetition of the section in that the vocal line never has to overlap itself. Instead, the vocal line of the first statement ends on the first beat of the measure, and the second statement begins a beat or two later. The nearly breathless quality of the overlap in each of the instances shown in example 1.10 contributes to the impression in these particular cases of the singer's earnestness.

1.9. A delayed beginning in the first phrase of Chicago's "(I've Been) Searchin' So Long," as shown in (a) transcription and (b) a metrical chart.

1.9 a.

"(I've Been) Searchin' So Long". Written by James Pankow. © 1974 Make Me Smile Music/Big Elk Music (ASCAP). All Rights Reserved. Used By Permission.

1.9 b.

As my life . . .   Somehow . . .

| 1   2   3   4 | 2   2   3   4 | 3   2   3   4 | 4   2   3   4 | 1   2   3   4 | etc.

The second compositional means of allowing immediate repetition of a section ending in overlap finds the section (usually a verse in this case) beginning with an isolated first note (see below). In the second statement of the section, this long first note also serves as the cadential note of the first statement. Example 1.11 shows portions of Stephen Bishop's "It Might Be You" (the theme from *Tootsie*).

A similar example is provided by the Beatles' "Here, There, And Everywhere" (1966), by Lennon and McCartney. The first verse begins with the single word "here," the second verse with the word "there." After a bridge, the third verse starts, as expected, with the word "everywhere." But while the pattern established by the title and the beginning of each of the first two verses (in conjunction with the harmonic structure, of course) makes it clear that the word "everywhere" marks the beginning of a verse, grammatically the word belongs to the last line of the bridge: "But to love her is to need her everywhere."*

Because of overdubbing, a studio technique in which two or more recordings by a singer are combined and heard simultaneously, the purely physical, logistical problems of melodic overlap become moot.[4] Taking advantage of the

---

*Here, There And Everywhere. Words and Music by John Lennon and Paul McCartney. Copyright © 1966 Sony/ATV Songs LLC. Copyright Renewed. All Rights Administered by Sony/ATV Music Publishing, 8 Music Square West, Nashville, TN. 37203. International Copyright Secured All Rights Reserved

1.10. The repetition of sections involving a combination of extension-overlap and delayed start in (a) Billy Joel's "A Matter Of Trust," and (b) James Taylor's "B.S.U.R. (S.U.C.S.I.M.I.M.)."

1.10 a.

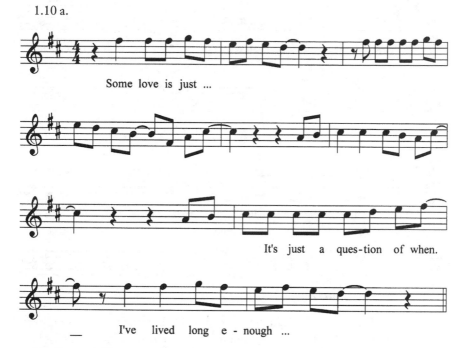

1.10 b.

1.11. Overlap by means of an isolated first note in Stephen Bishop's *Tootsie).* How is this listed on the music? "It Might Be You" (theme from *Tootsie).*

IT MIGHT BE YOU, by Alan Bergman, Marilyn Bergman, and Dave Grusin. © 1982 EMI Golden Torch Music and EMI Gold Horizon Music. All Rights Reserved. Used by Permission. WARNER BROS. PUBLICATIONS U.S. INC., Miami, FL 33014

possibility, many pieces incorporate repeats of a section (usually a chorus in this case) in which the last note or notes of one statement sound simultaneously with the first note or notes of the following statement. Example 1.12 presents two examples.

FIRST-DOWNBEAT MODEL

We have noted examples of vocal phrases ending on the third downbeat of four (2 + 2 model) and of vocal phrases extending to the fifth downbeat, or the first downbeat of a succeeding hypermeasure (extension-overlap model). It is also common to find pieces in which a short vocal phrase ends on the first downbeat of a hypermeasure. Such melodic phrases can be a measure or more long but often consist of no more than a single word of perhaps two syllables,

1.12. Melodic overlap achieved through overdubbing in (a) the Bee Gees'
"Run To Me" and (b) Chicago's "Look Away."

1.12 a.

Run To Me. Words and Music by Barry Gibb, Maurice Gibb and Robin Gibb.

1.12 b.

1.13. The short first phrases in (a) the Everly Brothers' "Lucille," (b) Foreigner's "Luanne," (c) the Beatles' "Girl," and (d) John Lennon's "Woman."

1.13 a.

Lu - cille,———

Lucille. Words and Music by B.B. King. Copyright © 1968 by Careers-BMG Music Publishing, Inc. and Universal—Duchess Music. Corporation. Copyright Renewed. International Copyright Secured All Rights Reserved

1.13 b.

Lu - anne,———

"LUANNE" (GRAMM/JONES). © 1981 Somerset Songs Publishing, Inc.

1.13 c.

Girl,———————

Girl. Words and Music by John Lennon and Paul McCartney. Copyright © 1965 Sony/ATV Songs LLC. Copyright Renewed. All Rights Administered by Sony/ATV Music Publishing, 8 Music Square West, Nashville, TN. 37203. International Copyright Secured All Rights Reserved

1.13 d.

Wo-man,

Woman. Words and Music by John Lennon. © 1980 LENONO.MUSIC. All Rights Controlled and Administered by EMI BLACKWOOD MUSIC INC. All Rights Reserved International Copyright Secured Used by Permission

or even only one. Example 1.13, which provides the opening statements of group of thematically related songs, demonstrates just how short these phrases can be. Although many songs begin with a statement of the title line using a first-downbeat phrase, the technique is by no means limited to opening lines. Many songs use the model exclusively, or almost so, among them Chuck Berry's "No Particular Place To Go," and Three Dog Night's "Never Been To Spain." But perhaps most often, the first-downbeat model serves as the basis of only one section of a song, as it does in the choruses to Blondie's "Call Me" (the theme from *American Gigolo*), the Cars' "Shake It Up," the Beach Boys' "I Get Around," and Bob Dylan's "Like A Rolling Stone" (1965).

ELISION MODEL

Although vocal phrases in rock do not exhibit a common length as consistently as do phrases of traditional songs, many are similar in that they incorporate a cadence on a hypermetrically strong downbeat. But, as noted above, the standard of cadences on strong downbeats accounts for a mere majority—not an overwhelming majority—of cases; traditional cadence placement, on the fourth downbeat, appears side-by-side with the newer model in many songs. But even in the case of the cadence on a weak downbeat, rock normally maintains its distinctiveness from traditional song styles. We'll now examine two of the idiomatic ways rock uses the fourth-downbeat cadence: the elision model and the 1 + 1 model.

The pattern of strong-downbeat cadences is so much a norm that even in many cases involving a traditional cadence placement—that is, on a fourth downbeat—an elision occurs: what is considered a weak downbeat in relation to the previous material proves upon further listening to have become a strong downbeat. As in an overlap, this elision involves a melodic phrase coming to a close at the same time as the beginning of a new four-bar hypermeasure. But in the case of an elision, the fourth measure of the first unit is the same as the first measure of the second; the end result is as if a measure has been left out, that is, elided. (The term *elision* seems preferable to Rothstein's lengthier "metrical reinterpretation.")[5] The elision model is easiest to hear when the downbeat in question coincides with the beginning of a new melodic idea, as in Elton John's "Goodbye Yellow Brick Road." (See example 1.14.) Most often, however, the point of elision simply marks the beginning of either two or four measures of melodic rest, as in the Doobie Brothers' "China Grove." (See example 1.15.)

1.14. Elision involving two melodic ideas in Elton John's "Goodbye Yellow Brick Road" as shown in (a) transcription and (b) a metrical chart.

1.14 a.

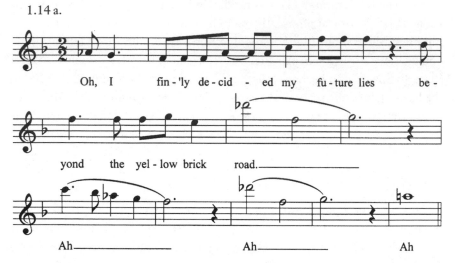

Oh, I   fin - 'ly de - cid - ed my   fu - ture lies   be -

yond   the yel - low brick   road._____

Ah_____   Ah_____   Ah

GOODBYE YELLOW BRICK ROAD, by Elton John and Bernie Taupin.
© 1973 Dick James Music Ltd. Universal/Dick James Music Ltd, 77 Fulham
Palace Rd., London W6. All Rights for U.S. and Canada controlled and
administered by Universal—Songs of Polygram. International, Inc. All Rights
Reserved. International Copyright Secured. Used by Permission. WARNER
BROS. PUBLICATIONS U.S. INC., Miami, FL 33014. Used by permission
of Music Sales Ltd.

1.14 b.

```
                        road.       Ah . . .
Oh, I . . .              ┌───┐      ┌──────┐
┌──────────────────────┐
|1   2 |2   2 |3   2 |4  2 |
              |1   2 |2   2 |3   2 |4   2 |  etc.
```

1.15. Elision involving an extra measure of melodic rest in the Doobie Brothers' "China Grove," measures 9–16 of verse.

```
┌────────┐  ┌────────┐                    ┌──────────────┐
|1  2  3  4 |2  2  3  4 |3  2  3  4 |4  2  3  4 |
              |1  2  3  4 |2  2  3  4 |1  2  3  4 |2  2  3  4 |3  2  etc.
```

1 + 1 MODEL

Even when a melodic cadence arrives on the downbeat of the fourth measure of a unit and no elision occurs, a phrase structure different from traditional models is often present, a structure termed here the "1 + 1 model." In traditional song, a musical phrase often corresponds to two textual phrases:

I've been working on the railroad
All the live long day.

Mary had a little lamb.
Its fleece was white as snow.

Oh, give me a home where the buffalo roam,
Where the deer and the antelope play.

Way down upon the Swanee River
Far, far away.

Rock also commonly pairs textual phrases but often separates the pair by melodic rest equal in duration to that following the second textual phrase: the first textual phrase comes to a close on the second downbeat of a four-bar unit, and the second phrase (usually starting near the beginning of the third measure) comes to rest on the fourth downbeat. With regard to the two textual phrases and the cadence on a fourth downbeat, the structure appears to be traditional. The structure differs from that of a traditional phrase, however, in the lack of continuity caused by the melodic rest in the second measure. In addition, the harmonic pattern in such cases is often two measures long and, as a result, supports the perception of two two-measure units. Little reason other than the expectation of a four-measure standard remains for calling such a four-measure passage a phrase in the traditional sense of the word with a traditionally located cadence in the fourth measure.[6] The 1 + 1 model pervades Bob Dylan's "All Along the Watchtower," the Doors' "Light My Fire," Credence Clearwater Revival's "Up Around The Bend," and the chorus of Tom Petty's "Into The Great Wide Open." (By counting half as many beats in a measure, a listener can interpret such examples, of course, as being based on the 2 + 2 model. Such an interpretation, however, does not alter the judgment that the phrase structure is nontraditional.) Pieces consisting mostly of 1 + 1 models frequently deny the traditional standard further through placement of the final cadence of the chorus or refrain on an odd-numbered downbeat. Such is the case, for instance, in Elton John's "Goodbye Yellow Brick Road" and Eric Clapton's "Tears In Heaven."

V-I MOTION BETWEEN UNITS

Although the topic of harmony belongs primarily to later chapters (see especially Chapter 4, "Chord Type and Harmonic Palette," and Chapter 5, "Harmonic Succession"), we must deal here with one aspect of nontraditional harmonic practice in rock, namely, a common pattern in the way harmonies are used to begin and end the morphological units corresponding to the traditionally termed phrase. We have noted already that the I chord commonly begins each unit. In many songs, the V chord may end most or even all units. (See Chapter 3, "Cadences," for a discussion of this.) This pattern is especially easy to find in rock songs from the 1950s and 1960s, songs usually based on a simple, repeating harmonic pattern. Examples include the 4 Seasons' "Sherry," "Twist And Shout" (recorded in 1962 by the Isley Brothers and in 1964 by the Beatles), and Buddy Holly's "Words Of Love." But many harmonically more complex songs, as well—the Beatles' "Michelle," for instance, and the Eagles' "Hotel California"—feature continuous repetition of harmonic patterns ending with V without ever resolving to I. In pieces such as these, the V chord at the end of a unit normally precedes the I, since the tonic harmony commonly begins units. Dominant-to-tonic motion is, of course, traditional and would seem to require no special notice here. But in the type of piece under consideration here, this V-I motion always happens at the juncture of units rather than at the end of one. The tonal resolution provided by the harmonic formula, therefore, does not line up with the metrical resolution traditionally associated with the end of a phrase. Joel Lester, in his argument against excessive recognition of the notion of hypermeter, points out as one difference between a phrase and measure that the last measure of a phrase functions as an ending while the last beat of a measure acts as an anticipation of the next measure.[7] In the many rock pieces like "Sherry" and "Hotel California," however, this distinction does not exist (which is one reason I have avoided using the term *phrase* for these morphological units). The harmony of the last measure of every unit in these cases always, because of the lack of tonal resolution, invites anticipation of the following morphological unit, acting as the last beat of a measure in this respect and thus suggesting the virtual equation of hypermeasure and formal unit in these pieces.

Composers occasionally make affective (and effective) use of the anticipatory nature of the cadence on V by extending its length, increasing the sense of anticipation even more than usual. Example 1.16 presents two instances. In each case, the idea of waiting for a resolution or answer that may or may not come is a central theme of the lyrics. The first is, of course, Carly Simon's

"Anticipation." In the chorus of this song, the second phrase ("Anticipation is making me late")* comes to a cadence one and a half beats into the fifth measure of the chorus, that is, one and a half beats later than the normal time for a cadence in an overlapped phrase. The singer and most of the instrumentalists are then kept waiting for a measure and a half by a syncopated drum fill. In the next phrase ("Is keeping me waiting"), after a false restart by the band, it is the vocalists who keep the instrumentalists waiting with a long melisma on the syllable "wait." Then two extra beats are added before the tonic harmony arrives with the beginning of the subsequent verse. (The first two beats of measure 5 as shown could be considered the extra beats, in which case measure 6 would begin with the arrival of the dominant harmony.)

The second case shown in example 1.16 is Foreigner's "I Want To Know What Love Is." At the end of this song, the singer, joined gradually by more and more voices, each voice desperately lonely in the midst of the crowd, repeats several times his desire to learn about love. Every plea, each covering two measures, ends on the V chord; every fourth melodic cadence is extended by one extra measure of the dominant harmony, expressing more clearly the sense of yearning for an answer.

Two traditional signals of closure, then—the rhythmic closure associated with melodic cadences and the tonal closure prompted by dominant-to-tonic harmonic motion—are in rock dissociated from traditional gestures of formal closure. That is, they are often relocated in rock from their traditional position at the end of a formal unit to a point of inception, the beginning of a hypermeasure. As a result, many rock songs proceed through a long series of overlapping propelling gestures. During the last measure of a four-measure unit, the standard time for closure in traditional music, harmonic forces, and sometimes melodic forces (e.g., in an extension-overlap model), carry the music into the next measure. This next measure, however, does not represent a point of metrical repose: the hypermetrical downbeat in its turn implies the succession of three more measures. Then, at the end of this new hypermeasure, the cycle begins again. In this way, the normal language of rock makes no provision for final resolution, has no way to end. For this reason, the fade-out, far from being the studio musician's easy solution to not being able to think of an ending, is ac-

*ANTICIPATION, by Carly Simon. © 1971 (Renewed) Quackenbush Music, Ltd. All Rights Controlled and Administered by Universal Polygram International. All Rights Reserved. Used by Permission. WARNER BROS. PUBLICATIONS U.S. INC., Miami, FL 33014

1.16. Durational lengthening of anticipatory V in songs dealing with anticipation and longing: (a) Carly Simon's "Anticipation" (the chorus and beginning of verse) and (b) Foreigner's "I Want To Know What Love Is."

1.16 a.

Anticipation,   Anticipation . . .

```
┌──────────────────┐    ┌──────────────────────────┐
| 1   2   3   4 |2   2   3   4 |3   2   3   4 |4   2   3   4 |
| IV              |IV            |I              |I              |
```

```
┌──────────────┐    ┌──────────────────────┐  ┌──────┐
| 1   2   3   4 |2   2   3   4 |3   2   3   4 |4   2   3   4 |5   2 |
| ii     V       | (drum fill) | ii     V        | (V)           | (V)   |
```

```
┐
| 1   2   3   4 |  etc.
| I             |
```

1.16 b.

```
I          vi  | V            | ii       vi  | V                |

I          vi  | V            | ii       vi  | V          | V          |
```

tually the only way to end most rock while respecting the integrity of the style's phrase structure.

Having noted the common occurrence of V-I motion at the juncture of two units as well as the standards represented by the five models of phrase structure described above, let us now examine a rather complex example, appreciating the truly idiosyncratic without being distracted by structures that, though they may look unusual with regard to traditional practice, are actually standard in the rock style. The verse of Billy Joel's "She's Always A Woman" (example 1.17) is represented by a chart of the harmonic scheme, with phrasing marked in brackets above. The piece was charted in a quick triple time in order to avoid the problems involved in talking about half measures.

As mentioned above, formal units are normally defined in rock by harmonic patterns; in this piece, the harmonic pattern of the opening measures conforms to a four-measure standard. As a result, the first phrase seems to start with pickups to the fourth measure of a unit. The tonic harmony in the ninth measure of the song (the second measure of the vocal phrase) marks the beginning

1.17. Harmonies and phrasing of Billy Joel's "She's Always A Woman."

Eb: I | I^{sus} | I | V | I | IV$^6_4$ | I |: V |

I |^{10} V | I | I | I | IV | IV^7 | IV^{add6} | IV^7 |

V | I |^{20} V | V/vi | V/vi | vi | vi^2 | IV^7 | V |

𝄋

I | V^{11} | I   :|^{30} I^2 | vi   Bb: ii | ii^2 | V$^6_5$ | V^7 |

I | I^2 | vi   Eb: I^7 | IV |^{40} IV^2 | ii^7 | V | IV^7 |

I | V^{11} | I | I$^6_4$ | eb: i | i^2 | IV$^6_5$ |^{50} IV^7 |

VII | VII$^2_{(maj7)}$ | v^7 | III^7 | VI | VI^7 | V$^6_5$/V | V^7/V |

V |^{60} V^{add6} | V^7 | V | Eb: I | V | I | I |

I | IV | IV^7 |^{70} IV^{add6} | IV^7 | V | I | V | V^7/vi |

2nd x to ⊕

V^7/vi | vi | vi^2 | IV^7 |^{80} V | I | IV | I^6 | V |

I | V | V/vi | V/vi | vi |^{90} vi^2 | IV^7 | V |

I | V^{11} | I | V^6 | D.S. 𝄋 al CODA

⊕ CODA

vi | vi^2 | IV^7 |^{100} vi$^6_4$ | ii | V | I | V^{11} | I |

V | I | V | V^7/vi |^{110} V^7/vi | vi | vi^2 | IV^7 | V |

I | I^{sus} | I   ‖

of the next unit. This first vocal phrase (consisting of the two textual phrases "She can kill with a smile / She can wound with her eyes")* comes to a cadence

*"She's Always A Woman," written by Billy Joel. © Copyright 1977 Impulsive Music. All rights reserved. Used by Permission.

on the downbeat of the third measure of the unit; the V–I harmonic motion occurring simultaneously confirms the sense of resolution on the strong downbeat. Everything about the first phrase, then, seems normal according to rock standards, except perhaps the long anacrusis.

This is an important exception, however, because the anacrusis spans enough time to make the vocal phrase four measures long, one measure longer than the typical phrase having a cadence on the third downbeat; this feature causes some ambiguity in subsequent phrases. The expectation of regular continuation of the four-measure unit assumes that measure 13 marks the beginning of the next formal unit. This measure also bears the beginning of a new vocal phrase, a phrase coming to a cadence on the fourth downbeat of the unit and followed by two measures of melodic rest. The structure could be seen simply as an instance of the elision model. But the equivalence of the rhythmic structure of the first two vocal phrases—three measures of motion followed by two measures of melodic rest—raises questions. If the first downbeat of the previous unit coincides with the second downbeat of the vocal phrase, should not the same be true of the second? Could we not consider the third formal unit to be five measures long, the fourth unit then beginning in measure 14 rather than measure 13? The delay of harmonic motion until the second measure of the vocal phrase strengthens the case. On the other hand, the oddity of such a long anacrusis weakens the case.

The next five measures (mm. 18–22), present a similar dilemma. If measures 13–17 are viewed as an instance of the elision model, 18–22 will likely be also. But if measure 13 is viewed as a formal pickup to measure 14, measure 18 (the first full measure of the third vocal phrase) will likely be heard as a pickup also, the strong downbeat arriving in measure 19 (the second measure of the vocal phrase) with the tonic harmony.

After two measures of V/vi (mm. 21 and 22), the arrival of the vi chord indicates the beginning of the next formal unit in measure 23. The simultaneous inception of a new vocal phrase, an instance of the extension-overlap model common at the end of sections, confirms that interpretation. The start of a unit in m. 23 leaves twenty-two measures preceding, and twenty-two measures cannot be divided evenly into four. If they are to be divided into units, it seems two five-measure units must be recognized somewhere. The question of where need not be settled definitively. The passage can be interpreted validly in two ways (at least); the features normally associated with strong measures just do not line up neatly enough to suggest strongly a single interpretation. Consequently, an individual's parsing of the passage may change with the conditions of each hearing; the listener might even voluntarily change the parsing. In fact, the noncoordination of clues might even suggest a reading that denies division at definite points and accepts a more gradual, fluid transition from one unit to the next. The structural ambiguity (or even vagueness) is inherent in the composition and can be accepted as a virtue: first, because of its creative departure from the rigid norm; second, because of the delight of the multiple readings it invites; and third, because of its perfect correspondence to the woman described in the lyrics:

> She can kill with a smile
> She can wound with her eyes
>
> . . . .
>
> Oh—and she never gives out
> And she never gives in
> She just changes her mind
> She will promise you more
> Than the Garden of Eden
> Then she'll carelessly cut you
> And laugh while you're bleedin'
> But she'll bring out the best
> And the worst you can be
>
> . . . .
>
> And the most she will do
> Is throw shadows at you
> But she's always a woman to me.

In the bridge of the song (mm. 31–62), the phrase rhythm becomes less ambiguous as the harmonies become more interesting (of note: the move from a minor key to its parallel major through tritone root movement in mm. 56–57, appropriately accompanying the words "She just changes her mind"). The bridge does, however, exemplify the rock standard by its exclusive use of four-measure units and by means of phrases of the extension-overlap and first-downbeat models, vocal cadences on a first downbeat. Also of note later in the song is the overlapped, seven-measure phrase found in the coda; its origins can easily be seen easily in the standard five-measure, extension-overlap phrase starting in measure 23.

PHRASE STRUCTURE AND POSTMODERNISM

The history of Western civilization is often divided into three periods: antiquity, the Middle Ages, and the modern era. It is in this broadly conceived modern era that, as J. B. Bury and others have pointed out, the idea of progress

25

came about.[8] In his work on Chaucer, G. K. Chesterton notes that in the medieval age "life was conceived as a Dance," or motion around a central object, whereas "after that time [i.e., in the modern era] life was conceived as a Race," or as progress toward an object.[9] Now, writers such as Jean-François Lyotard, Charles Jencks, and Umberto Eco in a sense suggest expanding the classical scheme in order to recognize a new era, the postmodern. One unifying feature in their approaches to the meaning of *postmodernism* is the acknowledgment of the end of progress as the result of the loss, for various reasons, of historically accepted goals. Lyotard, in his essay "Defining the Postmodern," points to a loss of faith; for instance, after Auschwitz, the goal of the emancipation of humankind seems to have been a mirage. On a related subject, he says, "The development of techno-sciences has become a means of increasing disease, not of fighting it. We can no longer call this development by the old name of progress."[10] Anthony Giddens explains that the term *postmodernity* refers, in part, to the idea that "'history' is devoid of teleology and consequently no version of 'progress' can plausibly be defended."[11] Suzi Gablik argues, in her *Has Modernism Failed?*, that the goal of modern art, namely, constant innovation, has become impossible. As she says,

> Neither science nor art in our era has been content with what has been believed before, associating traditional beliefs with backwardness and a lack of momentum. . . . Beliefs had to be continually changed, replaced, discarded—always in favor of newer and better ones, which would only be rejected in turn. . . . The reflex of negation, in the effort to perpetuate itself as a mode of thought, has ended up destroying not only tradition, but also the art of the previous avant-garde. At this point, the possibilities for stylistic innovation seem, paradoxically, to have reached a limit. . . . All this has led, in the last few years, to a disaffection with the terms and conditions of modernism—a repudiation of the ideology of progress and originality.[12]

What I have been calling traditional phrase structure, which by the way is only about four hundred years old, mirrors the typical modern belief in progress: the last event in a chain of events—the final measure of a phrase, for instance—should conclude a pattern, satisfy a need, solve a problem. In rock, however, what sound to the traditional ear like endings (melodic rest and V-I harmonic motion) often occur at points of beginning; a chain of events leads not to resolution but simply to the inception of another chain of events. The musical situation, in other words, shares postmodernism's rejection of progress toward a goal. The correspondence may not be accidental; many rock lyrics reveal a common philosopher's postmodernism, reflecting a lack of faith in the idea of progress or exhibiting a belief in eternity or in a never-ending cycle of life. These lyrics often incorporate the image of the wheel through the use of such words as *wheel*, *turn*, and *roll*. Here are some examples:

From Journey's "Wheel In The Sky":

> Don't think I'm ever gonna make it home again
> . . . .
> Wheel in the sky keeps on turning
> I don't know where I'll be tomorrow.*

From Rod Stewart's "Forever Young":

> In my heart you will remain forever young.†

From Carly Simon's "Coming Around Again":

> I know nothing stays the same
> But if you're willing to play the game
> It will be coming around again.‡

From Otis Redding's "(Sittin' On The) Dock Of The Bay":

> Sittin' on the dock of the bay
> Watching the tide roll away,
> Sittin' on the dock of the bay
> Wastin' time.§

And in the Byrds' "Turn, Turn, Turn," the use of King Solomon's

"To everything there is a season
and a time for every purpose under heaven."

The lyrics of Fleetwood Mac's "Over My Head" provide a fascinating case:

Your mood is like a circus wheel
It's changing all the time
Sometimes I can't help but feel
That I'm wasting all my time.*

This song has both a fade-in and a fade-out. Similarly, the singer's situation is in a continuous cycle. Like the song itself, it has no discernible beginning, no discernible end, no history, no goal.

In subsequent chapters, I present a number of stylistic norms concerning tonality, harmony, and melody in rock. But all seem to build on the foundation of phrase structure. For instance, harmonic successions, which are normally quite different from common-practice norms, must be understood as leading to resolution at a nontraditional moment, if they are to be seen as leading *to* anything at all. It is perhaps better to view them as continually leading away from the hypermetrically accented tonic harmony that normally begins each four-measure unit. It should come as no surprise that certain rhythmic features are foundational to the language of rock. But, as noted in the introduction, we must not assume, as Robert Walser and others have, that scales, keys, harmonies, and cadences do not matter in this music. Distinct patterns, in most cases different from common-practice patterns, do indeed exist in all these areas. We therefore turn next to the important subject of pitch.

2

key and mode

In 1978 I joined a dance band that I played with for about four years. I had never rehearsed with the members or even heard them before playing my first job with them. They had no written music, so all evening, every time the leader called out a new song, I turned to the bass player for a little information. He'd tell me, "This is a disco tune in C," or "We do this one in E♭." Then the drummer would count off, and we'd begin. But I was amazed (and not a little embarrassed) at how often I started on the wrong chord. Neither my ear nor the bass player's was deficient, however. We just had different methods of identifying keys in pop music.

Keys, like any other interpretive frameworks, do not necessarily work the

29

same way in any two given minds. So defining a method for determining keys in rock is a delicate problem. Two other pitfalls impede the path to a solution. The first is the scarcity of material on the subject of key determination in any music. Although virtually all educated musicians will agree on the key of most passages of common-practice music, music theorists have written little about how keys are established. As a result, musicians have no standard, agreed-upon understanding of the problem. Second, because the harmonic practice of rock does not align with the common practice, the key of a piece in rock will not mean the same as it does in other styles. In rock, as in common-practice music, to be sure, determination of a key will (1) identify a hierarchy in which one note and, in most cases, an associated harmony are considered more important than others and (2) imply a set of structures (pitch sources, cadences, harmonies, harmonic successions, etc.) that might be expected to be found in that key. But in rock the tonic harmony may or may not be the major or minor triad of the common-practice era and probably will not appear at all the structural moments expected by common-practice standards; similarly, the scales, harmonies, and cadences accompanying the tonic may or may not be those of the common practice (most likely not), and they probably will not function the way they do in traditional tonal music. So with little or no explicit agreement or methodology, especially with regard to the stylistic peculiarities of rock, I imagine that readers will sometimes disagree with some of the judgments of key made in this chapter.

Despite the problems, the issue of keys cannot be avoided; they must be named in order to discuss melodic and harmonic function in later chapters. Disagreement on particular cases, however, should not change the main point: for instance, where the harmonic succession of a given passage is said to be contrary to the common practice, it is highly unlikely that the succession will be recognized as one traditionally associated with any key whatsoever.

We begin the task of establishing a method of key determination by examining some of the literature on the subject. Most of the published material comes from computer scientists and psychologists with a secondary interest in music. As an example of the former, H. C. Longuet-Higgins and M. J. Steedman, of the Department of Machine Intelligence and Perception at the University of Edinburgh, report their efforts to program a computer to determine the key of the subject of each of the fugues of Bach's *Well-Tempered Clavier*. They attempt to find the major or minor scale that best fits the notes of the melody in question. They proceed from the assumption that our perception of key crystallizes progressively: "As a fugue subject proceeds the listener's ideas about its meter and key become more and more definite." Thus, notes occurring early in a melody do little to establish a key. According to their system, the first note only narrows the field of twenty-four possible keys down to four-teen.[1] Their system must examine on average about eleven notes of a fugue subject in order to identify its key, and it apparently does not recognize modulation that occurs in the *Well-Tempered Clavier* subjects.

Carol L. Krumhansl, of the Department of Psychology at Cornell University, has conducted numerous experiments in musical perception, including one in which subjects were asked to determine the strength of relationship between an established tonic and each of the twelve pitches of the chromatic scale. The system of resultant scores for each pitch, which Krumhansl calls the "tonal hierarchy," forms the basis of her key-determination method, which again is tested on the forty-eight fugue subjects from the *Well-Tempered Clavier,* among other melodies. Each pitch in a given passage is weighted according to its duration; the resulting list of scores for each pitch is compared with the tonal hierarchy for each of the twenty-four keys, and the key of the passage is determined to be the one that provides the highest correlation. This method requires an average of 5.11 notes.[2] Krumhansl admits certain errors in one version of the algorithm and a serious flaw in another version.[3] Like Longuet-Higgins and Steedman, she does not acknowledge the presence of modulation when it occurs in the fugues.

In addition to making mistakes in determining keys, these methods are all flawed in that they do not model correctly the process they are meant to explain. Human beings do not, before surmising the key of a musical passage, wait for the completion of a pitch source or wait for enough notes on which to base a comparison between durations and tonal strengths of pitches. A listener picks up clues from the very first sound she hears, interpreting it in relationship to her vast stores of tonal memories. David Butler, in a critique of Carol Krumhansl's work, says, "According to the theory that statistical distributions of tones exert some control over our perception of tonality, it must be assumed that a listener could identify the key of a piece of music with full certainty only after having heard and summed the durational weightings of all the tones in the composition—that is, after the performance was over."[4] Yet, as Butler points out later, "Everyday musical experience tells us that tonally encultur-ated listeners can recognize the tonal center in an unfamiliar tonal composition almost instantly, and without visible effort." In fact, he offers the notion that the very first note can at least suggest a key: "*Any tone will suffice as a perceptual anchor—a tonal center—until a better candidate defeats it.*"[5]

Although no satisfactory system has been developed of explaining how a key is perceived, the picture seems to be something like this: listeners perceive patterns that their musical memories teach them to associate with a particular key. The first notes heard, even the very first note, suggest as a tonality the key in which they are the most structural members; subsequent notes either confirm the original impression or supersede it with another by perhaps presenting tonally suggestive pitch collections (the one cue examined by Longuet-Higgins and Steedman), favoring the most structural pitches of a given key (the one cue examined by Krumhansl), employing special harmonies or cadential formulas normally associated with only one key, and the like. When all these factors point toward the same key, the sense of tonality is sure; when they don't or when such clues are mostly absent, the sense of key is vague or ambiguous.

The writers discussed above examine tonal pieces from the eighteenth and nineteenth centuries, but rock is generically no different: opening pitches and chords, harmonic combinations, melodic pitch sources, cadential formulas, and other features all suggest keys. The specific patterns employed in rock, however, are not always the same as the traditional patterns. Vestiges of traditional tonality do survive in this music. But just as Picasso takes two eyes, two ears, a nose, a mouth, and a chin and finds a new order for them, rock, when it employs traditional pointers to key, usually rearranges them into new structures. In the case of Picasso's paintings, most of us will always see the faces as distorted representations of what nature provides as a standard, but listeners accustomed to rock can learn to accept the new combinations simply as normal features of a new form of tonality.

That a key can be suggested by so meager an offering as one chord was recognized by Arnold Schoenberg in his acknowledgment that the atonal composer must eschew traditional structures because of their associations with traditional tonal styles.[6] In the case of rock, although many traditional uses of common-practice elements are normally abandoned, the retention of many of the elements (i.e., traditional scales, triads, and seventh chords) suggests in most cases a key, confirming Schoenberg's contention. This chapter (1) shows how key is suggested in a few simple cases by the presence of traditional features, (2) determines which traditional features most often operate in this body of music to provide clues to the listener (and which don't), (3) identifies some nontraditional features of keys in rock that may provide additional clues to key identity, and (4) outlines some common patterns of modulation.

INDICATORS OF KEY: BEGINNINGS VS. ENDINGS

In some harmonically conservative pieces, authentic cadences can be reliable indicators of key. Bob Seger and the Silver Bullet Band's "Old Time Rock And Roll" offers the perfect example: the main theme of the lyric is a celebra-

2.1. Conservative harmonic succession used for verse and chorus in Bob Seger
& the Silver Bullet Band's "Old Time Rock And Roll."

E | | A | | B | | E | :|

tion of musical conservatism. In this song the chords B and E come at the end of every verse and every chorus. (See example 2.1.) The two chords share a root relationship of a 5th and can be interpreted as V and I in the key of E. Other information corroborates the identity of E as tonic: for instance, the melody of each section ends on the pitch E. In this case, then, traditional interpretation of the last two chords as an authentic cadence yields accurate identification of the key.

Although in conservative cases, such as "Old Time Rock And Roll," a V-I cadence can act as a reliable indicator of key, looking for these cadences is not normally the best way of determining key. First, as indicated in Chapter 1, much rock does not have V-I cadences. Consider "Hey Joe," by the Jimi Hendrix Experience: the harmonic content of the song consists almost entirely of repetitions of a five-chord pattern, C-G-D-A-E. (See example 2.2.) This harmonic scheme does not contain any two successive chords that may be interpreted as constituting an authentic cadence. In cases such as this, therefore, examination of cadences cannot contribute to key determination, at least not when identification of a traditional authentic cadence is the goal of the examination.

2.2. The repeating harmonic scheme with no authentic cadence in Jimi Hendrix's "Hey Joe."

C G | D A | E | E   :|

But does rock employ a different cadence as a standard? Might we, having discarded our anachronistic expectations of finding authentic cadences, still look at cadential moments for clues to the identity of the key? The standard blues progression used in much early rock (and rather frequently in later pieces as well) ends with a plagal cadence. The IV-I cadence, in fact, turns up with some frequency in rock; it is found, for example, in "Hey Joe." Consequently its presence can suggest the identity of a key. Caution must be exercised, however: with no other input into the problem, what is to prevent the conclusion that A is in some unfamiliar way the key of "Hey Joe" and that the constantly recurring cadence is a half cadence?

These problems suggest that looking at cadences should not be the primary way of determining a key and should be used at best as a way of confirming an interpretation based on other information. The source of the problems is that a cadence is a logically inappropriate place to begin looking for clues to the identification of key; doing so—even where the appropriate cadences are present—places the analytical cart before the perceptual horse. A passage in a given key is not so because of its cadence; just the reverse, the cadence has structure and meaning because the passage preceding it is in a given key. Paul Hindemith's (and the typical college sophomore's) idea that, if all else fails, the root of the final harmony of a piece is the tonic, is just not true;[7] a piece by Schoenberg does not become tonal if a V-I cadence is added at the end, and a piece by Mozart does not become atonal or change keys if the performance is interrupted before the arrival of the final cadence. A key is the result of an interpretation of musical structures, an interpretation in which, in Carl Dahlhaus' words, a tone or chord "receives its 'colouring' or 'character' . . . primarily through its association with [the tonic]."[8] Definitions such as this imply that the tonic of any given passage is necessarily established early in the passage. If anything, the opposite of Hindemith's maxim is true: the first root heard is likely to be interpreted as a tonic. In David Butler's words, "The skilled musical listener actively engages with music by improvising inductively, making choices—usually unconsciously—of most-plausible tonal center, based on whatever pitch information is at hand."[9] If the pitch information at hand is only a single major or minor triad, the listener can recognize the root of that triad as the most plausible tonic and will entertain that interpretation unless other information contradicts it. All subsequent material is then perceived in light of this supposition: bodies of phrases are perceived as either confirming the tonic or moving away from it, and cadences are perceived as providing a certain degree of rest given the context of the key that has been at least suggested by the preceding passage. If analysis of key is to mirror the perception of tonal music, the process must then begin by looking at beginnings. And in fact, this approach proves fruitful in rock: in most pieces, one particular chord will be used to start most phrases, and other features of the piece normally confirm the identity of this chord as tonic.

A METHOD OF KEY DETERMINATION

In rock, if one chord can be said to be more stable than others, it is usually the first; in many pieces the same chord is used as the first chord of each hypermetrical unit in the first section, if not in the entire song. Such a harmony will be referred to as an "initiating harmony" or a "persistently initiating harmony."[10] For instance, in Steve Winwood's "Back In The High Life Again," every phrase of both verse and chorus begins with a D major triad, making it the persistently initiating harmony. In most cases, other features of a piece will confirm that a persistently initiating harmony is the tonic harmony, the I chord. (An exception, occurring just often enough to confirm the rule, involves the use of ii as an initiating harmony, as in the Guess Who's "These Eyes" and the Buckinghams' "Kind Of A Drag.")

The listener accustomed to this practice learns to interpret *the first chord of the piece* as the tonic harmony unless or until further evidence suggests another interpretation or a change of pitch center. As a result, the listener can have a fairly secure sense of a key from the first chord in a piece, just as David Butler suggests.

Most tonal music begins with tonic harmony. But three significant points make rock distinct. First, this initial harmony often begins every phrase, as in Mr. President's "Coco Jamboo," the Temptations' "My Girl," and Steve Miller's "Rock'n Me." The second difference involves evidence that may be thought to contradict the assumption that the first harmony is tonic. As seen above, lack of cadential resolution on the harmony that opens a piece does not necessarily mean that the chord is not the tonic harmony. And, as will be explained below, neither does the absence of a leading tone. The third difference is that the tonic harmony in rock may be a major seventh, minor seventh, or dominant seventh chord as well as a major or minor triad.

The features confirming the identification of the root of the first harmony as a tonic are often melodic features traditionally associated with the identity of a tonic pitch. For instance, if the melody emphasizes two notes a fifth or fourth apart, these features will indicate key in a traditional way. That is, given two structural pitches a P5 apart, the lower note will normally serve as tonic (or the top note of a structural P4).

In Bill Haley and the Comets' "Shake, Rattle, & Roll," for example, the first two phrases emphasize F by making it the first and highest pitch and by repeating it; within the same early phrases, C is emphasized by skipping to and from it, by making it the last accented pitch, and by repeating it. (See example 2.3; N.B.: rock transcriptions generally employ key signatures traditionally associated with a key even when they do not accurately indicate the actual pitches.) The two notes being a P4 apart, the top note, F, is the suggested tonic. This information aligns perfectly with the use of an F-major triad as the first chord of the verse; F clearly serves as tonic in this song.

2.3. The P4 between structural pitches indicating tonic in Bill Haley & the Comets' "Shake, Rattle, And Roll."

Shake, Rattle And Roll. Words and Music by Charles Calhoun. Copyright © 1954 by Unichappell Music Inc. Copyright Renewed. International Copyright Secured All Rights Reserved

In addition to serving structurally in many phrases, the tonic often fulfills its traditional role as the final melodic note in many sections. This is often true even when the tonic *harmony* does not coincide with the melodic cadence, as at the end of the verse in the Lovin' Spoonful's "Do You Believe In Magic." (See example 2.4.)

2.4. A melodic resolution on tonic despite the lack of harmonic resolution in the Lovin' Spoonful's "Do You Believe In Magic." (The pickups to m. 6 begin the second verse.)

Do You Believe In Magic. Words and Music by John Sebastian. Copyright © 1965 by Alley Music Corp. and Trio Music Company, Inc. Copyright Renewed. International Copyright Secured All Rights Reserved. Used by Permission

So far, the method of determining key in a piece of rock is as follows:

(1) Identify the root and quality of the first chord and assume that the chord is the tonic harmony.
(2) Confirm or question this assumption by noting one or more of the following features:
    (a) The first harmony initiates phrases persistently.
    (b) Structural pitches are P4 or P5 apart in the melody.
    (c) The last melodic pitch in major sections is the same as the first.

SCALE AS MELODIC PITCH CONTENT

The relationship of the tonic and the pitch source of the melody tends to fall into one of a few categories. Because of the rather limited possibilities, the identification of this pitch source can aid in the identification of key. It cannot be used as a primary method, of course, for all the reasons outlined earlier in the chapter. But the structure of the pitch source can be used to confirm—or cast doubt on—the key indicated by the first chord and the structural pitches of the melody.

Three basic sets, as outlined below, commonly serve as pitch sources for melodies; in each case, the relationship between the set and the tonic usually defines one of three scales. (Scale can be defined as a set of pitch classes interpreted in the light of the identification of one of its notes as a tonic. Thus, the C major and D Dorian scales involve the same set of pitch classes but indicate a different hierarchy within that set.) This simple scheme is complicated slightly by the possibility of blue alterations of the third scale degree in pieces with major tonic triads: in many rock styles, it is common in melodies to tune the third scale degree so low that it forms a m3 with the tonic.[11]

The simplest of the common melodic pitch sources is the pentatonic scale. Given a [02479] pentachord as the pitch source of a melody, either [0] or [9] will usually be identified as the tonic.[12] In other words, given that the notes C, D, E, G, and A form the pitch source of a melody, either C or A or likely acts as tonic. The first possibility results in a scale that can be expressed as an ascending order by [02479]; the second results in the scale [0357T]. (See example 2.5.) The Alan Parson Project's "I Wouldn't Want To Be Like You" establishes C as tonic, with the C pedal presented by the introduction. The priority of C is confirmed by the C minor seventh chord that the introduction eventually settles on and by the resolution of the melody on C at the end of the refrain. How do the pitches used in the melody relate to this established tonality? The pen-

2.5. The prime form of the standard pentatonic set and its two most likely arrangements as scales.

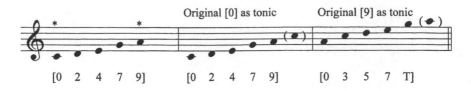

tatonic set E♭, F, G, B♭, and C perfectly represents the pitch source of the vocal melody (prime form [02479], where E♭ = [0]). Thus, in a piece with a minor tonic harmony, the tonic is pitch [9] of the pentatonic set forming the melodic pitch source. Starting this pitch collection on the tonic, C, yields the scale C, E♭, F, G, B♭, or [0357T]. (Remember that when the abstract prime form is re-ordered to start on tonic, [0] represents that tonic.)

In the Beach Boys' "Barbara Ann," F♯ major is clearly established as the tonic harmony: it is both the initiating and concluding chord of each verse. All the pitches of the melody come from the pentatonic set F♯, G♯, A♯, C♯, D♯. Thus, in a piece with a major tonic harmony, the tonic pitch is [0] with respect to the prime form of the pentatonic set serving as the pitch source to the melody.

Hootie and the Blowfish's "Hold My Hand" provides a good example of how the standard relationship is affected by the blue alteration of the third scale degree. The song uses F♯, G♯, B, C♯, and D in its melody and establishes B major as the tonic triad. The D in the melody can therefore be seen as an alter-ation of the third degree expressed in the triad. When this transformation is recognized, the basic pitch source proves to be a standard pentatonic set (B, C♯, D♯, F♯, G♯), and the tonic is PC [0] in relation to the set's prime form.

Other songs with major tonic harmonies that use a pentatonic scale as a pitch source include Credence Clearwater Revival's "Midnight Special," Steve Miller's "Take The Money And Run," Huey Lewis and the News' "Stuck With You," Rod Stewart's "Maggie May," the Lovin' Spoonful's "Do You Believe In Magic," and Melissa Etheridge's "Come To My Window." Other songs with major tonic harmonies whose melodies employ a pentatonic pitch source with blues transformation include Buddy Holly and the Crickets' "That'll Be The Day," Jim Croce's "Bad, Bad Leroy Brown," and Elvis Presley's "Hound Dog." Other songs with *minor* tonic harmonies that employ a pentatonic scale as melodic pitch source include Eric Clapton's "Cocaine," the Temptations' "I Can't Get Next To You," and Electric Light Orchestra's "Evil Woman."

In many cases, the diatonic set [013568T], or a six-note subset of the dia-

2.6. The prime form of the standard diatonic set and its three most likely arrangements as scales.

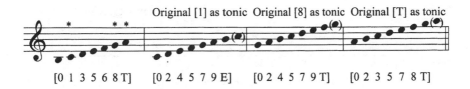

tonic set, serves as the pitch source for the melody. When a melody uses the diatonic set, the tonic is usually either [1], [8], or [T], resulting in a major, Mixolydian, or natural-minor scale, respectively. In other words, if a melody contains the notes B, C, D, E, F, G, and A, the tonic is almost certainly C, G, or A. (See example 2.6.) Because only one of the three scales is associated with common-practice music (the contention of first-year textbooks that the natural-minor scale has something to do with common-practice music cannot be supported by examination of the music itself), we could for consistency's sake use the modal names for all three of these scales. Thus, rock melodies are usually based on either an Ionian, an Aeolian, or a Mixolydian scale.[13]

In REO Speedwagon's "Take It On The Run," for instance, the identification of the key is a straightforward matter: the verse's harmonic succession G-C-D-G is clearly to be analyzed as I-IV-V-I in G, while the melody's emphasis on G and D as well as its resolution on G clearly confirms the identification of G as tonic. The vocal melody of the song as a whole forms a perfect expression of the G Ionian scale: every note of the scale is present, and only notes of that scale are present. The Moody Blues' "Nights In White Satin" uses exactly the same pitches in its melody, yet here E is promoted as tonic by the appearance of E-minor chords in the strong measures of the introduction and in the first two strong measures of each verse; this interpretation is confirmed by the prolongation of B at the beginning of the vocal melody and by the resolution on E at the end of both the verse and refrain. The vocal melody perfectly expresses the E Aeolian scale. Other songs with diatonic sets as pitch sources include the Shirelles' "Will You Love Me Tomorrow" (Ionian), Gordon Lightfoot's "Carefree Highway" (Ionian), the Gin Blossoms' "Follow You Down" (Ionian), Blondie's "Call Me" (Aeolian), Chicago's "25 Or 6 To 4" (Aeolian), Supertramp's "The Logical Song" (shifting between Ionian and Aeolian), the Beatles' "Norwegian Wood" (Mixolydian), and the Allman Brothers Band's "Ramblin' Man" (Mixolydian with blues flavoring).

The most common six-note subset of the diatonic set used as a melodic

2.7. The prime form of the most common hexatonic pitch source and its two most likely arrangements as scales.

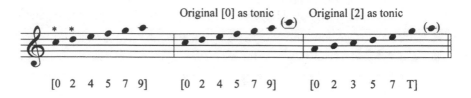

pitch source is [024579]. In a context with a major triad as a tonic structure, this pitch source tends to be arranged so that [0] is the tonic; with a minor tonic triad, [2] is almost always the tonic. In other words, if the pitch content of a given melody is G, A, B, C, D, and E, the tonic will likely be either G or A, suggesting in the former case either an Ionian or Mixolydian scale and an Aeolian scale in the latter.[14] (See example 2.7.) These very notes in fact serve as the pitch source for the melody of Bruce Hornsby and the Range's "On The Western Skyline." The use of a G major triad as the initial harmony of both verse and chorus of the song establishes G as the tonic pitch. Thus, in this song having a major triad as the tonic harmony, the tonic pitch, G, is pitch [0] of the hexatonic pitch source [024579]. Led Zeppelin's "Stairway To Heaven" uses the very same six pitch classes in its melody. But here the use of an A minor triad as the initial harmony of the first and last of the song's several recurring harmonic patterns promotes A as tonic. As a result, the tonic pitch, A, is pitch [2] of the [024579] hexachord. Other examples in which the [024579] hexachord combines with a major tonic harmony include "Loco-Motion" (recorded by Little Eva in 1962 and Grand Funk in 1973), Fleetwood Mac's "Second Hand News," the Beatles' "Eight Days A Week," Eric Clapton's "Wonderful Tonight," and Tom Petty's "You Don't Know How It Feels." Examples in which the [024579] hexachord combines with a minor tonic harmony include Jefferson Airplane's "Somebody To Love," Pat Benatar's "Treat Me Right," and Vicki Sue Robinson's "Turn The Beat Around."

Although [0] and [2] usually prove to be tonic in cases where this hexachord serves as pitch source, other relationships between this hexachord and tonic occur occasionally. For instance, in the Greg Kihn Band's "Breakup Song (They Don't Write 'Em)," the tonic, A, is established by the use of an A minor triad as an initiating harmony in the verse. But A is PC [9] in relation to the prime form of the hexachord used as a melodic pitch source: C, D, E, F, G, and A. A is also the tonic in Ben E. King's "Stand By Me"; but here it supports a major triad, and the [024579] hexatonic pitch source of the melody involves the pitches E, F♯, G♯, A, B, and C♯. In this case, the tonic A is PC [5] in relation to the prime form of the hexachord.

Any book proposing to outline standards and generalities will necessarily overlook certain exceptions and complications. Although the diatonic patterns described above are certainly the standard in rock, melodic pitch sources in rock pieces are sometimes more complex. A couple of examples will suffice to show some of the complexities that can arise even in simple cases. First, Elton John's "Sorry Seems To Be The Hardest Word" demonstrates the use of the leading tone in a piece with a minor tonic triad. The G minor tonality of the song is established by an initiating harmony, and most of the melody employs notes of the G Aeolian scale. But a nod to the common practice is made by the use of F♯ as the penultimate note of the final cadence. Thus it could be said that the song actually uses the traditional melodic-minor scale with its variable scale degrees.

The second example also employs two versions of the seventh scale degree, but in this case the tonic triad is major. In the Who's "Squeeze Box," use of G as an initiating harmony establishes that chord as the tonic triad. Most of the melody confirms the identity of this triad as tonic by the use of a G Ionian pitch source. In the bridge, however, both the normal F♯ and F♮ are found. The result can be viewed as the mixture of the standard Ionian and Mixolydian scales.

Again, having once recognized the standards concerning the pitch content of melodies, we may include information concerning the pitch content of a melody as data in determining the key. Given that the vast majority of clear cases use an Ionian, Aeolian, or Mixolydian scale, the analyst may be justified in interpreting slightly differently a passage whose tonic is otherwise vague or which otherwise seems to support one of the other modal scales.[15] For instance, Fleetwood Mac's "Dreams" begins as if it were in a Lydian mode. The pitch source of the melody of this piece (and of the chords) is G, A, B, C, D, and E: the [024579] hexachord. According to the norms described earlier, the tonic should probably be either G or A, possibly C or E. But the harmonies strongly suggest F as the key pitch: the harmonic scheme consists almost entirely of repetitions of the harmonic pattern F—G11, with F coming on the strong downbeats. If F were truly the tonic, the melody would have to be seen as being based on a Lydian scale, with no tonic pitch present! Recognizing this entire situation as highly unusual for this genre, the analyst may, with justification, hear the opening of this piece as an exception to the general rule concerning tonic chords initiating hypermeasures. The notes most likely to be identified as tonic in this case are A and C. Either interpretation satisfies ex-

2.8. Melodic figures pointing to A and C as tonic in Fleetwood Mac's "Dreams."

Dreams. Words and Music by Stevie Nicks. Copyright © 1977 Welsh Witch Music. All Rights Administered by Sony/ATV Music Publishing, 8 Music Square West, Nashville, TN. 37203. International Copyright Secured All Rights Reserved

pectations concerning scale: the pitch source could represent a portion of either the A Aeolian or the C Ionian scale.

Each interpretation finds some support in specific melodic figures. (See example 2.8.) The one instance of a harmony other than F and G, an A minor chord, favors A as tonic. Otherwise, the chords point more strongly to C than to A: IV and V are more common than VI and VII.[16] The melody also ultimately favors C by ending each section on C.

We need not decide ultimately whether the tonic is C or A; it may float between these two relative keys (see "Multiple Keys," below), an appropriate situation in light of the subject matter of "Dreams" and the sometimes surreal grammar of its lyrics. The point here is that an F Lydian hypothesis suggested by the harmonies must be abandoned once the melody begins.

THE PHRASE "IN A KEY"

I have avoided until now saying that these pieces are in a key—and in fact have avoided referring to keys. I have also avoided saying that the pieces are in major or minor. I have instead pointed out that for a particular piece, one note acts as a tonal center and that note serves as the root of a major or minor harmony. The primary reason is that declaring a piece to be in a major or minor key implies the presence of patterns from a previous era. The cumbersome phrase "having as its tonic triad a G major chord" will, from here on, give way to the slightly problematic "in the key of G." The reader accustomed to using the phrase with regard to music in other styles will do well to remember that the phrase carries only those connotations suitable to the music to which it is applied.

For instance, many writers have pointed to the importance in tonal music of the tendency of the seventh scale degree (raised form in minor) to resolve up, a tendency whose force is heightened when the pitch's tritone relationship with the fourth scale degree is made explicit. This tendency is recognized in the seventh scale degree's frequently used moniker, leading tone. Most of the standard melodic systems of rock afford no place for this tendency. Viewed as abridged forms of the "complete" diatonic set, the pentatonic scales leave out precisely the two notes that form the tritone; for example, the pentatonic set C, D, E, G, and A would become a C major scale if F and B were added. In the standard major-mode arrangement ([0] of [02479] as tonic), these omissions remove the leading tone from play. In the standard minor-mode arrangement ([9] of [02479] as tonic), a seventh scale degree is present, but it is the lower form, or subtonic, that is, a whole step below tonic rather than a half step. The hexatonic standards add (with respect to the pentatonic scales) one member of the tritone but still include no leading tone. And of the diatonic standards, only the Ionian scale includes a leading tone; both Mixolydian and Aeolian scales have subtonic pitches instead. As much as some would like to believe that rock follows common-practice standards, examination of the facts just does not support the claim.

ISOLATED PROBLEMS

The Monkees' "Last Train To Clarksville" begins with a guitar repeating the motive found in example 2.9. If common-practice ears and common-practice analytical methods were able to ignore the (for them) uncharacteristic rhythm, they would have to interpret the motive as a partial arpeggiation of a dominant-seventh chord, the embellishment of a dominant-function G. Ears and analytical methods accustomed to rock (and not surprised at all by the syn-

2.9. A tonally ambiguous guitar riff from the Monkee's "Last Train To Clarksville."

copated rhythm) would agree with the recognition of G as the root of the implied harmony but would disagree with the interpretation of the pitch as fulfilling dominant function. The method for key determination proposed above would assume that this root is also the tonic and will retain that function until later evidence outweighs the interpretation. The F, also emphasized in the vocal melody beginning in measure 9, does not hinder this interpretation despite being a minor seventh above the proposed tonic as opposed to the major seventh traditionally expected; it simply establishes a Mixolydian scale as the pitch source of the melodic material. The common-practice ear predicts correctly that this dominant-seventh chord will resolve to a chord on C; but an analysis according to the rock paradigm is justified by the simultaneous resolution, at the end of each section, of both the melody and the harmonic pattern on G.

That pitch content of harmonies alone does not suffice for the identification of key—especially given traditional assumptions only—is clear in the case of a song such as Bob Seger's "Mainstreet." (See example 2.10.) The pitches involved in the repeated harmonic pattern of the introduction form a perfect one-sharp diatonic set. Traditional thought would suggest that the pitch content points to G as a tonic. But the key of the song is clearly D major. The analyst familiar with rock musicians' tendency to use Ionian, Mixolydian, and Aeolian modes would recognize D major as one possible interpretation of the pitches but would not, on the basis of pitch content alone, be able to explain why D is correct and the other two possibilities, G major and E Aeolian, are not. Only by looking at the order of the chords and at the melody and its prominent notes does it become clear how D is established as a tonic: the D major triad coming first, it is assumed to be the tonic in absence of evidence to the contrary, and the P5 formed by D and A, the first and last pitches of the introduction's saxophone riff, confirms D as tonic.

2.10. The introductory chord succession and saxophone riff in Bob Seger's "Main Street."

MAIN STREET, by Bob Seger. © 1976 Gear Publishing Co. All Rights Reserved. Used by Permission. WARNER BROS. PUBLICATIONS U.S. INC., Miami, FL 33014

2.11. Contrasting tonal interpretations of virtually identical harmonic successions on the basis of melody in (a) Lynyrd Skynyrd's "Sweet Home Alabama" and (b) Warren Zevon's "Werewolves Of London."

2.11 a.

SWEET HOME ALABAMA, by Ed King, Ron Van Zant, and Gary Rossing-
ton. © 1974 Universal—Duchess Music Corporation, Universal—On Backstreet Music, Inc., and. EMI Longitude Music. All Rights Reserved. Used by
Permission. WARNER BROS. PUBLICATIONS U.S. INC., Miami, FL
33014

2.11 b.

"Werewolves Of London," written by LeRoy P. Marinell, Waddy Wachtel,
and Warren Zevon. Copyright © 1978 Tiny Tunes Music, Leadsheet Land
Music, and Zevon Music. Copyright © 1997 Zevon Music. All rights reserved.
Used by Permission.

Sometimes the melody does provide evidence contrary to that supplied by
the identity of the opening harmony. The point is made by a comparison of
Lynyrd Skynyrd's "Sweet Home Alabama" and Warren Zevon's "Werewolves
Of London." In each song, the most commonly repeated harmonic pattern (it
actually constitutes the whole Zevon song) involves three major triads with
roots moving down by a major second and then down by perfect fourth. (See
example 2.11.) In "Sweet Home Alabama," the position of the D major triad at
the beginning of the song and of each two-measure group for the remainder of
the song points to that chord as the tonic triad. The shape of the melody, by
centering around the pitch D and coming to a cadence on D every four mea-

sures, confirms this interpretation. The harmonic succession is to be interpreted I-VII-IV.

In "Werewolves Of London," on the other hand, the harmonies and melody do not work together in the same way. Whereas the harmonic pattern suggests D major as the tonic by beginning on the harmony, most of the notes of the melody are Gs. This melodic concentration on G outweighs the importance given to D by its being the first harmony. Therefore, the song is in G, and the succession is to be interpreted V-IV-I.

In certain cases with harmonic successions more complex than those of the songs just discussed, melodic factors play an even stronger role, establishing a key whose tonic harmony need not come first in the piece, or even very often, for that matter. Consider the case of Diana Ross' "Ain't No Mountain High Enough." The first chord of the song is a B dominant seventh. The presence of this chord devoid of any previously established tonal context suggests two possibilities as to key: B, in which the chord would be the tonic harmony, and E (or E minor), in which the chord would act as a V7. The next chord, however, is $B^\flat 11$, followed by $B^\flat 7$. The use of such combinations as embellishments and prolongations of the dominant is so frequent in traditional tonal music that, for the listener accustomed to that music, the impression of $E^\flat$ as pitch center ($B^\flat$ is the dominant, or fifth scale degree, in $E^\flat$) is overwhelming. The B7 harmony appears in retrospect to have been a harmonic embellishment of the true dominant.

Once the drum beat and singers join in, however, the key appears to be neither B, E, E minor, $E^\flat$, or even $B^\flat$. The harmonies support none of these possibilities: the first four of the chords listed above do not appear in the ensuing passage, and $B^\flat$ appears only in the unstable third inversion. The repeated vocal motive, however, by beginning on C and ending on G, points to C as tonic, and the harmonic succession confirms the suggestion by employing C minor seventh as the final chord of its repeated pattern. (See example 2.12.) Thus, the key seems tentatively at this point to be C minor. After this vocal portion of the introduction, a key having been weakly established, the tonic harmony disappears. During the spoken verses, the four-chord pattern, doubled in length now, abandons the C-minor harmony in favor of a C dominant 7. The key is presumed to be C minor still, the C7 acting as a secondary dominant (although, typically, unresolved; see Chapter 5). None of the other chords in the pattern has any claim on being the tonic harmony, and the absence of melody precludes establishment of a new key by melodic means. Thus, although several chords appear multiple times in the introduction and verse of the song, minimal melodic information (the P4 outlined by the singers in the introduc-

2.12. The suggestion of C minor as tonic in the introduction of Diana Ross's "Ain't No Mountain High Enough."

Ain't No Mountain High Enough. Words and Music by Nickolas Ashford and Valerie Simpson. © 1967, 1970 (Renewed 1995, 1998) JOBETE MUSIC CO., INC. All Rights Controlled and Administered by EMI APRIL MUSIC INC. All Rights Reserved International Copyright Secured Used by Permission

tion) establishes a key whose tonic harmony is one of the most infrequently heard chords of the passage (C minor appears only three times), being entirely absent during the verse. For those who disagree with the interpretation that the key changes from E♭ to C minor with the introduction of the voices, the point is even stronger: no E♭ harmony appears until 1 minute 55 seconds into the song. (The song ends, by the way, in the key of E major. Some readers may delight in interpreting the opening B7 chord as a foreshadowing of the final key of the piece and may even wish to entertain the notion that the entire C minor–E♭ episode—the bulk of the song—acts as a long, topsy-turvy embellishment of the overall V-I progression in E.)

As all the examples of this section demonstrate, in cases of doubt or ambiguity with regard to key, melodic patterns carry more weight than harmonic patterns. Although the listener may take the identity of the first harmony as a strong suggestion of key—in that most rock pieces begin with the tonic harmony—any ensuing conflict should (1) be relished as interesting and (2) be decided (if at all) in favor of the key pointed to by melodic patterns.

MULTIPLE KEYS

The ways a key can be established having been discussed, it is now possible to examine some cases that involve more than one key. As will be seen, although many rock pieces involve something akin to the modulation of the common practice, some passages promote two keys almost simultaneously. It is even legitimate at times to recognize that a given rock piece is not in a key if common key-defining features are not strongly present.

Many times one section of a song is clearly in one key, and another section in another. For instance, the verse and the chorus or bridge may be in different keys. In such cases, where each key is clearly established and the change in key is clearly supported by a formal distinction, it is safe to speak of modulation. The key relationships involved in rock tend to fall into five categories: relative major and minor, parallel major and minor, fourth relationships, chromatic third relationships, and chromatic second relationships, the last two probably being the most common.

Songs employing relative keys for the two main keys include Gary Wright's "Dream Weaver" (verse beginning in C♯ minor, chorus in E major), Fleetwood Mac's "Rhiannon" (verse in A minor, chorus in C), Cheryl Crow's "My Favorite Mistake" (verse in B minor, chorus in D), and Collective Soul's "The World I Know" (verse in B minor, chorus in D). Songs emphasizing parallel keys include the Grass Roots' "Temptation Eyes" (verse in B♭ minor, chorus in B♭) and Lipps Inc's "Funkytown" (A section in C major, B section in C minor). Songs employing a fourth relationship include the Buckinghams' "Kind Of A Drag" (chorus in G, verse in C), the Corrs' "Breathless" (verse in B, chorus in E), and Paul Simon's "Kodachrome" (verse in E, chorus in A). Songs whose main sections juxtapose keys of a chromatic third relationship include Steve Winwood's "While You See A Chance" (verse in D, bridge in B♭), the Doobie Brothers' "What A Fool Believes" (verse in D♭, chorus in E), the Sanford/Townsend Band's "Smoke Of A Distant Fire" (verse and refrain in A, bridge in F), Chicago's "(I've Been) Searchin' So Long" (A section in C, B section in A), the Beatles' "Something" (verse in C, bridge in A), the Guess Who's "Hand Me Down World" (verse in B, chorus in G), Diana Ross' "Upside Down" (chorus in G minor, verse in B♭ minor), and Duran Duran's "Hungry Like The Wolf" (verse in E, chorus in C). Songs whose major sections juxtapose keys sharing a chromatic second relationship include the Beach Boys' "Don't Worry, Baby" (verse in D, chorus in E♭), Bread's "It Don't Matter To Me" (verse in D, bridge in C), the Bee Gees' "I've Got to Get a Message To You" (verse in B♭ and chorus in C), and Huey Lewis and the News' "Stuck With You" (verse in C, chorus in D).

Some rock pieces tend to float back and forth between two keys. This phenomenon occurs when a feature that allows multiple interpretations of key (usually a diatonic set as pitch source) is accompanied by other, more precise evidence in support of each possible interpretation (such as use of one note as the root of the initiating harmony and persistent use of another note as pitch of melodic resolution and root of the final harmony of each phrase). The most common key relationship in such a case involves relative major and minor keys, in that they can share a melodic pitch source: C Ionian, for instance, involves exactly the same pitch classes (all the natural notes) as A Aeolian.

2.13. An ambiguous chord pattern in Dan Fogelberg's "Face The Fire."

Am | Dm | G | C   :|

Consider the case of Dan Fogelberg's "Face The Fire." (See example 2.13.) Each four-chord pattern begins with an A minor triad, but many end with a C major triad. A key is an interpretation based on familiar stylistic features, and listeners familiar with Western music other than rock cannot help hearing this many cadences on C major without ascribing some sort of stability to the chord. The use of a G major triad before each C only strengthens that sense. In some instances involving a cadence on C, the melody also comes to a close on C. The case is closed, then; C major is tonic. Or is it? This same listener must acknowledge that the cultural sensibilities that latch on to C as tonic are uncomfortable with the persistent use of anything other than tonic as an initial harmony. Perhaps it is better to say the piece is in constant oscillation between the two keys. This solution, however, doesn't take into account the extreme brevity of some of the areas in each key and the seamless ease with which the song goes from one to the other. The case demands a rejection of the insistence on a safe, simple, single answer: the song is in some sense in both keys.

The listener may hope for a final cadence to clear up the interpretation of all the music that went before. Two factors frustrate this hope. First, most rock recordings fade out. (Chapters 1 and 3 suggest an aesthetic justification for the ubiquitous fade-out.) In these instances, one cannot look to a final cadence for the answer. Even when such a cadence exists, however, the rock composer's aesthetic apparently recognizes no need for this cadence to conclude with the tonic harmony. The G major tonality of America's "Lonely People" is clear from the beginning, but the song ends on an E-minor triad, hinting at the unity some composers must feel exists at some level between relative keys. Chicago's "Searchin' So Long" includes a section in C and a section in A (see above), but it ends on a B♭ chord.

Other songs that float back and forth between relative keys or even promote both virtually simultaneously include the Rolling Stones' "Under My Thumb," the Beatles' "And I Love Her," the Animals' "Don't Let Me Be Misunderstood," and 10,000 Maniacs' "Noah's Dove." The Moody Blues' "The Story In Your Eyes" provides an example in which the two keys continuously promoted are not relative keys: each verse begins in E minor and ends in D.

In many songs, a similar ambiguity arises with reference to pieces in which a single identity for the tonic pitch is clear but the mode is not distinctly major or minor. This ambiguity arises originally from the conflict in blues-flavored pieces between the normal, major third scale degree in the tonic harmony and the lowered third scale degree in the melody. (The variability of the third scale degree in melodies seems to happen only when the tonic triad has a major third.)

Introduced to the genre through the blues-based conflict, this ambiguity of mode appears in other instances not otherwise associated with blues or unstable pitches, most notably, in the form of tonic harmonies that have no thirds. (See Chapter 4.) The distortion normally applied to these chords in hard rock and heavy metal, where they are common, slightly emphasizes the major third as the acoustically natural sum tone of two notes a P5 apart.[17] As a result, the chords have something of the flavor of major triads. In most of these cases, however, the melodies employ a minor third scale degree. Examples include Deep Purple's "Smoke On The Water."

But even where distortion is not present to strengthen a suggestion of a major third, open-fifth chords frequently occur in situations in which the mode freely alternates between major and minor. Marvin Gaye's "I Heard It Through the Grapevine" provides an interesting example. The song begins with a pattern of open-fifth chords primarily on E♭ and G♭. (See example 2.14.) Although the lack of a third in the E♭ chord leaves the question of mode open, the prominence of G♭ in the bass line strongly suggests the minor mode. The use of G♭ in the melody strengthens the suggestion. The presence of a minor third scale degree in the melody, however, does not rule out the possibility of the major mode in rock where blues inflections often alter that scale degree. The quality of the third in the tonic triad provides the most pertinent evidence

2.14. Ambiguity of mode in the introduction to Marvin Gaye's "I Heard It Through The Grapevine."

I Heard It Through The Grapevine. Words and Music by Norman J. Whitfield and Barrett Strong. © 1966 (Renewed 1994) JOBETE MUSIC CO., INC. All Rights Controlled and Administered by EMI BLACKWOOD MUSIC INC. on behalf of. STONE AGATE MUSIC (A Division of JOBETE MUSIC CO., INC.). All Rights Reserved International Copyright Secured Used by Permission

toward establishment of a mode, evidence absent in this case. Neither does the presence of a chord built on a minor third rule out the possibility of the major mode. Chapter 4 describes more fully a harmonic system, commonly used in rock, in which a major tonic triad is accompanied by triads built on the notes of the natural-minor scale. Consequently, the listener accustomed to rock norms does not rule out the notion that every instance of G♭ is to be interpreted as an altered form of a major third scale degree. This reservation of judgment is justified when, at the end of the verse, a passage of "complete" triads begins with a C minor chord, a chord that, because of its G♮, points to the major mode. At the entrance of the refrain, the instruments make the harmonic situation even clearer by playing an E♭ major chord. The intonation of the third scale degree in the melody, however, continues to be shaded toward G♭. In summary, while E♭ is never in doubt as the tonic pitch, the mode is not entirely clear. During the refrain, both major and minor modes present themselves in separate ways.

Some pieces will seem not to settle in a key. For instance, REM's "Try Not To Breathe" consistently uses the notes of the one-sharp diatonic collection but promotes as tonic sometimes D, sometimes G, sometimes E. (See example 2.15.) The piece opens with several repetitions of the four-chord pattern D-Am-C-G. Because the D major harmony comes first, and because the lead guitar opens the song by playing D and A together with the bass, thus emphasizing the tonally suggestive P4, D major seems at the beginning of the song to be a strong candidate for the tonic harmony.

2.15. Harmonic patterns in REM's "Try Not To Breathe."

D	Am		C	G		D	Am		C	G		:|
|: Am		| Am		| C		| C		| G	D	| G	D	:|
|: Em		| Em		| Am		| Am	:|	C		| C		|

However, in the second section of the song (whose harmonic pattern is listed in the second line of example 2.15) all D major harmonies come on weak beats, the G major harmonies come on strong beats, and G becomes a prominent melodic pitch. The key seems rather clearly to be G major. When the A section returns, the interpretive situation becomes quite interesting: while in its first appearance the section appeared in the key of D, it is heard the second time only after G major has been established. Once the mind has settled on a framework within which to interpret stimuli, evidence of some compulsion is required for it to abandon the framework in favor of another. The notion of a key is just such an interpretive framework, and the mind will retain the notion that the music is in the key of G unless compelling evidence prompts it to change the interpretation. The pitch content of the passage can be interpreted as G Ionian as well as D Mixolydian. The only real evidence favoring the interpretation of D as tonic—besides, of course, the memory of having heard the passage as being somewhat weakly in D the first time—is the consistent appearance of D major at the beginning of every two-measure hypermeasure. But once a key is established, rock often employs a harmony other than tonic to begin subsequent sections. (See Chapter 6, "Form".) This interpreter, at any rate, finds it very hard to hear the second appearance of the A section as strongly in one key or another. One later passage (whose harmonic pattern is notated as the third line in example 2.15) makes things even more interesting. By abandoning both D major and G major harmonies altogether for several measures and presenting E minor chords in hypermetrically strong positions, the passage promotes E minor as tonic. The effect is that of clearing the palate, leaving the question of key deliciously and freshly ambiguous upon the final return of the A section. (The B section comes last, concluding the song on a G major harmony.)

Although many ambiguous cases arise, we are left with the useful notion that the root of the first chord usually proves to be the most stable pitch, based on traditional melodic structures or use of the opening chord as the persistently initiating harmony.

The beginnings of phrases have been the focus of this chapter; we now turn to endings.

3

cadences

The word *cadence* comes from the Latin *cadere*, meaning primarily "to fall." Since the fall of a thing often indicates its end, *cadere* was used sometimes figuratively to mean "to end" or "to close." We speak, for instance, of the fall of Rome.

The English word *cadence* draws upon both senses when it refers to the fall of the voice at the end of a sentence.[1] Because the first clearly documented musical phrases of Western history—the chants of medieval monasteries—were conceived as stylized speech patterns, both these definitions come into play again: a fall in pitch generally marks the end of each phrase. (Although this feature of chant is thought to imitate patterns of speech, both actually stem rather naturally from the physiological need to breathe.) In music, then, the term *cadence* refers either to the end of a phrase or to the melodic, harmonic, or rhythmic formula that occurs there.

The typical musical cadence from the common practice is marked by one or more of the following formulas: (1) a rhythmic pause in the melody as the result of a long note, a rest, or a combination, emulating the breathing points in speech (or actually providing a breathing point in a melody for voice or wind instrument), (2) a melodic descent, (3) a harmonic pattern ending with V, V-I, vii°-I, or V-vi (in roughly that order of likelihood), and (4) the simultaneous arrival of the final chord, the final note, and the downbeat of the final measure of a phrase (the fourth measure in the typical four-measure phrase). Because cadences copy patterns of speech, they occur much more frequently in songs and instrumental forms based on songs than in purely instrumental works such as symphonies, sonatas, and concertos.

It comes as no surprise, in light of this history, that many textbooks on theory compare cadences to punctuation. Heinrich Christoph Koch offered this explanation in 1787:

> Certain more or less noticeable resting points are generally necessary in speech and thus also in the products of those fine arts which attain their goal through speech, namely poetry and rhetoric. . . . Such resting points are just as necessary in melody if it is to affect our feelings. . . .
>
> By means of these more or less noticeable resting points, the products of these fine arts can be broken up into larger and smaller sections. Speech, for example, breaks down into various sentences [*Perioden*] through the most noticeable of these resting points; through the less noticeable the sentence, in turn, breaks down into separate clauses [*Sätze*] and parts of speech [*Redetheile*]. Just as in speech, the melody of a composition can be broken up into periods by means of analogous resting points, and these, again, into single phrases [*Sätze*] and melodic segments [*Theile*].[2]

One hundred ninety years later, Ralph Turek offers a similar explanation: "Most phrases end with a *cadence*. Like a grammatical punctuation, a cadence serves to separate ideas. . . . Melodic cadences are usually supported by harmonic cadences and may be conclusive, producing an effect similar to that of a period at the end of a sentence, or inconclusive, producing an effect similar to that of a comma."[3]

As Turek points out, cadences are often categorized in terms of the degree of finality. In general, the tonic chord or tonic pitch (or both) at the end of a phrase makes a cadence sound more closed, or complete, whereas other chords and pitches make a cadence sound open, or incomplete. As Koch points out, this distinction (he calls the more complete cadences simply "more noticeable") mirrors the patterns of spoken language. In English, a fall of pitch and a pause in the rhythmic flow generally accompanies the end of a statement and command (and, in many British dialects, a question as well).

But this fall of pitch and rhythmic pause also usually marks the end of subordinate clauses of a sentence. Consider the following string of words: "Yesterday when I went to the grocery store." Any English speaker will find it natural to read or hear the phrase with a drop in pitch over the last two words (followed, perhaps, by a slight rise in pitch at the end of the last syllable) and to expect a slight pause after the phrase before any other words are spoken. So the phrase has some degree of completeness or integrity; its end has some degree of finality or closure. Consider how much less final the phrase sounds if stopped sooner: "Yesterday when I." These three words sound odd when read with a drop of pitch through "when" and "I." The same effect holds with "Yesterday when I went," "Yesterday when I went to," and "Yesterday when I went to the." In each case, the clause would sound complete enough to bear a drop in pitch, a cadence, with the addition of just one word. (Try "exercised," "downtown," "Milwaukee," and "bank.") The urgent expectation of perhaps just one word causes the sense of incompleteness in these phrases. In addition, the original clause is grammatically incomplete. It requires an entire independent clause to follow it, however, not just one word. "Yesterday when I went to the grocery store, I noticed a sale on strawberries," for instance. The sentence then has two cadence points, the first carrying a sense of partial closure, and the second a sense of thorough closure.

Similarly, in common practice songs, a phrase with an open cadence is usually followed by a phrase with a closed cadence. The typical arrangement, known as a period, most often consists of a phrase ending with a half cadence followed by a phrase ending with a perfect authentic cadence.

It is essential to the idea of resolution that the harmony and the melody arrive on the tonic not just together but also at the right time: at the end of a phrase. Because stability depends on meter and rhythm as well as on harmony, the tonic harmony provides resolution only when it appears at the end of a phrase. Consider the well-known hymn in example 3.1. The chord on beat 1 of measure 5 (marked with an "x") is the tonic harmony in root position with the tonic pitch in the melody, and it follows the V chord; if pitch patterns alone can create resolution, then this chord should sound perfectly stable. But try playing through the piece and stopping on the chord marked "x"; the chord does not in fact provide a satisfying feeling of closure. If all the pitch patterns indi-

3.1. Tonic chords with no sense of finality, showing that resolution depends on rhythm and not on pitch alone, in William Croft, "St. Anne," 1708.

cate resolution but the chord still does not feel resolved, rhythmic considerations must be responsible for the sense of unrest. Specifically in this case, where tonic harmony follows a dominant chord that ends a phrase, the tonic functions not to resolve either the previous phrase or the V that ends it but to launch the next phrase. The chord marked "y," also a root-position tonic chord with the tonic pitch in the melody, sounds even less satisfying as a final chord. The primary reason is again rhythmic: the chord's placement on the second beat of the measure. So for a I chord to act as a resolution, it must come on a strong beat at the end of a phrase. In music with some consistency of hypermeter, this must occur at the end of a hypermeasure, normally on the fourth downbeat.

Such is the nature of cadences in traditional thought, but we will find in rock no such assumption of a necessity for all aspects of a piece to lead to simultaneous resolution. Information in other chapters has already suggested that the traditional notion of cadence as a coordination of melodic, harmonic, and metrical resolution in one of a limited set of simple patterns does not apply in rock. Melody and harmonic pattern seldom come to some degree of rest at the same time, and when they do, the time is often not at the end of a formal unit or hypermeasure, but at the beginning. In this chapter we will observe that when cadences do occur, they frequently do not follow the formulas of earlier music. The traditional perfect authentic cadence, for instance, rarely occurs, although a wide variety of patterns fulfills its function. An even wider variety of patterns is found among open cadences. We will also see that open cadences are more frequent than closed cadences, the latter being entirely absent in many cases.

Even though the definition of *cadence* is tricky in rock, we can say we have a cadence in two conditions: one based on rhythmic notions traditionally associated with cadences, and the other on harmonic patterns. First, we can state that a cadence occurs when the melody comes to rest at the end of a textual line on the fourth downbeat of a four-bar hypermeasure (or *near* the fourth downbeat —allowances must be made for syncopations and for weak-syllable endings coming after the downbeat). Fourth-downbeat cadences, as we will see, do not always involve the I, V, or vi chord. Second, we can speak of a cadence when the melody comes to a rest at the end of a textual line and the accompanying harmony is I or V. A harmonically driven cadence of this type might occur on the third downbeat of a hypermeasure, on the fourth downbeat of a hypermeasure (in which case the two categories of cadence overlap), in a situation where hypermeters are not present, or even at the beginning of a hypermeasure (as in the extension-overlap model of phrase structure—see Chapter 1).

One other problem arising from the lack of coordination among harmony, melody, and hypermeter deserves attention. If cadence is to be used to refer to a total harmonic-melodic gesture, the chord accompanying the final melodic note should be the last chord before the beginning of the next vocal line. For instance, in the Beatles' "Please, Please Me," the first vocal phrase ends in the third measure on a I chord. (See example 3.2.)[4] But the chords continue to change before the next melodic line begins. How can the tonic chord be *the* cadential chord when the passage as a whole ends with a V? In a case like this, the melody and harmony act independently enough that we can't speak of cadence as a unified gesture. We must instead refer to the melodic cadence (in measure 3) and the harmonic cadence (in measure 4).

3.2. Continued harmonic motion after a melodic cadence in the Beatles'
"Please, Please Me."

E: I | I | IV   I | III   IV   V |

A similar situation arises when the final harmony enters one or more measures before the melody. Most commonly, the final harmony of the line begins on the third downbeat, while the melody continues to the fourth downbeat, as in Elton John's "Saturday Night's Alright For Fighting." (See example 3.3.) In

3.3. Continued melodic motion after a harmonic cadence in Elton John's "Saturday Night's Alright For Fighting."

G: I		I		VII		VII		

| IV | | IV | | I | | I | | |

cases such as this, we can identify the chord accompanying the last note of the melodic phrase as the cadential chord, thereby providing some small sense of melodic and harmonic coordination, but we cannot say that the harmonic cadence occurs in measure 4 with the melodic cadence.

HARMONIC POSSIBILITIES AND FUNCTIONS

The fourth-downbeat type of cadence occurs several times in America's "Sister Golden Hair." (See example 3.4.) The rhythm of the melody line as well as the grammatical structure and rhyme scheme of the text clearly establishes the four-bar hypermeter. Fourth-downbeat cadences occur in measures 4, 8, 12, 20, and 24. The harmonies involved are iii, iii, IV, I, and I, respectively.

The variety suggests that open cadences can occur on almost any chord in rock, and this is in fact true. Fourth-downbeat cadences occur on ii in Billy Joel's "Innocent Man" (first phrase), iii in Elton John's "Your Song" (first phrase), IV in the Bee Gees' "To Love Somebody" (second phrase), VI in Gary Wright's "Dream Weaver" (first phrase), vi in Peter Cetera's "One Good

3.4. A harmonic chart and the vocal phrase rhythm of America's "Sister Golden Hair."

		. . . depressed				. . . undressed		
E: I		I		iii		iii		IV		I		iii		iii		

		. . . times				. . . mine		
IV		ii		vi V		IV		ii		IV		I		I	:|

		. . . air				. . . care		
V		V		IV		I		V		V		IV		I		

ii		iii		IV		IV		

Woman" (first phrase), VII in Styx's "Fooling Yourself (Angry Young Man)" (second part of chorus, at 2 minutes 34 seconds and 3 minutes 55 seconds into the track), V/V in Madonna's "Borderline" (first phrase of chorus), and V/vi in both Nilsson's "Without You" (first phrase) and the Hollies' "Air That I Breathe" (first phrase).[5]

Despite the variety possible, I and V appear at most fourth-downbeat cadences. Here the fourth-downbeat category overlaps with the harmonically driven category, cadences in which the melodic line comes to rest at a V or I chord. How do cadences of this second category function? Two cadences from "Sister Golden Hair" fit this second category (three if the placement of the end of the fourth vocal phrase is considered a rhythmic transformation of a more normal placement on the downbeat of its third measure; see below). In each case, the final chord is the tonic harmony, I. But because these cadences come early in the chorus, ending the first two phrases, they assume a degree of incompleteness. So even the I chord can be used in open cadences.

The most common chord at open cadences in rock is the V chord. In fact, the V chord ends most or all of the phrases in many songs such as Little River Band's "Help Is On Its Way" (excluding the bridge), Culture Club's "Karma Chameleon" (excluding the first two phrases), "Twist And Shout" (recorded by the Isley Brothers and by the Beatles), and the Tokens' "The Lion Sleeps Tonight." (Other examples are listed in Chapter 1.) As a result, these songs never resolve; that is, they never reach tonal closure. The tonic chord begins most phrases in these songs, and so most of these cadential V chords are followed by the I chord. Might not this motion to tonic bring about a sense of closure? No. As example 3.1 shows, the tonic at the beginning of a phrase is not a goal but rather an inception. In these songs, the phrases move not toward the tonic but repetitively away from it.

These cases are not exceptional, because most rock songs don't ever reach closure. Several methods are used to keep the pieces from resolving. The first is the open cadence, whether it involves the V chord or not, especially at the ends of sections. For instance, in Tina Turner's "What's Love Got To Do With It," the verse ends on v, the chorus on VII. In the Turtles' "Happy Together," the verse ends on V, the chorus on III. And in Supertramp's "Logical Song," the verse ends on IV7 of C minor, while the chorus ends on VII of E♭. A second method involves the melodic line, but not the harmony, coming to rest on the tonic. Such is the case with Elton John's "Crocodile Rock," where the melody of the chorus ends on tonic (with a doubly repeated upper neighbor) over the IV chord. (See example 3.5.) The chorus of Joan Osborne's "One Of Us" presents a similar situation. In a third scenario, both melody and harmony do re-

3.5. Melodic resolution without harmonic resolution in Elton John's "Crocodile Rock."

CROCODILE ROCK, by Elton John and Bernie Taupin. © 1972 (Renewed) Dick James Music Ltd. Universal/Dick James Music Ltd, 77 Fulham Palace Rd., London W6. All Rights for U.S. and Canada controlled and administered by Universal—Songs of Polygram. International, Inc. All Rights Reserved. International Copyright Secured. Used by Permission. WARNER BROS. PUBLICATIONS U.S. INC., Miami, FL 33014. Used by permission of Music Sales Ltd.

solve, but at the beginning of a hypermeasure, where metrical factors don't allow a feeling of rest. This pattern arises in Buffalo Springfield's "For What It's Worth," where the harmonic and melodic resolution of the chorus always coincides with either the beginning of a repeat of the chorus or the return of the introduction.

Songs such as these make it clear that open cadences in rock, even those involving V, should not be called by the anachronistic term "half cadence." If period structures or other patterns ending with closure are not necessary, open cadences won't be perceived as marking a halfway point toward any greater resting point. (For more information, see Chapter 5, under "Antiperiodic Structure.") Differences in finality among cadences are not normally used to imply where a piece is going. That is, an open cadence doesn't prompt the listener to wait for a more complete cadence at the end of the next phrase, and the listener should not expect ultimate resolution in this music. Differing degrees of finality, if they have significance at all, serve only to highlight the lyrics at the moment or to lead directly into the next phrase or section (with no expectations about how that next passage will end). Otherwise, they simply combine in an array of patterns, sometimes with the most open cadence coming last, as in the chorus to "Sister Golden Hair"; sometimes with every cadence being open, as in "Help Is On Its Way"; and sometimes with every cadence having a degree of finality, as in "Superstar," from the rock opera *Jesus Christ Superstar*.

Although resolution is not necessary in rock, it is not uncommon to find closed cadences employing the I chord. The V-I cadence, however, with all its traditional features, almost never occurs. Although V-I motion does occur, it most often involves the V at the end of one phrase and the I at the beginning of the next, that is, between two phrases rather than at the end of one. We have discussed this pattern already in "The Lion Sleeps Tonight" and other songs, and have noted that such a pattern cannot constitute any kind of closure or cadence, coming as it does at the wrong time for a closing gesture. Many times, however, the tonic harmony does finish a phrase; but at these times the penultimate harmony is usually either a V11, avoiding the leading tone and its half-step melodic resolution, or a chord other than V. The fourth, fifth, and sixth phrases of "Sister Golden Hair" all use a IV-I cadence, one of the most common possibilities. (Chapter 5 lists others.)

RHYTHMIC TRANSFORMATION OF MELODIC CADENCES

Before examining what happens in melodies at cadences, we must deal with the issues of syncopation and rhythmic transformation. Before the seventeenth century, when composers began to think about harmonies as elements with separate identities and properties, all harmonies came about as the result of combining melodic lines. (See also Chapter 4, under "Melody and Harmony.") These lines had to be combined in such a way as to produce harmonious intervals most of the time. And when three or more lines were involved in a composition, three-part harmonies, which modern-day musicians would identify as triads, were most often the result (in the fifteenth and sixteenth centuries, at any rate). But these harmonies were totally subservient to the melodic line. No one thought about naming the various chords in a piece or examining their order. Chords changed when it was right for the melody to change, and, since chords were solely the product of the melodic lines, they had no choice but to contain the primary notes of the melodic lines.

But in rock, as indeed in any music in which some parts or instruments present chords while others carry the melody, the melodic and harmonic aspects are much more loosely connected. As a result (1) melodic notes need not fit the chord played by the harmonic instruments, and (2) the melody and the chord need not move at the same time. The second case concerns us here (Chapter 4 examines the first).

Consider the melody to "Mary Had A Little Lamb." (See example 3.6.) This song is well known, but primarily by its melody. Anyone recording it is free to arrange the harmonic accompaniment in any way. (Performers of Beethoven's Symphony no. 5 are also free in a sense to change the parts. The point here is that while virtually every performer essentially follows the parts on that piece, it is doubtful whether any arranger has ever consulted a written

3.6. Last phrase of "Mary Had A Little Lamb."

score of "Mary" to see what the accompaniment ought to be.) The last five notes of that melody follow the pattern $\hat{2}$-$\hat{2}$-$\hat{3}$-$\hat{2}$-$\hat{1}$. The third scale degree in this cadence is generally thought of as an embellishment; the essential melodic motion is from $\hat{2}$ to $\hat{1}$. The harmonic cadence must almost certainly consist of a V chord, accompanying the second scale degree, and a I chord, supporting the tonic pitch. The melody resolves to $\hat{1}$ on the downbeat of the fourth measure; the change to the I chord should occur at that time, too. While it is hypothetically possible for the chords and melody not to align, it is still stylistically appropriate that they do so.

Now consider "Invisible Touch" by Genesis. (See example 3.7.) This song is also well known, but here we have a definitive version of the harmonic accompaniment: the one found on the recording. The cadence of the first line of the chorus uses a similar melodic formula: $\hat{1}$-$\hat{3}$-$\hat{2}$-$\hat{1}$. And again, the final two chords are V and I. But beyond these similarities, differences abound. For one, the I chord comes in an odd-numbered measure; in this song harmonic resolution comes not at the end of a hypermeasure but at the beginning. As we have seen in other songs, this odd-numbered measure with the tonic chord (and other measures like it throughout the song) must serve as both harmonic resolution of what comes before and metrical impetus of what follows. As a result, the vocal rhythm follows a pattern, described in Chapter 1, in which the vocal phrases begin after the downbeat, leaving room for the resolution of preceding

3.7. End of the first phrase and beginning of the second phrase of the chorus of Genesis's "Invisible Touch."

material at the beginning of the measure; the vocal phrases of the chorus each begin on the second half of the first beat of their respective measures—the "and" of 1. Partly to leave even more room before these only slightly delayed entrances, the last note of the line we are examining comes not on the downbeat but on the "and" of 4. In this way, the last note of the phrase, the tonic pitch, occurs before the tonic chord. In fact, the tonic pitch is so short, it and the tonic chord are never heard together; the tonic pitch sounds only in conjunction with the V chord.

Note that the tonic pitch is not a member of the V chord. In some situations, it could represent a stable added fourth in the harmony (see Chapter 4, under "Chord Types"). But in this situation, it clearly functions as a resolution to the phrase. That is, it functions in the melody as the tonic chord does in the harmonies. It is appropriate, therefore, to hear the tonic pitch as associated with the I chord, not the V chord. What happens at this cadence represents a rhythmic transformation of a model cadence in which the second scale degree moves to the first at the same time that the V chord moves to the I. (See example 3.8.) The transformation is a common one in rock: placing the textually accented note just ahead of the downbeat, not directly on it. Such a transformation occurs in almost all the examples to follow; most often the note of resolution is early (marked as "anticipated" in the examples below), as in "Invisible Touch"; at other times it is delayed.

3.8. V-I cadences: (a) model in which melody forms part of the chords and (b) typical rhythmic transformations.

3.8 a.

3.8 b.

MELODIC POSSIBILITIES

Having defined some standard rhythmic variations at cadences, we stand ready to discover and record any standard melodic patterns at cadences. But here a problem of numbers arises. With any given harmonic cadence, several melodic patterns might occur. But so many possible harmonic combinations would make the melodic possibilities unmanageable. Therefore, the following discussion is limited to certain frequent harmonic combinations ending on the tonic chord: namely, IV-I and V-I in major or minor, and V11-I in major. The melodic possibilities might be expected to be somewhat limited by a tendency for the melody to end on the tonic pitch in functional coordination with the harmonic motion. If any standard patterns of melodic cadence exist, they are found in these circumstances.

With a IV-I cadence, the pitch content of the chords suggests the smoothest possible approach to the tonic: from the tonic pitch itself. And in fact the $\hat{1}$-$\hat{1}$ cadence appears in many songs, including the Beatles' "Dear Prudence," John Denver's "Take Me Home, Country Roads" (with upper neighbor), Rod Stewart's "Maggie May," and Paul McCartney's "My Love." The arrival of the tonic pitch before the metrical resolution at the end of a line plays a prominent role in English folk song (see example 3.9) and may have made its way to rock through that important stylistic source.

3.9. Arrival of the final pitch before the rhythmic close of a phrase in the traditional English folk song "Banks Of The Newfoundland."

The opportunity for this melodic formula afforded by the frequent presence of the IV-I cadence may be simply a happy coincidence of ideas, or the IV-I cadence itself may have been suggested by the melodic practice. In either case, it is clear that in the cadences described here, melody and harmony work together to express a unified musical ideal. In most periodic styles of traditional tonal music, where the note of resolution in the melody is delayed to the very end (the Germanic source of much of traditional tonal style suggests a link with the practice of placing the verb at the end of the sentence in German),[6] it is appropriate that that note not be present anywhere in the penultimate chord. But rock, in pursuing a different ideal, places a premium on chord successions in which the root of one chord is present in the preceding chord. (See Chapter 5.) So in the cadences in question, both melody and harmony present the tonic pitch well ahead of the metrical point of resolution.

As we have seen, musical phrasing and linguistic structures have a long-standing, acknowledged connection, one that permeates even the terminology of musical phrase structure. This connection, when considered in connection with the melodic and harmonic structures of the cadences in "Dear Prudence" and the like suggests that at least some of the differences between rock style and earlier popular styles can be explained as an abandonment of a Germanic ideal for an English one. Can statements involving such slippery notions as national character be made? Can we reliably say that musical structures embody philosophies in ways that are passed down by cultural streams of influence roughly bounded by national borders?

Could it be that the people whose goal-oriented traditions of thought helped them conquer Roman Europe, produced Hegel's theory of directed history, prompted some less-than-admirable expansive exploits in this century, and are responsible for the world-famous promptness of their trains find expression of that tradition in the periodic custom of delaying notes of resolution? And could it be that the island-bound people who took the time on a trip to Canterbury to share lengthy tales, who sat by the fire with the family on cold winter evenings reading of the Cratchits also sitting by the fire, who made an art out of growing hedgerows, and whose greatest literary figure praised his country as

> This precious stone set in the silver sea,
> Which serves it in the office of a wall
> Or as a moat defensive to a house,
> Against the envy of less happier lands;[7]

—could these people find expression of that domestic, almost timeless mentality in the melodic custom of arriving at the pitch of resolution ahead of the rhythmic close of a phrase? And could it be that the American society that, beginning with the youth of the 1960s, gave up (perhaps the best of) the German ideal of a goal-directed life for (perhaps the worst extension of) the English ideal of enjoying the present recognized that the Beatles had found in the musical traditions of their island the philosophically perfect counterpart to the physical excitement of Elvis and Little Richard?

It is an interesting theory, and valuable—as far as it goes. In their histories, however, the Germans have produced timeless fairy tales, and the English have been noted for a distinct streak of imperialism. Human activity is much too richly complex for any neat explanation. The influence of English folk song through English groups such as the Beatles may account for the $\hat{1}$-$\hat{1}$ cadence. But a bewildering array of other combinations presents itself at IV-I cadences: $\hat{6}$-$\hat{1}$ occurs in Journey's "Faithfully," $\hat{4}$-$\hat{1}$ in the Verve Pipe's "The Freshmen," $^\flat\hat{7}$-$\hat{1}$ in Credence Clearwater Revival's "Fortunate Son," $^\flat\hat{3}$-$\hat{1}$ in Fatboy Slim's "Praise You," $\hat{1}$-$\hat{3}$ in the Beatles' "Yesterday," $\hat{4}$-$\hat{5}$ in the Who's "Won't Get Fooled Again," $\hat{6}$-$\hat{5}$ in Michael Jackson's "Billie Jean," $\hat{4}$-$\hat{3}$ in the Rolling Stones' "You Can't Always Get What You Want," and $^\flat\hat{3}$-$^\flat\hat{3}$ in the same group's "It's Only Rock 'N Roll (But I Like It)." In some cases, it should be noted, the melodic notes don't even fit the harmonies.

Most often in V-I cadences, the melody finds the second scale degree resolving to the first. This happens, for instance, in Rod Stewart's "I Was Only Joking" (verse, melodic cadence anticipated), John Lennon's "(Just Like) Starting Over" (refrain, melodic cadence delayed), and the Byrds' "Mr. Tambourine Man" (chorus, melodic and harmonic cadences simultaneous). The $\hat{7}$-$\hat{1}$ motion in the melody at V-I cadences is rare but not impossible to find. Examples include James Taylor's "Sweet Baby James" (chorus, melodic cadence anticipated), Buddy Holly's "That'll Be The Day" (melody and harmony anticipate strong beat; on Linda Ronstadt's remake, melody, harmony, and bass all anticipate the strong beat), and the Beatles' "Hey Jude" (verse, melodic cadence delayed).

In V11-I cadences the melody often resolves on $\hat{1}$. In this situation, the melody approaches the tonic pitch in a variety of ways, partly because the V11 contains so many notes. A look at the pitch content of the V11 chord shows that the hypothetical possibilities include the second, fourth, fifth, sixth, and even first scale degrees. (See example 3.10.) The V11 is sometimes extended to a V13sus by the addition of the third scale degree; so $\hat{3}$ becomes a possible penultimate note as well. In practice, all but the $\hat{4}$-$\hat{1}$ combination can be found. The $\hat{2}$-$\hat{1}$ combination occurs in Elton John's "Little Jeannie," $\hat{3}$-$\hat{1}$ in Marilyn

3.10. The chords (a) V11 and (b) V13sus and (c) typical melodic patterns found at cadences involving these chords.

McCoo and Billy Davis, Jr.'s "You Don't Have To Be A Star (To Be In My Show),"$\hat{5}$-$\hat{1}$ in the final cadence of the Eagles' "Desperado," and $\hat{6}$-$\hat{1}$ in the same group's "Lyin' Eyes." Because rock follows only loosely any rule that structural pitches must be part of the chord accompanying them, there is no reason $\hat{7}$ couldn't act as the penultimate note in a V11-I cadence except that $\hat{7}$-$\hat{1}$ is a rare cadential formula in rock no matter what the chords involved are. But this combination in fact happens in Bread's "If."

The most common melodic pattern at V11-I cadences, however, is $\hat{1}$-$\hat{1}$, partly because the tonic note is such a distinctive feature of the V11 chord, and partly, again, because of the nonperiodic ideal described above. Examples include England Dan and John Ford Coley's "I'd Really Love To See You Tonight" (chorus, melodic cadence anticipated), Elton John's "Don't Let The Sun Go Down On Me," Billy Joel's "Piano Man," and Carole King's "Home Again."

The lists above often note cadences in which the melody and harmony resolve at slightly different times, and cadences in which melodic pitches and harmonic pitches don't correspond. The independence of melody and harmony is often even greater, however. In the cadences in example 3.11, the melody moves near the downbeat to some note in the tonic harmony and then steps or skips to $\hat{1}$. In such cases, while the resolution of harmony and melody come at about the same time, the timing is skewed enough to show that melody and harmony need not work together in coordinated fashion. They may have shown up for their appointment, but they didn't arrive in the same car.

In many cadences the notes of the melody have little to do with either the timing or the pitch content of the harmony except that the melody and the harmony both reach resolution on the tonic at approximately the same time at the end of a phrase. As the cadences in example 3.12 show, the relatively independent melodic cadence generally consists of notes from a pentatonic scale.

The conclusions to be drawn about cadences are mixed. On the one hand, cadences seem to be decidedly unimportant in this repertoire as a whole—they are by no means a given in rock. In many pieces, melody does not work together with harmony and rhythm to create unified gestures called phrases that tend toward points of resolution called cadences. Instead, in many cases melody moves in short surges toward hypermetrically strong downbeats. In Chubby Checker's "The Twist" (also recorded by composer Hank Ballard), Foreigner's "Juke Box Hero," and others like them, the voice acts more as a rhythm instrument than as a bearer of sustained gestures. Then, where cadences do occur, they follow a wide variety of harmonic and melodic formulas and don't necessarily fall into any patterns ending with tonal closure.

3.11. Independent melody and harmony in cadences from (a) Elton John's "Rocket Man," (b) James Taylor's "Handy Man," and (c) Hootie and the Blowfish's "Only Wanna Be With You."

3.11 a.

ROCKET MAN (I Think It's Gonna Be A Long Long Time), by Elton John and Bernie Taupin. © 1972 (Renewed) Dick James Music Ltd. Universal/Dick James Music Ltd, 77 Fulham Palace Rd., London W6. All Rights for U.S. and Canada controlled and administered by Universal—Songs of Polygram. International, Inc. All Rights Reserved. International Copyright Secured. Used by Permission. WARNER BROS. PUBLICATIONS U.S. INC., Miami, FL 33014. Used by permission of Music Sales Ltd

3.11 b.

HANDY MAN, by Otis Blackwell and Jimmy Jones. © 1959 (Renewed) EMI Unart Catalog Inc. All Rights Reserved. Used by Permission. WARNER BROS. PUBLICATIONS U.S. INC., Miami, FL 33014

3.11 c.

Only Wanna Be With You. Words and Music by Darius Carlos Rucker, Everett Dean Felber, Mark William Bryan and. James George Sonefeld. © 1994 EMI APRIL MUSIC INC. and MONICA'S RELUCTANCE TO LOB. All Rights Controlled and Administered by EMI APRIL MUSIC INC. All Rights Reserved International Copyright Secured Used by Permission

3.12. Even greater independence of melody and harmony in cadences from (a) Alanis Morissette's "Hand In My Pocket" and (b) Oasis's "Don't Look Back In Anger."

3.12 a.

HAND IN MY POCKET, by Alanis Morissette and Glen Ballard. © 1995 Songs of Universal, Inc., Vanhurst Place, Universal—MCA Music Publishing, a. Division of Universal Studios, Inc., and Aerostation Corporation. All Rights for Vanhurst Place Controlled and Administered by Songs Of Universal, Inc. All Rights for Aerostation Corporation Controlled and Administered by Universal MCA Music. Publishing, a Division of Universal Studios, Inc. All Rights Reserved. Used by Permission. WARNER BROS. PUBLICATIONS U.S. INC., Miami, FL 33014

3.12 b.

Don't Look Back In Anger. Words and Music by Noel Gallagher. Copyright
© 1995 Sony Music Publishing United Kingdom and Creation Songs Ltd. All Rights Administered by Sony/ATV Music Publishing, 8 Music Square West, Nashville, TN. 37203. International Copyright Secured All Rights Reserved

This common avoidance of cadential closure, when viewed with several other features of rock style, presents a clearly nonteleological message. These songs do not seem static; they move. But the movement is less often progression—that is, motion toward a goal—than it is cyclical motion. If this music follows a path, the path does not start at one point and end at another. Its shape is more like an athletic track, that of a "6"; once started on such a track, one soon returns to previously trodden passages and begins a never-ending loop. A person doesn't travel such a loop in order to reach a particular place but to traverse a particular distance, sometimes attempting to do so more quickly than others, as when racing; often (and this makes the analogy more germane) one makes the loop simply for the benefits of the traveling itself, as when training or exercising.

Similarly, rock for the most part has no harmonic or melodic goal that, once reached, signals the end of the piece. But herein arises a problem. A CD, a song on the radio, and a live performance must each cease playing at some point. How is this to be achieved? To tack on a closed cadence in a piece where such cadences don't play a part would be to spoil the integrity of the style. The most common solution for recordings is ideal for this music: the fade-out. Far from being just an easy way out of a problem for crude, uneducated musicians who are too lazy to think of an ending, the fade-out is actually the only way for this music to end with preserved stylistic integrity. In live performance, where fade-out is impractical, musicians often end such songs simply by choosing, according to what is considered an appropriate length for the piece, one of the chords and marking that chord as the end of the piece by sustaining it, much as a runner will continue on a track until, according to the length of the race, a tape is placed across the path to signify the end point.

On the other hand, the very lack of closure in most rock makes cadences potentially significant when they do occur. The frequently recurring, totally coordinated resolution in Stevie Wonder's "I Just Called To Say I Love You," for instance, while keeping the song from the sustained drive and harmonic variety of some of his more interesting compositions, leaves the listener no room to doubt the sincerity of the line "I love you from the bottom of my heart."*

The effect becomes clearer when compared to the insincerity clearly present at the end of each verse in John Waite's "Missing You," as the singer tells the woman who has left his life that he doesn't miss her at all. The harmony and melody may both reach tonic at the end of the line, but the end of the line comes at the beginning of a hypermeasure. This hyperdownbeat's impulse for continuation provides the perfect setting for the line: if the statement really represented the singer's last word on the subject, why would the music have to keep going, and why would the singer have to repeat the line again so soon? Methinks John Waite and his nonteleological constructions do protest too much. But, of course, that is the whole idea of the song. (Does the absence of the negative in the title represent merely abbreviation of the refrain or rather an "unintentional" slip?)

In Fleetwood Mac's "I'm So Afraid," closure represents not sincerity but fi-

*I Just Called To Say I Love You. Words and Music by Stevie Wonder. © 1984 JOBETE MUSIC CO., INC. and BLACK BULL MUSIC c/o EMI APRIL MUSIC INC. All Rights Reserved International Copyright Secured Used by Permission

nality of life itself. In the first verse, the persona sings of a life of loneliness and despair. The history doesn't take long to tell because it is cut entirely of one cloth; as he says in the second half,

I never change
I never will.

His emotional response to this life of never-changing loneliness is, as the title suggests, fear: "I'm so afraid the way I feel." But fear suggests an eventual change. As Mr. Buckingham sings the chorus of the song in a wavering, fear-filled falsetto tone, he explains the object of that fear. Reverting to infantile grammar, he ends the chorus with

So afraid
Slip and I fall and I die.*

A strong, closed cadence could not be more appropriate; remember the two definitions of *cadere* offered at the beginning of this chapter. And in fact the end of the line offers the first cadence of the song in which melody, harmony, and rhythm converge in a coordinated fashion: the final word (sung on the tonic) and the final tonic harmony occur together on the downbeat of the third measure of the third hypermeasure of the chorus. All instruments simply hold the notes of the chord until the drummer signals a cutoff with an ominously low series of strokes on a tom-tom. The feared death offers no relief, no reward, merely cessation.

The singer's fear extends to the imminence of his death as well. The timing of this clearly closed cadence gives it the sense of being early when compared to the other cadences of the song. The vocal phrases of the verse all end halfway through the fourth measure. Each of the first two phrases of the chorus ends halfway through the third measure. (One short fragment ends on the first downbeat of the second hypermeasure). The position of the end of the chorus then, on the downbeat of the third measure, completes a pattern in which cadences come earlier and earlier. If the life presented by this song has any tendency at all, it is toward an early demise.

Note, however, that the singer seems to prefer the life of never-ending despair to death: it is death he fears, not the continuation of life. After the second chorus, "I'm So Afraid" offers us a picture of the brave, continuing struggle.

The singer, having exhausted even the minimal verbal ability displayed in the chorus, now expresses his despair through an improvised guitar solo. (Mr. Buckingham, portraying the song's persona, both sings and plays the guitar part on the recording.) The extended solo, full of long, soft, wailing tones, takes place over repetitions of the harmonic pattern of the introduction. The first hypermeasure of this pattern ends on v, the second on VII. The lack of resolution offered by either chord makes a fade-out musically appropriate. This fade-out takes on special significance, though. Its unusually great length, encompassing many repetitions of the unresolved harmonic pattern, tells us that although the singer fears sudden and utter annihilation as the only way out of his cycle of despair, he may be doomed not to see his fear fulfilled.

So far we have sketched an outline of the basic rhythmic units of rock, defining those units and examining the ways these units begin and end. We will now attempt to add color and depth to the outline by examining what happens in between, turning first to the specifics of the harmonic content of rock.

4

Chord type and harmonic palette

Tone systems used in melodies and tone systems used in harmonies are not necessarily the same. Although we have seen that chromaticism occurs in melodies only as an embellishment of a basic diatonic system, all of rock's harmonic systems have at least some potential for chromaticism—and some have a great deal.

In traditional tonal music, chord quality generally depends on tone system: some chords are major and some minor because of the way they lie in the scale. In rock the situation is generally reversed: although some pieces seem to use chord qualities chosen to fit a certain scale, the harmonic tone systems generally result from a combination of harmonies. Rock borrows its basic harmonies from earlier tonal music (major and minor triads, seventh chords, etc.), but it combines these harmonies in a novel way. Given a tonic chord, the other chords tend to cluster in one of three ways, or systems. The range of harmonic choices provided by each system is called a "palette," in that, like an artist's palette, it provides the composer with a ready set of colors from which to choose.

The task of describing the precise chord qualities commonly used in rock is complicated slightly by changes in chord-quality preference over the course of history, as well as by the acceptance of some new chord types suggested by rock's distinctive interplay of melody and harmony. The resulting chord qualities and the chromaticism possible in each of the three harmonic systems display a surprising complexity.

MELODY AND HARMONY

The harmonies used in rock are almost all major and minor triads, or chords based on them. The most frequent alterations involve various extensions and added tones, alterations that spring from two sources: (1) the distinctive way melody and harmony interact in rock and (2) the use of pedal points in instrumental parts, often by means of open strings in guitar chords.

The interaction of melody and harmony in rock is best understood in relation to melody and harmony in Western music over the ages. Historically, melody came first. Most European music from the time of ancient Greece through the early Middle Ages seems to have had only one melodic line at a time, a texture known as "monophony."

Then around 900, Parisian musicians began to play two or more melodies at a time, such that the two notes heard simultaneously at structurally significant moments blended well, a texture known as polyphony. A pair of notes that blended harmonically was called a consonance, meaning "sounding [well] together."

By the 1500s, melodies were being combined in such a way that three-note sonorities formed of combinations of consonances—thirds, fifths, sixths, and octaves—filled most pieces. The primary stuff of composition, however, was still melody; composers recognized few conventions dictating which harmonies were to appear at which points and which patterns of succession harmonies should follow. Notes forming dissonant intervals were used but had to be treated as obvious melodic embellishments of notes forming consonances, that is, they were generally preceded and followed by steps.

Starting around 1600, composers began thinking about these consonant combinations, which they called harmonies or chords, as primary units of composition and devised conventions concerning which chord types were to be used when, and how chords might succeed one another. For the next 350 years, many pieces were written in a texture known as homophony, in which certain parts were devoted to chords, while a melody moved above them. This primary melody now had to use notes from the current chord most of the time, with notes outside the chord allowed only as melodic embellishments of the harmonic pitches.

In rock, although it is homophonic, all these assumptions are loosened. Melody is allowed to interact with harmony more freely, and just as the combination of melodies in the Renaissance suggested the chords used in the homophonic music of the following centuries, the interplay of melody and harmony in rock suggests new harmonies as standard. Sonorities created by the combination of guitar (or keyboard) and voice parts enter the musicians' ears and appear in later years as integrated harmonies in the instrumental parts alone.[1] The types of chords used in rock therefore change as history unfolds.

Much of the time, rock follows the traditional custom: a note is considered stable (i.e., not an embellishment and not requiring resolution) only if it fits the current harmony. But at times in rock, certain pitches of the scale are treated as stable despite the harmonic context. In Chuck Berry's "Rock And Roll Music," for instance, the lowered seventh scale degree is treated as stable whether the chord is I, IV, or V.[2] (See example 4.1.) It is the highest note of the chorus, is repeated often, begins most of the vocal phrases (thus requiring no preparation), and occurs on strong beats: it cannot be an embellishment.

Nearly forty years later, we see much the same thing happening with the first and second scale degrees in the chorus of Soul Asylum's "Runaway Train." (See example 4.2.) The first vocal phrase concludes in measure 2 on a D. This pitch, being the last of the phrase, has no resolution and as a result cannot be an embellishment; it is treated as stable. Yet the pitch does not fit the C major harmony occurring at that time. The second vocal phrase, although similar to the first, ends on a C. So here C is treated as melodically stable, and yet it, like the D at the end of the first phrase, clashes with the harmony—in this case the E minor harmony of measures 3 and 4. C is in fact clearly treated as stable throughout these two measures despite the harmony: it is the first pitch and the highest pitch, lasts four full beats, and is followed by a leap. The case is similar in measures 7 and 8, where the melodically stable C clashes with the G major harmony.

In a third example, the Beatles' "A Hard Day's Night," the fifth and lowered third scale degrees are treated as stable at moments when they do not fit the harmony. (See example 4.3.) The stability of the fifth scale degree, D, could

4.1. A lowered seventh scale degree as a stable nonharmonic pitch in Chuck
Berry's "Rock And Roll Music."

not be clearer than it is in measure 1: it lasts the full duration of the measure
and part of the next. And yet the harmony beneath it changes to a chord that
contains no D. D is also treated as melodically stable in measure 3, despite the
F major harmony at the time. The lowered third comes in at the end of the
chorus, where it fits neither the C major nor the G major harmony heard
against it.

These three examples involve a conflict between instrumental harmonies
and a single melodic pitch. When vocal harmonies occur, the conflict can be
even more drastic. For instance, in the Eagles' "Take It To The Limit," the vocal harmonies marked "x," "y," and "z," simple triads themselves, clash with the
instrumental chords they occur against. (See example 4.4.) None of the vocal
structures can be explained as merely a passing combination of traditional embellishments. Chord x, besides dominating the measure in duration, is fol-

4.2. First and second scale degrees as stable nonharmonic pitches in Soul
Asylum's "Runaway Train."

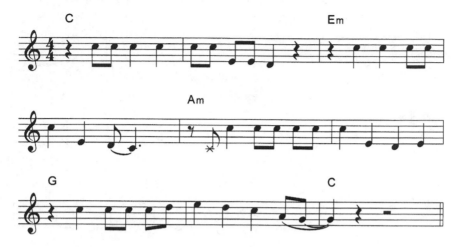

RUNAWAY TRAIN, by David Pirner. © 1992 WB Music Corp. and LFR
Music. All Rights Administered by WB Music Corp. All Rights Reserved.
Used by Permission. WARNER BROS. PUBLICATIONS U.S. INC.,
Miami, FL 33014

lowed by a rest, not a resolution, while chords y and z have no preparations and
leap in all voices to the following sonorities.

Occasionally, the same combination of clashing chords occurs with instruments alone, as in the second half of the verse to Boston's "Long Time." The
guitar sustains an F major triad while the organ plays against it F, C minor, B♭-
sus, and B♭ chords.

The second source of triad extension in rock is the use of pedal points in
instrumental parts. A clear example occurs in the Supremes' "You Keep Me
Hangin' On." (See example 4.5.) During the chorus, one electric guitar plays
a rhythmic figure exclusively on the pitch E (actually two Es separated by an
octave), while the other instruments play A major, G major, and F major
chords. The guitar's E fits the first of these chords but not the second or
third.

In many other examples, a single guitar sustains one or more pitches
through several chords by means of open strings. Consider the introduction to
John Denver's "The Eagle And The Hawk," in which the top two strings of the
guitar, B and E, are left open for five consecutive chords: B major, A major, G
major, F major, and E major. (See example 4.6.)

4.3. Fifth and lowered third scale degrees as stable nonharmonic pitches in the Beatles' "A Hard Day's Night."

A Hard Day's Night. from A HARD DAY'S NIGHT. Words and Music by John Lennon and Paul McCartney. Copyright © 1964 Sony/ATV Songs LLC. Copyright Renewed. All Rights Administered by Sony/ATV Music Publishing, 8 Music Square West, Nashville, TN. 37203. International Copyright Secured All Rights Reserved

Although the notes of the open strings form a natural part of the last chord, they contribute to each of the first three sonorities one note outside the basic triad, and two notes to the F major chord. Similar examples can be found in, among other pieces, Tom Petty's "Free Falling" and "Name," by the Goo Goo Dolls. (See example 4.7.)

As "Name" demonstrates, these pedal points can be so consistent that the movement of the bass note alone constitutes harmonic change. The bass normally therefore bears the burden of harmonic identification, while the structure of the other pitches merely provides color. As a result, most rock harmonies are in root position, that is, the root of the chord is in the bass. Inversions are infrequent enough that when they do appear, they generally are integral to the character of the music, as in much of the music of Phil Collins (e.g., "Against All Odds," with its prominent second-inversion chord at the

4.4. Clash between vocal harmonies and instrumental harmonies in the Eagles' "Take It To The Limit."

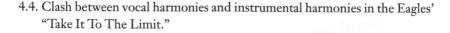

TAKE IT TO THE LIMIT. Written by Don Henley, Glenn Frey, and Randy Meisner. © 1975 Cass County Music/Red Cloud Music (BMI)/Nebraska Music (ASCAP)

beginning of the chorus), Peter Cetera (Chicago's "You're The Inspiration," with the numerous first-inversion triads at the end of the verse), and Elton John ("Rocket Man," with its inverted chords at the cadences, or "Someone Saved My Life Tonight," with the second-inversion tonic chord in its introduction).

As the examples given above suggest, the most common tones treated as stable regardless of the harmonic context are the first and fifth scale degrees. Early in rock history, the lowered seventh also frequently acts as stable, and in blues-influenced pieces, the lowered third. Less common is the stable use of the second scale degree. Rarely are the fourth and sixth scale degrees treated as stable.

4.5. A pedal point as a source of complex harmonies in the Supremes' "You Keep Me Hangin' On."

You Keep Me Hangin' On. Words and Music by Edward Holland, Lamont Dozier and Brian Holland. © 1966 (Renewed 1994) JOBETE MUSIC CO., INC. All Rights Controlled and Administered by EMI BLACKWOOD MUSIC INC. on behalf of. STONE AGATE MUSIC (A Division of JOBETE MUSIC CO., INC.). All Rights Reserved International Copyright Secured Used by Permission

4.6. Open guitar strings as a source of complex harmonies in John Denver's "The Eagle And The Hawk."

The Eagle And The Hawk. Words by John Denver. Music by John Denver and Mike Taylor. Copyright © 1971; Renewed 1999 Cherry Lane Music Publishing Company, Inc. (ASCAP) and. DreamWorks Songs (ASCAP). Worldwide Rights for DreamWorks Songs Administered by Cherry Lane Music Publishing. Company, Inc. International Copyright Secured All Rights Reserved

The first and fifth scale degrees work so well as stable pitches because they are acoustically the most stable pitches of the scale. As a result they suggest a strength and confidence that contributes expressively in certain cases. For instance, in Alanis Morissette's "You Learn," the alternation of scale degrees one and five in the melody of the chorus occurring against a constantly changing harmonic background mirrors perfectly the message of the text—that in all of life's events, good or bad, knowledge steadily grows, making all that happens worthwhile:

> You grieve you learn
> You choke you learn
> You laugh you learn
> You choose you learn
> You pray you learn
> You ask you learn
> You live you learn.*

*YOU LEARN, by Alanis Morissette and Glen Ballard. © 1995 Songs of Universal, Inc., Vanhurst Place, Universal—MCA Music Publishing, a. Division of Universal Studios, Inc., and Aerostation Corporation. All Rights for Vanhurst Place Controlled and Administered by Songs Of Universal, Inc. All Rights for Aerostation Corporation Controlled and Administered by Universal—MCA Music. Publishing, a Division of Universal Studios, Inc. All Rights Reserved. Used by Permission. WARNER BROS. PUBLICATIONS U.S. INC., Miami, FL 33014

4.7. Pedal points as sources of complex harmonies in (a) Tom Petty's "Free Falling" and (b) the Goo Goo Dolls' "Name."

4.7 a.

FREE FALLIN', by Tom Petty and Jeff Lynne. © 1989 Gone Gator Music and EMI April Music Inc. All Rights Reserved International Copyright Secured Used by Permission. Used by Permission. WARNER BROS. PUBLICATIONS U.S. INC., Miami, FL 33014

4.7 b.

Name. Words and Music by John Rzeznik. © 1995 EMI VIRGIN SONGS, INC., FULL VOLUME MUSIC and SCRAP METAL MUSIC. All Rights Controlled and Administered by EMI VIRGIN SONGS, INC. All Rights Reserved International Copyright Secured Used by Permission

Similarly, the stable first and fifth scale degrees in the title line of Amy Grant's "Lead Me On" declare that faith in the never-changing God comforts and sustains even the cruelly enslaved or the politically oppressed awaiting genocidal execution.

CHORD TYPES

The most common chord types in rock are the major and minor triads. Although many other chords are possible, triads have functioned as primary harmonic structures throughout the rock era. Buddy Holly's "That'll Be The Day" (1957), the Beatles' "Hey Jude" (1968), Three Dog Night's "Joy To The World" (1970), and Bobby McFerrin's "Don't Worry Be Happy" (1988) demonstrate that popular songs from four successive decades use triads primarily. Triads, in fact, constitute the most common chord type in the era as a whole.

Just behind these triads in frequency lies a class of chords consisting of major and minor triads with added tones. These chords function as secondary, unstable structures in pieces where triads predominate. But in certain styles and periods, as noted below, some of these other chords take the primary role, occurring more frequently than triads and in some cases even functioning as tonic harmonies. These chords are strongly suggested by an emphasis on nonchord tones, as outlined in the previous section of this chapter. We need only look again at those examples to discover the most standard combinations.

In "Rock And Roll Music," the lowered seventh scale degree occurs with the I, IV, and V chords. (Please refer again to example 4.1.) In the case of the IV chord, A major, the D can be regarded as an embellishment, since it resolves immediately. But when sounding against the I and the V, no such interpretation is possible. Together with the I chord, E major, the D forms a dominant seventh chord. In the context of the V chord, B major, the pitch acts as a lowered third, clashing against the normal major third of the chord.

In fact, the chords suggested by this example occur frequently in rock, sometimes as moments of passing color, but often as primary harmonic structures of a piece: chords that pervade a piece and are found on several different scale degrees, including the tonic. The dominant seventh chord acts as a primary structure in many rock songs; in rock pieces following the blues harmonic pattern, for instance, the IV and V chords are almost always dominant seventh chords (or an extension of the dominant seventh such as the dominant ninth). In most blues-based songs, the tonic chord is simply a major triad, as in Bill Haley and the Comets' "Rock Around The Clock" and Buster Brown's "Fanny Mae." But in some blues-based pieces, such as Chuck Berry's "Back In

The U.S.A." and Loggins and Messina's "Your Mama Don't Dance," a dominant-seventh chord is used for the tonic harmony as well.

The chord predominates in other songs as well, appearing as a tonic har-
mony in many, including Little Richard's "Lucille" (1957), the Beatles' "I Saw
Her Standing There" (1963), Nilsson's "Coconut" (1971), Jim Croce's "You
Don't Mess Around With Jim" (1972), the Drifters' "On Broadway" (1963),
and Oasis' "Roll With It" (1995). As suggested by this list, rock musicians used
this chord as a primary structure mostly in the first fifteen years of the era;
"Roll With It," the most Beatlesque tune on Oasis' Beatlesque *(What's The
Story) Morning Glory?* album, sounds so retrospective partly because of the use
of the dominant seventh as a tonic harmony. (The resemblance of Liam Gallagher's voice to John Lennon's, the tone of the guitars, the opening ninth
chords à la "She's A Woman," and the Ringo-like open high hat add to that impression.) After 1970, however, extensions of the dominant seventh, such as
the dominant ninth and dominant thirteenth, emerged as stable tonic harmonies, mainly in the funk and disco pieces of that decade, such as White
Cherry's "Play That Funky Music."

Much more than dominant-structure chords, however, major seventh and
minor seventh chords became common choices for tonic harmonies starting in
the second half of the 1970s. These chords cut across many stylistic lines of this
disparate period, pervading soul, country rock, soft rock, MOR (middle-of-the-
road styles), jazz rock, funk, and disco. In soul and disco, a tonic minor seventh
harmony often alternated with a dominant seventh or dominant ninth chord on
$\hat{4}$, such as in LaBelle's "Lady Marmalade," and Chic's "Le Freak." In other
styles, major seventh and minor seventh chords generally mix (usually with
eleventh chords; see below) to create a diatonic composite in either major or
minor mode. Examples include the Eagles' "One Of These Nights" (minor),
Bread's "Make It With You" (major), America's "Tin Man" (major), Blood,
Sweat & Tears' "You've Made Me So Very Happy" (major), the third (and main)
part of Paul McCartney and Wings' "Band On The Run" (major), and Carly Simon's "The Right Thing To Do" (major). I dare not neglect the most famous
major seventh chord in the history of music, the one that opens Chicago's
"Colour My World," even though the song departs from the usual pattern described above by "colouring" the harmonic succession with several chromatic
chords. Still, seven of that song's fourteen chords, including the tonic, are major
sevenths or ninths, demonstrating the primacy of that chord type.

After a short-lived simplification of harmonic types achieved by the punk
and New Wave movements of the early 1980s, the major and minor seventh
chords returned as basic harmonic material in songs such as Frankie Goes to

Hollywood's "Relax," the Fixx's "One Thing Leads To Another," Gloria Estefan's "Words Get In The Way," and Bobby Brown's "My Prerogative."

The second extended harmony suggested in "Rock And Roll Music," a triad containing both a major and minor third, is sometimes called a "split-third chord." This chord is found only rarely as an integrated harmony, and only in guitar or keyboard parts; one example occurs in Paul McCartney's "Maybe I'm Amazed." Much more common, however, is a dominant seventh chord with added minor third. This chord is more commonly referred to in sheet music as a dominant seventh with sharp ninth, for example, C, E, G, B♭, and D♯ as opposed to C, E♭, E, G, and B♭. (See example 4.8.) It was used as a primary structure

4.8. A dominant seventh with raised ninth (a) as compared to a dominant
seventh with split third (b).

and tonic chord mainly in the funk and disco music of the 1970s, such as Heatwave's "Boogie Nights." As with the major seventh chord however, the seven-sharp-nine may forever be associated primarily with one song, one that powerfully hit the rock scene in 1966, the Jimi Hendrix Experience's "Purple Haze."

The split-third chord is also suggested by the last note and chord in "A Hard Day's Night." The beginning of that song's verse provides the germ of another important class of chords coming to the fore in the 1980s. In "A Hard Day's Night," the voice holds a D over a G-C-G harmonic succession. The note fits the G major chord, but it is a second above the root of the C major chord and therefore not part of the basic triad. When C, D, E, and G are played together *as a chord*, the result is known as an added-note chord.

One important traditional assumption of the theory of harmony is that standard chords are built in thirds. A C major triad, for instance, is formed of two overlapping thirds: C to E, and E to G. Chords with more members are formed by adding even more thirds onto a triadic foundation: B or B♭ (a third above G) is added to form a seventh chord, and D (a third above B) is added to the seventh chord to form a ninth chord. Around the turn of the century, however, Debussy and other composers began using chords that could not be arranged into a stack of overlapping thirds but could be seen as triads with additional notes. One common form, the chord from "A Hard Day's Night," is known as an added-second chord, since the notes can be described as those of a C major triad plus a second above C. The chord is notated in sheet music as "C(add2)" or simply "C2." It is also sometimes notated as "C(add9)," since D can be found a ninth above C as well as a second above. Academic textbooks, jazz sheet music, and rock sheet music all agree that a ninth chord and an added-ninth chord differ in that the ninth chord has a seventh, whereas the added-ninth chord consists simply of a triad plus one other note. As a result, C9 includes B♭, C(add9) does not. Added-second chords serve as primary, stable harmonies in many songs, including the Rolling Stones' "You Can't Always Get What You Want," Mr. Mister's "Broken Wings," Don Henley's "The End Of The Innocence," the Police's "Every Breath You Take," Cheap Trick's "The Flame," Lionel Richie's "All Night Long (All Night)," Men at Work's "It's A Mistake," DeBarge's "Rhythm Of The Night," Starship's "We Built This City," and Deniece Williams' "Let's Hear It For The Boy."

"Runaway Train" contains the suggestion of one other type of added-note harmony: the added-fourth chord. (Please refer again to example 4.2.) In measures 7 and 8 of the example, C is treated as a stable melodic pitch against a G major triad. The total sonority, including the triad in the guitar and the note in the voice, would have to be called an added-note chord since the notes cannot be arranged in stacked thirds. Because C is a fourth above the root of the triad, the chord is called an added-fourth chord. The particular chord described here would usually be notated in sheet music as "G(add4)." This chord type almost always appears on the fifth degree of the scale, the stable tonic pitch acting as the added tone. One instance is provided by the second chord in the verse to "Runaway Train." Another appears in the introduction to the Who's "Baba O'Riley." (See example 4.9.)

Measure 3 of "A Hard Day's Night," the second chord of "You Keep Me Hanging On," and the third chord of "The Eagle And The Hawk" suggest that the added-sixth chord appears fairly often in rock. In fact it occurs only occasionally, such as at the end of the Beatles' "She Loves You." McCartney reports that the chord, included at the suggestion of George Harrison, struck producer George Martin as "old-fashioned."[3]

Diminished triads and diminished seventh chords are rare in rock; as noted above, standard practice is to use only major and minor triads and extensions of them. But diminished chords occur just often enough to prove the rule. That is, the occasional diminished chord shows that rock musicians know how to play them but avoid them by compositional choice (whether consciously or unconsciously). One occurs in "Don't Look Back In Anger," by Oasis, and another in David Bowie's "Space Oddity." (See example 4.21, below). Two occur in the emotional phrase just before the refrain in Paul Young's "Everytime You Go Away."

4.9. Added-note chords resulting from stable use of $\hat{1}$ and $\hat{5}$ in The Who's "Baba O'Riley."

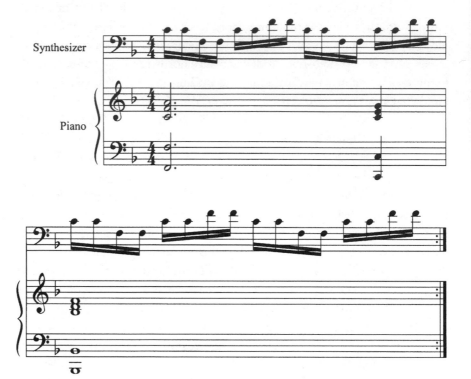

4.10. Use of an augmented triad as linear harmony.

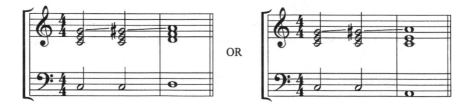

OR

The augmented triad (notated as "aug" or "+") is even rarer than the diminished and occurs almost always as a linear embellishment linking an opening tonic chord with the next chord. When the tonic harmony is major, the augmented chord arises as the result of chromatic passing motion between the fifth and sixth scale degrees. (See example 4.10.) Such an example occurs in John Lennon's "(Just like) Starting Over," where the sixth scale degree forms part of the ii chord. The chord arises from *descending* passing motion leading *to* the tonic harmony in the Beatles' "All My Loving"; the harmonic succession is vi-I+-I.

Infrequent, but worthy of mention because of its unusual character, is the minor triad with major seventh (e.g., F, A♭, C, E). The chord is virtually always found on the fourth scale degree in the major mode. (The example just given would occur in C major.) The seventh of the chord is therefore the third scale degree. Given the propensity of the third scale degree to be lowered as a blues alteration, it is striking that it so frequently stays stubbornly fixed in this situation, producing as a result a historically rare chord type. Examples can be found in Lesley Gore's "It's My Party," the Chiffons' "One Fine Day," Mariah Carey's "Vision Of Love," and the Beatles' "Magical Mystery Tour."

Rock uses three chord qualities that do not represent triads or extensions of them. The first is the dominant-eleventh chord. Although eleventh implies that the chord is constructed simply by superposing another interval of a third above the ninth of a chord, such a chord virtually never occurs in actual music. (See example 4.11a.) Most texts explain that since the eleventh of such a chord would clash with the third, the latter is left out. The absence of a third in a chord, however, seems to constitute abandonment of the principle of building chords in thirds. Although some sheet-music publishers preserve the theoretical name of the chord in example 4.11b, calling it C11, many refer to the chord

4.11. The eleventh chord (a) as theoretically conceived and (b) as it appears in actual music.

descriptively as Gm7/C.[4] Songs using this chord prominently include Billy Joel's "Just The Way You Are," Paul McCartney and Stevie Wonder's "Ebony And Ivory," and Mariah Carey's "Love Takes Time." The eleventh chord is almost always found on the fifth scale degree of a major key; the chord shown above in example 4.11 would normally be found in the key of F. It is, however, sometimes found in a minor key. An eleventh chord is found on the fifth scale degree in C minor in Carole King's "I Feel The Earth Move."

The second type of harmony not constructed from extending a triad is the open-fifth chord. The sonority is the standard harmony in much heavy metal, such as Deep Purple's "Smoke On The Water." Usually in this subgenre, the harmonic complexity lacking in the chord's construction is supplied by various techniques of distortion, which generally add high harmonics or enhance those already present. The open-fifth chord is also common in other rock styles from the 1980s, for instance, in the Cars' "You Might Think." In such genres, rather than enhancing the chord through distortion, players often emphasize the austerity of the chord by muting the strings and plucking the chord repeatedly. Some sheet-music publishers retain the traditional notion of chords built in thirds and indicate a harmony consisting of C and G, for example, as C(no 3). Others indicate this chord as C5.

The third class is so-called suspended harmony. This chord is generally thought of as a triad with a fourth instead of a third: C, F, and G, for example. This particular sonority would be indicated in sheet music as Csus4 or simply Csus. The name comes from the traditional idea that, in the chord just mentioned, F would be held over (i.e., suspended) from the previous chord and would be expected to resolve down to E. In rock, the term is used to indicate only the harmonic structure, with no implications about what comes before or after. The fourth of the chord is traditionally prepared only about as often as it is unprepared. The chord is usually resolved in a traditional manner, with some exceptions. For instance, the last chord of the first bridge in the Police's "Every Breath You Take" is an unresolved suspended chord. The introduction and chorus of Shocking Blue's "Venus," contains one unresolved suspended chord, and the introduction to Chicago's "Make Me Smile" contains two different suspended chords with no traditional resolution.

Suspended chords may have sevenths (virtually always minor sevenths) and even ninths. A 9sus chord, however, is identical to an eleventh chord (see above) and may be labeled in that way instead. Another possible variation, infrequently found, is the sus2 chord: a chord with a second instead of a third.

NATURAL-MINOR SYSTEM

Having delineated the basic types of harmonies, we can move on to the combinations of harmonies rock composers normally use within a given composition, the palettes they use to paint their harmonic landscapes. The simplest of these we shall call the natural-minor system, which carries the following defining features: (1) the use of only major and minor triads (or seventh chords

4.12. The harmonic palette of the natural-minor system.

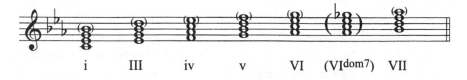

i   III   iv   v   VI   (VI^{dom7}) VII

made out of them) and (2) keeping the natural-minor scale pure as the aggregate pitch content. As a result, it involves minor triads on $\hat{1}$, $\hat{4}$, and $\hat{5}$, and major triads on $\hat{3}$, $\hat{6}$, and $\hat{7}$. (See example 4.12.)[5] It is clear that following the two defining features consistently allows no form of chord on the second scale degree: either a major or a minor triad would involve a pitch outside the natural-minor scale, whereas the chord that fits the scale, a diminished triad, would depart with the standard of using only major and minor triads.

The natural-minor system, though the simplest of the harmonic systems used in rock, is also the least common. Enough examples exist, however, to recognize it as a standard harmonic system of the style. Pieces employing the natural-minor system include Billy Ocean's "Caribbean Queen" (see example 4.13), REM's "Losing My Religion," Styx's "Blue Collar Man (Long Nights)," K. C. and the Sunshine Band's "That's the Way (I Like It)," the Romantics' "Talking In Your Sleep," the Animals' "Please Don't Let Me Be Misunderstood," Fleetwood Mac's "I'm So Afraid," and Bill Withers' "Ain't No Sunshine."

4.13. A harmonic chart of the chorus of Billy Ocean's "Caribbean Queen,"
showing use of the natural-minor harmonic palette.

Dm: i | VII | VI7 | III⁶ | iv7 | VI7 VII | i7 v7 | i7 v7 |

The simple triadic symbols displayed in example 4.12 are not intended to suggest that the system uses only triads; any triad indicated, even the tonic, may be represented in an actual piece by a triad, seventh chord, ninth chord, and so on. (The same assumption applies to the other palettes described later in this chapter.) Triads in this palette, when extended to seventh chords, normally use the form of the seventh appearing in the natural-minor scale, just as the defining features of the system would suggest. One prominent exception involves the VI7, which often employs the lowered fifth scale degree, making the chord a dominant seventh and thereby adding a touch of chromaticism to the palette. A prominent example occurs in Eric Clapton's "I Shot The Sheriff." The piece, in G minor, uses G minor seventh, C minor seventh, and D minor seventh chords, clearly locating the harmonic scheme within the natural-minor system. Also included, however, is a VI chord, sometimes as a major seventh and sometimes as a dominant seventh.

A few cases introduce a bit of chromaticism with a major triad built on the lowered second scale degree. Such a chord may be indicated by its traditional symbol, N (for "Neapolitan"—it seems such a chord was popular in Naples at one time), although no traditional functional connotations accompany the symbol. Examples include Fleetwood Mac's "Save Me," Journey's "Who's Crying Now," and the Rolling Stones' "Mother's Little Helper."

CHROMATIC-MINOR SYSTEM

Whereas the construction of the natural-minor system involves the consistent use of a scale at the expense of variety in triad qualities, the chromatic-minor system involves consistent use of a particular triad type—the major triad—at the expense of purity of scale. The chromatic-minor system consists of major triads based on every step of the natural-minor scale, with one exception: the tonic triad may be either major or minor. On occasion, a major triad built on the lowered second scale degree replaces the normal II. (See example 4.14. Because this harmonic system is unlike any traditional tonal system, the chord built on the second scale degree is called II. In the major system, described below, such a chord will be labeled V/V.)

4.14. The harmonic palette of the chromatic-minor system.

I or i   (N)   II   III   IV   V   VI   VII

In rock, the mode of the piece depends on nothing but the tonic triad. This system may therefore serve either major keys or minor keys. It is called a minor system simply because the chords are built on the pitches of a minor scale. It is called the *chromatic*-minor system because, unlike the natural-minor system, which allows chromaticism only in a few cases, the fundamental principle involves ignoring purity of scale in favor of uniformity of chord quality. In the pitch content of the system as a whole, chromatic variants are found on the third scale degree (see, for instance, I and III), fourth scale degree (II and IV), sixth scale degree (IV and VI), and seventh scale degree (V and VII). When seventh chords appear, they are usually dominant sevenths. The appearance of these chords creates further chromaticism; use of the VI7, for instance, results

4.15. A harmonic chart of the Rolling Stones' "Brown Sugar," showing use of
the chromatic-minor harmonic palette without II.

Introduction
C: III | I | VI VII | I   :|

Verse
I | I | IV | IV | I | I | VII | I |

Chorus
V | V | I | I | V | V | I | I |

in the presence of two versions of the fifth scale degree (normal $\hat{5}$ in I7, III7,
and V7, but lowered $\hat{5}$ in the VI7).

As a rule, II and VI are not used in the same piece, perhaps because the tritone between their roots leaves the two chords too distant. Use of the chromatic-minor palette without II can be seen in the Rolling Stones' "Brown
Sugar." (See example 4.15.) The Beatles' "Sgt. Pepper's Lonely Hearts Club
Band" uses the chromatic minor system without VI. (See example 4.16.) Other
examples, generally using most of the chords in the chromatic-minor system,
include the following (since this palette is so different from traditional harmonic systems, numerous examples are given in order to show that (1) it is not
an anomaly and (2) its expressive purposes are varied): Eddie Floyd's "Knock
On Wood" (major tonic); the Beatles' "Here Comes The Sun" (major tonic);
the Turtles' "Happy Together" (minor tonic chord in the verse and major tonic
chord in the chorus); R.E.O. Speedwagon's "Ridin' The Storm Out" (minor
tonic); the Rolling Stones' "Paint It, Black" (minor tonic); the Clovers' "Love
Potion No. 9" (minor tonic); "Green Onions" (open 5th as tonic harmony), by

4.16. A harmonic chart of the Beatles' "Sgt. Pepper's Lonely Hearts Club
Band," showing use of the chromatic-minor palette without VI. (All
harmonies dominant-seventh chords.)

Verse
G: I   II | IV   I | I   II | IV   I |

II | IV | I   IV | I |

IV | VII | IV | V | V |

Chorus
I   III | IV   I | IV | I |

I   III | IV   I | II | V | etc.

Booker T. and the MGs; the Animals' "House Of The Rising Sun" (minor tonic); Jefferson Airplane's "Somebody To Love" (minor tonic); Tom Petty's "Refugee" (minor tonic); the Who's "Pinball Wizard" (major tonic) and "I Can See For Miles" (quality of tonic harmony changes); the Bangles' "Walk Like An Egyptian" (major tonic); Bachman-Turner Overdrive's "Roll On Down The Highway" (major tonic); Eric Clapton's "Cocaine" (major tonic); the Partridge Family's "I Woke Up In Love This Morning" (minor tonic); Grand Funk's "We're An American Band" (major tonic); Devo's "Whip It" (major tonic); the Go-Gos' "We Got The Beat" (with VI and II but no V); and Harry Chapin's "Cat's In The Cradle" (major tonic).

Examples of songs using the chromatic-minor system with the Neapolitan (see above, under "Natural-Minor System") include Joni Mitchell's "Help Me," the Mamas and the Papas' "Monday, Monday," "Carry On Wayward Son" (with one exceptional chord in the introduction) by Kansas, and the Moody Blues' "Nights In White Satin." Songs using the chromatic-minor system with VI(dom7) include Linda Ronstadt's "You're No Good," and Aerosmith's "Toys In The Attic."

The equivalence of the two forms of the tonic triad is demonstrated in two versions of Eric Clapton's "After Midnight." In the version on the album *Eric Clapton* (1970), the tonic chord clearly includes a major third. (The minor seventh is also present.) The succession at the beginning of each chorus is I-III-IV-I; the second half of each chorus follows the pattern I-IV-V. The slower version found on *Crossroads* uses essentially the same harmonic pattern, except that the tonic chord is minor. Thus, in two versions of the same song by the same performer, this same chromatic harmonic system works with either a major or minor tonic triad.

MAJOR SYSTEM

The full major system is a chromatic system involving variable qualities (major and minor) of several chords whose roots are built on the notes of the Mixolydian scale. (See example 4.17.) Rarely, however, will all the choices of-

4.17. The harmonic palette of the major system.

I	ii	V/V	iii	V/vi	iv	IV	v	V	vi	V/ii	VII or ♭VII

4.18. The diatonic subset of the major system.

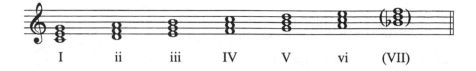

fered by this palette appear in a single composition. Many songs in fact use only the diatonic chords of the major system: I, ii, iii, IV, V, and vi. The ♭VII sometimes appears in an otherwise diatonic harmonic pattern, even though the lowered seventh scale degree clashes chromatically with the raised form found as the third of the V chord.[6] As in the natural-minor system, no combination of major or minor triads could be arranged on all seven notes of the scale while preserving the diatonic integrity of the aggregate pitch content; the only solution that would produce a purely diatonic pitch content would involve a diminished chord, a type usually avoided in rock. But the chromatic chord (here, almost always VII) arises much more frequently than it does in minor (there, generally a Neapolitan). Infrequently, the minor v appears in an otherwise diatonic harmonic setting. (See example 4.18.)

Songs using the six diatonic chords of the major system (or a portion of them) include the Young Rascals' "Lonely Too Long" (see example 4.19), Aerosmith's "Angel," the Byrds' "Turn! Turn! Turn! (To Everything There Is A Season)," and Stephanie Mills' "Never Knew Love Like This Before."

Songs using the diatonic chords (or a portion of them) plus VII include A-ha's "Take On Me" (see example 4.20), Gordon Lightfoot's "If You Could Read My Mind," Amy Grant's "Good For Me," Aretha Franklin's "(You Make Me Feel Like) A Natural Woman" (also recorded by Carole King), Bread's "Everything I Own," Elvis Costello and the Attractions' "Everyday I Write The Book," and the Traveling Wilburys' "Not Alone Any More."

A small number of songs use I, IV, and minor v as harmonies, such as the Kingsmen's "Louie Louie," K. C. and the Sunshine Band's "Get Down Tonight," and "I Know What I Like" (verse only; the chorus uses different harmonies in a different key), by Huey Lewis and the News. Because only the ma-

4.19. A harmonic chart of the Young Rascals' "Lonely Too Long," showing use of the diatonic chords of the major palette.

D: I		vi7		I		vi7		I		iii7		IV		ii7	V	
vi7		ii7		vi7		ii7	iii7	IV	V		I	V11		I	V11		etc.

4.20. A harmonic chart of A-ha's "Take On Me," showing use of the diatonic chords of the major system plus VII.

Verse
A: ii7 | V7 | I | IV7 iii7 | ii7 | V7 | I | IV7 iii7 |

ii7 | V7 | vi7 | IV |

Chorus
I | iii$_4^6$ | vi | IV | I | iii$_4^6$ | vi | IV |

I | iii$_4^6$ | vi | IV | I | V^6 | IV | V |

Bridge
iii7 | iii7 | VII | VII | iii7 | iii7 | VII | VII |

ii7 | ii7 | V7 | V7 |

jor palette accommodates all three chords, it seems that such songs fall within that system.

In traditional tonal theory, only chords that fit the major scale constitute the harmonic palette of a major key. The other chords shown in example 4.17 are traditionally explained as brief forays into another key; an A-major triad in a passage in C usually leads to a D minor chord and as a result is called a V of D minor, or V/ii. In rock, however, traditional functions do not apply (see chapter V); the presence of an A major chord in the key of C does not imply the imminent approach of D minor or even its presence anywhere else in the piece. Therefore, it is inappropriate in rock to say that these chords are not normal components of the primary key. However, rock musicians who have no formal training in music theory often use the traditional names, calling major chords on $\hat{2}$, $\hat{3}$, and $\hat{6}$ V/V, V/vi, and V/ii, respectively.[7] It would also be convenient to have a symbol for the major chords on $\hat{3}$ and $\hat{6}$ that would distinguish them from the III and VI chords of the chromatic-minor system. (The chromatic-minor palette for C major, for instance, uses an E♭ major triad, whereas the major palette for the same key calls for an E major triad.) It seems excusable, therefore, to use the traditional terminology; but the reader familiar with traditional theory should bear in mind that these analytical symbols bear no more traditional functional connotations than do any other roman numerals in this chapter.[8]

Songs that employ both diatonic and chromatic chords from the full major system include David Bowie's "Space Oddity" (includes the full palette; see example 4.21); "Don't Look Back in Anger" (includes V/vi and iv), by Oasis;

4.21. A harmonic chart of David Bowie's "Space Oddity," showing use of the full major palette.

C: I		iii7		I		iii7		vi		V/V	:| V/V		V/V		V/V	
|: I		V7/vi		IV		iv	I		IV		iv	I		IV		:|
IV7		iii7		IV7		iii7		VII	vi		$^2_4$ V		$^4_4$ V		
I IV V V/ii		I IV V V/ii														
IV7		iii7		V/ii		I		V/V		V/vi				
I		V7/vi		IV		iv	I		IV		etc.				

Bryan Adams' "(Everything I Do) I Do It For You" (includes V/V and iv); Nilsson's "Without You" (includes V/vi and V/V); the Beatles' "Ask Me Why" (includes V/V, V/vi, iv, and I+) and "Day Tripper" (includes V/ii, V/V, and V/vi), both by John Lennon and Paul McCartney; Don McLean's "American Pie" (includes V/V); Roy Orbison's "Crying" (includes iv as well as I+); Jim Croce's "Bad, Bad Leroy Brown" (includes V/V and V/vi); and "I'm The Only One" (includes V/ii), by Melissa Etheridge.

Other, linearly derived harmonies occasionally appear within passages employing the major-system palette. One of the most frequent is a half-diminished seventh on the third scale degree, usually in second inversion. (See example 4.22.) The unusual quality and inversion show that the chord occurs as a result not of harmonic patterns but of linear motion, usually providing a linear connection between I and V7/ii. Examples occur in Eric Carmen's "All By Myself" (also recorded by Celine Dion) and Captain & Tennille's "Love Will Keep Us Together."

4.22. Typical use of half-diminished seventh as linear harmony.

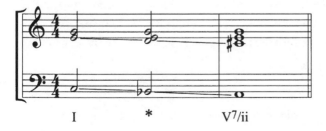

4.23. The three harmonic palettes and their common chords.

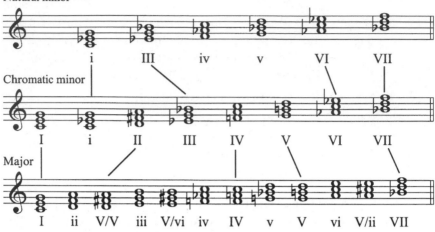

AMBIGUOUS CASES

The natural-minor system, the chromatic-minor system, and the major system are not, however, entirely distinct. (See example 4.23.) The natural-minor system and the chromatic-minor system coincide at the III, VI, and VII chords, as well as on the tonic harmony (in cases where a piece using the chromatic-minor system employs a minor tonic triad). The chromatic-minor system and the major system coincide on the II, IV, V, and VII chords, as well as, perhaps, on the tonic harmony. In the case of a piece that uses only the chords shared by two systems, it is impossible to determine which palette the song is drawing from. Pieces using only the chords i, III, VI, and VII include the Jimi Hendrix Experience's "All Along The Watchtower" (also recorded by U2), Van Morrison's "Wild Night," Men at Work's "Down Under," and Tom Petty's "Breakdown." These songs can be identified as using either the natural-minor or the chromatic-minor system. Pieces that employ only the chords I, IV, V, and VII include the Beatles' "You've Got To Hide Your Love Away," Bad Company's "Can't Get Enough," Gordon Lightfoot's "Sundown," and Credence Clearwater Revival's "Fortunate Son." These use either the chromatic-minor or the major system.

MIXED SYSTEMS

Although the harmonies of rock compositions tend to settle into one of the three systems described above, some pieces are not faithful to a single palette.

In some, the palette changes to correspond with formal divisions: different sections of a song employ different harmonic systems. Examples include Supertramp's "Take The Long Way Home" (chromatic-minor on verse, major on bridge); Lesley Gore's "It's My Party" (major including I+ on chorus; chromatic-minor on verse); the Rolling Stones' "Angie" (chromatic-minor on chorus, natural-minor on bridge); "Dust In The Wind" (natural-minor on verse, chromatic-minor on chorus), by Kansas; Paul McCartney and Wings' "Rock Show" (major on verse and chorus, chromatic-minor on second bridge); Seals and Crofts' "Summer Breeze" (chromatic-minor on verse, major on chorus); Van Halen's "Jump" (major on verse and chorus, natural-minor on solo); Eric Clapton's "Let It Grow" (chromatic-minor on verse, major on chorus); Credence Clearwater Revival's "Proud Mary" (chromatic-minor on introduction, major on verse); Peter Cetera's "Glory Of Love" (chromatic-minor on verse, major on chorus); Spice Girls' "Wannabe" (chromatic-minor on rap interlude, major on verse and chorus); and Lynyrd Skynyrd's "Free Bird" (major on first part, chromatic-minor on second part).

Some exceptional pieces, however, simply provide an array of harmonies that do not fit neatly into one of the three systems. In pieces with a minor chord as tonic, the harmonies tend to settle into either the natural-minor or the chromatic-minor system. But a few examples exist that contain both the minor iv and v from the former and the major IV and V from the latter. In some cases, the variant forms appear next to one another, making the mixture of systems clear. For instance, in the Band's "The Night They Drove Old Dixie Down" (also recorded by Joan Baez with a slightly different harmonic scheme), iv and IV appear one after the other at the end of the verse. (See example 4.24a.) And in Paul McCartney and Wings' "Mrs. Vanderbilt," v and V appear together. (See example 4.24b.)

4.24. A mixture of minor-mode systems in (a) the Band's "The Night They Drove Old Dixie Down" (note iv and IV), and (b) Paul McCartney and Wings' "Mrs. Vanderbilt" (note v and V).

4.24 a.

Analysis:	i^6_4	| VI	| III	| iv	| IV	|
Harmonies:	Am/E	| F	| C	| Dm	| D	|

4.24 b.

Analysis:	i	| v	| V7	| i	|
Harmonies:	Am	| Em	| E7	| Am	|

4.25. A mixture of major-mode systems in (a) the chorus of Elton John's "Goodbye Yellow Brick Road," (b) the verse of the Doobie Brothers' "China Grove," and (c) the chorus of Boston's "More Than A Feeling."

4.25 a.

```
F: I         | V7/vi   | IV      | I       | V7/ii   | ii7     | V7      | I  V⁶
   1           2         3         4         1         2         3         4
```

```
vi         | V7/vi   | IV      | VI      | VI  VII |
1            2         3         4
                                 1         2
```

```
I    V⁶    | vi  vi₂⁴ | IV  V   | iv  etc.
1            2          3         4
```

4.25 b.

```
E: I         | I         | VII  IV⁶ IV | I     | I         | I         | VII  IV⁶ IV | I    |
   1           2           3             4       1           2           3             4
```

```
vi         | V         | IV      | VI      | VI      |
1            2           3         4         2
                                  1
```

```
I          | VII  IV⁶ IV | I     | VII  IV⁶ IV | I    | VII  IV⁶ IV | I    | I    |
1            2             3        4             1      2             3      4
```

4.25 c.

```
G: I  IV  | vi  V  | I  IV  | vi  V  |
```

```
I  IV  | vi  V  | I  IV  | VI      |
```

```
G: vi7
D: ii7     | V       | IV      | IV  I⁶  ii7 | I
```

98

In pieces with a major chord as tonic, the harmonies tend to settle into either the major system or the chromatic-minor system. But a few pieces mix harmonies from the two palettes. Those that do, commonly use the major system for most of the song and insert VI from the chromatic-minor system at the end of the penultimate phrase of a section. In such cases, the composition generally calls for holding the chord two bars, emphasizing the peculiarity of the chord. Excellent examples are found in Elton John's "Goodbye Yellow Brick Road," the Doobie Brothers' "China Grove," and Boston's "More Than A Feeling" (see example 4.25); the first two involve VI at a point of elision (as described in Chapter 1), thus calling even more attention to the singular moment. Other chords from the minor palette can be found, however. "Hip To Be Square" by Huey Lewis and the News uses I, IV, and v from the major palette and III from either minor palette. Of course this set of harmonies can also be viewed as I, III, and IV from the chromatic-minor palette and v from one of the other two.

Having ascertained the harmonic choices available in rock, we now examine the order in which these chords normally occur.

5
harmonic
succession

The patterns of harmonic succession in rock are grossly misunderstood. "It's just the same three chords" is uttered so frequently—as both praise and condemnation—that it has become a cliché.[1] This chapter will disprove that statement.

Music theorists are rarely guilty of making this statement. But if printed literature (and personal experience) is at all representative, most music theorists do hold another unfounded assumption, namely, that rock follows the standards of the common practice with regard to harmonic progression. Many writers confess this belief. Benward and White, for instance, state that "most jazz and popular music is structured around standard harmonic progressions," without singling out rock as an exception.[2] In *Music Theory for the Music Professional: A Comparison of Common-Practice and Popular Genres*, Richard Sorce says, "Popular-music practice is not significantly different from traditional practice." Sorce compares the two styles, analyzing not specific patterns of harmonic succession but only the number of harmonies used; he chooses as his common-practice example part of a Bach chorale (chorales being, as the reader knows, harmonically more dense than most genres of common-practice music), and as his popular example a passage by Paul Simon that uses only two harmonies.[3] Christopher Gordon, in his *Form and Content in Commercial Music*, teaches standard common-practice functional harmony and claims it is valid for popular music, explicitly including rock in his list of popular styles.[4] This belief is false.[5] Alongside vestiges of traditional patterns of progression, a new harmonic practice is found. This new practice, hinted at by the blues pattern common in the early years of rock, gradually expands both in complexity and in pervasiveness during the 1960s. The new style, in fact, becomes so pervasive that it may be called a new standard. This new standard does not rule despotically over the repertoire any more than does the common practice over eighteenth- and nineteenth-century music; it does not dictate rules of harmonic succession that are allowed to be broken only rarely. In fact, traditional successions are found in rock throughout its history. But (1) these traditional successions are in the statistical minority, and (2) when they do occur, their rhythmic deployment within the phrase structure is usually not the same as that associated with common-practice music. As Justin London has noted, "It might well be said that popular music has its own set of harmonic conventions, and that we commit an analytical error in construing pop harmony in terms of common-practice chord grammar."[6] It might well be said indeed, but hasn't been with any frequency. Recognizing these harmonic conventions is the purpose of this chapter.

As in other areas examined so far, the standard patterns of harmonic succession used in rock, though different from those of the common practice, are best understood when compared with the traditional norms from which they depart. So we begin by examining those norms. Books on common-practice harmony generally agree that although virtually any succession can be found somewhere in the standard literature, the frequency of some successions is so much greater than that of others that they are considered standard ("progressions"), and the others exceptional ("retrogressions," "elisions," etc.).[7] Most writers propose that the particular patterns involved in progressions in common-practice music are the result of one (or both) of two factors: function or classification of a chord dependent on its root's position in the scale (an explanation as old as Gottfried Weber), and root movement between successive chords (an idea as old as Jean-Philippe Rameau). Although not everyone agrees whether some of the less frequent successions are to be considered progressions (i.e., where the cutoff line lies between statistically normal and exceptional), the schemes given in examples 5.1 and 5.2 are not far from those that are found in any given standard harmony text.

5.1. A common-practice progression chart, showing minor-mode qualities. (Allowing for the differing qualities of the triads involved, all but the first of the following patterns are considered progressions in the major mode as well.)

VII	is normally followed by	III.
III	"	VI or iv.
VI	"	iv or ii°.
iv	"	V, vii°, or ii°.
ii°	"	V or vii°.
V	"	i or VI.
vii°	"	i.

5.2. A common-practice root-movement chart, showing the root movements normally involved in progression.

↑2   ↓3   ↑4

It is often stipulated that the tonic chord may be inserted between two chords forming a normal succession without constituting an exception, that is, without disturbing the effect of progression.[8] (Many writers describe IV-I motion as progressive. But IV-I as a cadence appears only in codas, as Piston points out,[9] and when it is found within a phrase, the I acts as an interruption.)[10] Many authors also mention that the tonic chord may begin a progression by leading to any other harmony.[11] Because the tonic chord begins and ends progressions and is often found inserted in progressions, it is usually the most frequent harmony, the V chord being the second most frequently occurring chord.

With regard to harmonic succession, as with cadence placement, rock has, from its beginning, used a style opposed to that of common practice, a style that became increasingly standard during the late 1950s and the 1960s. The twelve-bar blues pattern common to much of the early repertoire presents the new standard in a nutshell and was no doubt influential in the development and establishment of the new practice as a standard. (See example 5.3.)

5.3. A harmonic pattern for twelve-bar blues.

I | I | I | I | IV | IV | I | I | V | IV | I | I |

Looking at only the first eight bars of the twelve-bar blues progression does not allow us to say whether any particular standard of progression applies; the IV can be seen merely as an embellishment of the tonic harmony. But when the succession of nontonic harmonies finally begins, in measure 9, it is clear that a new standard is at work. Chords IV and V are used to lead to the final tonic harmony, but not in their traditional order: V is followed by IV, and IV leads to the final I in the pattern; both successions are instances of retrogression from the traditional point of view.

This, then, is the harmonic pattern that perhaps half of early rock 'n' roll and rhythm and blues is based upon, and it involves a fundamental structural departure from the common practice. True, not all songs utilizing the basic pattern include the IV in measure 10, upon which the whole argument hangs. But most do. Of eleven blues-based songs on the *American Graffiti* soundtrack album, for instance, eight include the cadential IV.

During the 1960s, as the harmonic palette of rock expanded (see Chapter 4), the rejection of traditional practice suggested by the blues pattern was gradually expanded to incorporate more than just the I, IV, and V chords. And as mentioned above, the new patterns became pervasive enough to be called a new standard. Again, this is not to say that traditional conventions disappeared altogether. They remained as an option to the composer. Rock composers sometimes turned to primarily traditional conventions in order to evoke a trouble-free or retrospective mood, and sometimes combine or blend the old standard and the new in a single piece.

Of what does this new standard suggested by the blues pattern consist? It might be expressed most succinctly by this negative formula: "Whatever successions are not normal in the Common-Practice are now normal and vice versa." In a positive mode, however, the rock harmonic standard is better sum-

5.4. The root movement of rock harmonic standard.

↓2   ↑3   ↓4

marized in a root-movement chart than in a progression chart. (See "Specific Successions," below, for further discussion.) The root-movement chart for the new style is diametrically opposed to that of common-practice music. (See example 5.4.) Successions involving these root movements form the staple of rock harmonic patterns. One also finds in rock pieces successions that involve traditional root movement but are nevertheless rare in the common practice, for example, vi-VII and V-iii. Carried over from the common practice to the new standard are the stipulations that the tonic harmony often begins phrases and, partially as a result, can lead to any other chord. Therefore, no particular instance of root movement from a tonic in the following examples can be cited in opposition to the proposed model, any more than the frequency of the I-vii° succession can weaken the statement that in the common practice, root movement by second is virtually always ascending.

Consider the harmonic scheme for the Bee Gees' "To Love Somebody." (See example 5.5.) It is clear in the first measure of the introduction that the piece follows rock standards in its harmonic palette; the second chord is the subtonic chord typical of rock. (See Chapter 4.) The chord's major seventh and ninth are products of the use of the pentatonic scale in the melody.

5.5. Rock-standard harmonic succession in the Bee Gees' "To Love Somebody."

Introduction
I VII9 | IV I | I | I |

Verse
|: I | ii | IV | I | VII | I | V | IV :|

Chorus
I | V | IV | I | V | IV | I |

But the piece follows rock standards in more than just harmonic palette: the VII chord in the introduction is followed by descending-fourth root movement to the IV chord, which then proceeds by descending fourth to a cadential tonic harmony. The passage continues following root-movement patterns from the new rock standard: every V is followed by a descending step to IV, every cadential I is preceded by a descending fourth from IV, and the ii chord in the verse (which is played four times during the song) is followed by an ascending third to IV. Other than incidental cases following a tonic harmony (most of the cases of motion from I actually happen inconsequentially to follow the new pattern), the only succession involving root movement contrary to the rock standard—the ascending second between the VII and I in measures 5 and 6 of the verse—nevertheless falls firmly within the boundaries of rock style because the use of the VII.

"Nights In White Satin," from the Moody Blues' 1967 album *Days of Future Passed*, provides a minor-mode example of consistent use of the rock standard, that is, root movement traditionally thought of as retrogressive. (See example 5.6.)

5.6. Rock-standard harmonic succession in the Moody Blues' "Nights In White Satin."

i		VII		i		VII		VI		III		N		i		:|
IV		IV		VI		VI		i		VII		i		VII		

The harmonies come from the chromatic-minor palette for E minor, including the optional Neapolitan (a major chord built on the lowered second scale degree; see Chapter 4). But again, the piece follows rock harmonic standards not just in its harmonic palette but in root movement as well. Measures 4–8 of the verse, for instance, feature three descending seconds and one descending fourth. The chorus, on the other hand, features ascending thirds, between IV and VI, and between VI and the cadential tonic. The only instances of traditional root movement (always ignoring motion away from the tonic chord) occur as VII resolves to i. And this is hardly a traditional progression: most writers on common-practice harmony note that in the minor mode the subtonic harmony normally progresses to the mediant, as indicated in example 5.1 above.[12]

Journey's "Faithfully" displays a similarly consistent use of rock's standard of harmonic succession. The song consists essentially of repeats, sometimes varied or altered, of a single stanza. (See example 5.7; approximate vocal phrasing shown with brackets.) The harmonic pattern of the first, elision-model unit begins as if it were a common-practice progression leading to a half cadence in the fourth bar. But the appearance of the tonic chord in the cadential measure changes the whole effect; undergraduate texts may teach the plagal cadence as one of three or four equally important types of cadences (authentic, half, plagal, and sometimes deceptive), but outside of codas, the plagal cadence is sim-

5.7. Rock-standard phrasing and harmonic succession in Journey's "Faithfully."

I		vi		IV		I		I		I		vi		IV		I⁶₄ V	

I | vi | I | IV vi | I | IV vi | I |

V   iii | V | ii   I⁶ | IV | I | vi | I⁶₄ | IV :|

ply not a part of the common practice. The second phrase, on the other hand, follows common-practice norms perfectly as a result of changing the inversion of the cadential tonic harmony and following it with dominant harmony.

The harmonic scheme of the third phrase of the piece, however, declares firmly its recognition of the rock standard by its use of successive ascending thirds. The resultant succession is not an exceptional quirk hidden in the middle of an otherwise traditional progression: the double repetition of the figure establishes it as an integral component of the piece's harmonic style.

The third line of example 5.7 begins with V and iii, two harmonies rarely found together in the common practice, in either order. "Faithfully" not only pairs the two harmonies; it provides both possible orders: V followed by iii, and iii followed by V. This harmonic pattern does not represent merely a contrapuntal embellishment of the V chord by means of an upper neighbor on the fifth of the chord; both chords are in root position. The harmonic scheme of the phrase continues with motion precisely opposite to traditional standards: V to ii, ii to IV (the I is a passing chord), and IV to I at the overlapped cadence.[13] The final few measures follow traditional practice, except (and it is a significant exception) for the final IV.

Similar cases can be found early in the rock period, although the harmonic palette of that time is often more restricted than music from the time of the Moody Blues and Journey. The most frequent use of the new root-movement standard in the 1950s is the V-IV-I succession. The first four bars of Buddy Holly's "Peggy Sue Got Married," for instance, present rock-standard motion involving only I, IV, and V7, although the rest of the verse proceeds traditionally. (See example 5.8.)

5.8. Rock-standard root motion in Buddy Holly's "Peggy Sue Got Married."

I		V7		IV		I		IV		I⁶₄ V		I IV		I		

5.9. Rock-standard root movement in Del Shannon's "Runaway."

i		i		VII		VII		VI		VI		V		V	:|
I		I		vi		vi		I		I		vi		vi	
I		I		vi		vi		I		I		vi		vi	
IV		IV		V		V		I		IV		I		V	

In the early 1960s, as harmonic palettes became more extensive, they were frequently controlled by the new standard as well. This can be seen as early as, for instance, Del Shannon's "Runaway"; in the verse of this song the new standard is used almost exclusively, although the common practice is called upon to bring the refrain to a close. (See example 5.9.)

Thirty-one years later, retrogressive root movement remains the standard, as can be seen in "Noah's Dove" by 10,000 Maniacs. (See example 5.10.) Although the song wanders between relative major and minor keys (see Chapter 2), to help one discern root relationships, example 5.10 is presented as if the major key were consistent throughout.

5.10. Rock-standard root movement in 10,000 Maniacs' "Noah's Dove."

vi		iii		IV		I		vi		iii		IV		I		
ii		vi		ii		V	:| V									
I		ii		vi		V		I		ii		vi		ii		vi	
ii		V		D.C.												

The following three songs each feature rock-standard root movement by a particular interval: Fleetwood Mac's "You Make Loving Fun" features descending seconds, the Animals' version of "The House Of The Rising Sun" is rich in ascending thirds, and the Rolling Stones' "Jumping Jack Flash" emphasizes descending fourths. (See example 5.11.) As with "Noah's Dove" in example 5.10, above, the scheme for "You Make Loving Fun" is given as if the major key were consistent throughout.

SPECIFIC SUCCESSIONS

The preceding examples demonstrate the harmonic successions of rock primarily through means of an examination of root movement. As mentioned

5.11. Songs featuring rock-standard root movement by a particular interval:
(a) descending seconds in Fleetwood Mac's "You Make Lovin' Fun";
asterisks indicate that the tones of tonic harmony have been added,
(b) ascending thirds in the Animals' "House Of The Rising Sun," and
(c) descending fourths in the Rolling Stones' "Jumping Jack Flash."

5.11 a.

| vi | | vi | | vi | | vi | | V | | V | | IV | | IV | :| |

| I | | I | | VII* | | VII* | | vi | | V* | | IV | | IV | :| |

*With the tones of tonic harmony added.

5.11 b.

| i | | III | | IV | | VI | | i | | III | | V | | V | |

| i | | III | | IV | | VI | | i | | V | | i | | V | |

5.11 c.

| I | | I | | I | | I | :|: III | | VII | | IV | | I | :| |

above, rock's harmonic practice is not easily or usefully summarized in a chart of typical successions. This is true for two principal reasons. First, the common practice is not entirely rejected in this music; many songs follow the earlier standard in some passages and the new standard in other passages (see Chapter 6), and many other songs simply make no distinction, infusing what is otherwise a traditional progression with rock-standard motion and vice versa. Second, any chart displaying all the successions frequently used would be complicated beyond usefulness. Just to show all the harmonies that might lead to I at the final cadence of a chorus or refrain, the chart would have to include the traditional V (as in, for instance, Bill Haley and the Comets' "Shake, Rattle And Roll" and the Monkees' "Last Train To Clarksville"),[14] III (Blondie's "Rapture"; see example 5.12c, below), IV (the already mentioned "To Love Somebody" and the Band's "The Weight"), vi (the Everly Brothers' "('Til) I Kissed You" and Credence Clearwater Revival's "Who'll Stop The Rain?"), and VII (the Righteous Brothers' "You've Lost That Lovin' Feelin'" and Tom Petty and the Heartbreakers' "Refugee").

The chords commonly found following IV are even more numerous; besides the traditional V (which is not ruled out, remember) and the cadential tonic mentioned just above, they include iii, vi (or VI), and VII. The pieces in

5.12. Nontraditional successors to IV in (a) Bob Dylan's "Like a Rolling Stone," (b) Rod Stewart's "Forever Young," (c) Blondie's "Rapture," and (d) Jefferson Airplane's "Somebody to Love."

5.12 a.

I	ii		iii	IV		V		V	:| IV		V		IV		V	
IV	iii		ii	I		IV	iii		ii	I		ii		ii	IV		V etc.

5.12 b.

I			IV		I		I	:| ii		IV		vi		IV	
I			IV$^6_4$		I		I		ii		IV		I		I	

5.12 c.

i		i		i		i		IV$^6_4$		IV$^6_4$		i		i	:	
N	IV		VI	i		N	IV		VI	III		i		i		etc.

5.12 d.

i			IV	VII		i			i	:|: III	VII		i	IV	:|
III	VII		i	IV		VII	IV		i							

example 5.12 provide instances of these uses of IV (and of other retrogressive successions as well).

The least common triad in the common practice, iii (or III), remains rather infrequent in rock. But it, too, normally precedes several different harmonies and contributes to the impracticability of a chord chart. Although occasionally followed by the traditional vi, it is more often followed by the other traditional choice, IV ("Like A Rolling Stone" and "Noah's Dove"; see above), as well as by ii (as in the Eagles' "Lyin' Eyes," shown as example 5.13a) and V (as in

5.13. Nontraditional successors to iii in (a) a chorus of the Eagles' "Lyin' Eyes" and (b) Billy Joel's "Matter Of Trust."

5.13 a.

I			V11		I	IV		I		vi		iii		ii		V	
I			V11/IV		IV		V/V		ii		V11		I		etc.		

5.13 b.

I			vi		I		vi		iii		iii		V		V	:|

"Faithfully," above, and Billy Joel's "Matter Of Trust," shown as example 5.13b).

NOT JUST THE SAME THREE CHORDS

The preceding examples show that the common remark about "the same three chords" reflects a mistaken understanding of the harmonic practice of rock. The restriction of some rock songs to only three chords does not indicate the limits of the harmonic possibilities of the style any more than does the similar restriction of some pieces by Handel and Mozart. These examples also demonstrate that the similar notion, expressed by Gordon and others, that rock simply perpetuates the basic formulas of the common practice is also wrong. Even when a rock song uses only three chords, their usage almost always departs from the common practice in at least one way. Often the three chords are not the primary triads. And when they are, they often do not follow traditional order. Even when they follow traditional order at the local level, they normally do not allow hierarchical organization of phrases at a higher level.

Lynyrd Skynyrd's "Sweet Home Alabama," for instance, uses only three chords almost exclusively; they are not, however, the I, IV, and V of common practice but I, IV, and VII. In addition, its repeating I-VII-IV pattern departs from the common practice in its descending-fourth and descending-second root movement.

Many songs indeed use only I, IV, and V, often called the "three primary triads" and probably the three chords referred to in the famous epithet. But most of these songs follow either the traditional blues pattern or some other scheme that follows the rock standard through use of the V-IV succession. Although most prevalent in the late 1950s, the standard blues pattern can nevertheless be found throughout the rock period, in Little Richard's "Long Tall Sally" (1956), Cream's "Strange Brew" (1967), Pink Floyd's "Money" (1973), U2's "I Still Haven't Found What I'm Looking For" (1987), and Michael Jackson's "Black And White" (1991). Credence Clearwater Revival's "Bad Moon Rising" provides an excellent example of a succession that, while not strictly the classic blues scheme, is clearly derived from it. (See example 5.14.)

5.14. Rock-standard use of I, IV, and V in Credence Clearwater Revival's "Bad Moon Rising."

I		V	IV		I			I			I		V	IV		I			I	
IV			IV			I			I			V			IV			I			I	

5.15. Rock-standard use of I, IV, and V in the Who's "Baba O'Riley."

I   V | IV | I   V | IV | etc.

The Who's "Baba O'Riley" provides an example using only I, IV, and V in what would traditionally be called retrogressive order without otherwise emulating the blues pattern at all. Most of the song consists of repetitions of this pattern. (See example 5.15.)

ANTIPERIODIC STRUCTURE

I have argued that the harmonic practice of rock opposes the common practice and that the blues pattern, which has strongly influenced the development of popular music since the 1950s, was a rejection of common-practice progression. But what of that other staple harmonic pattern of early rock, I-vi-IV-V? After all, this chord succession is declared normal and progressive by every description of the common practice, from Piston to Benward. And what about the many pieces that use only I, IV, and V, but in the traditional order? Surely the abundance of examples weakens the argument that the harmonic practice of rock rejects the common practice.

It is true that numerous rock pieces follow the common practice in local-level harmonic succession, though this may not dictate the overall form of the piece. But in most of these cases, the common practice is rejected in some other way, often in a nontraditional alignment of harmonic scheme and phrase rhythm. The new manner of deploying the harmonic patterns with regard to phrase rhythm often results in the rejection of the periodic structure associated with certain common-practice pieces such as strophic songs and dance melodies. In such pieces, the dominant harmony at the end of the first phrase is often followed by a tonic chord at the beginning of the second. But that first cadential harmony has more structural significance than merely leading to the next chord. It in fact implies the imminence of another whole phrase (at least) with an authentic cadence. The listener, upon hearing the first cadence, awaits or anticipates the final tonic chord much as a reader anticipates the second half of the verb at the end of a German sentence. Another way of putting the matter is that in such music, a V at the end of a hypermeasure points to and is resolved by a I at the end, not the beginning, of a subsequent hypermeasure. But in rock using traditional progressive harmonic patterns, that final tonic often never comes.

The Beatles' "Twist And Shout" (also recorded by the Isley Brothers) and the Tokens' "The Lion Sleeps Tonight" both use only the I, IV, and V of the

5.16. Antiperiodic structure with traditional root movement in (a) the Beatles' "Twist And Shout" and (b) the Tokens' "The Lion Sleeps Tonight."

5.16 a.

I   IV | V | I   IV | V | I   IV | V | etc.

5.16 b.

I | IV | I | V | I | IV | I | V   :|

common practice, and both arrange the chords using traditional root movement. But each song repeats a simple pattern leading to V so many times that that pattern cannot be said to end with a half cadence, a term that implies a hierarchy of stability at cadential points; a cadence given this name is supposedly unstable, suggesting that it represents the halfway point in a period that will end in a full cadence. But in these two songs, no full cadence ever occurs. (See example 5.16.)

Many similar examples use the I-vi-IV(ii)-V pattern common to the love songs and ballads of the early rock era. These songs normally repeat the pattern several times (seven times, for instance, in the case of the Dell-Vikings' "Come Go With Me") before it breaks and the tonic harmony is presented at other than the beginning of a hypermeasure. Such a situation comes the closest yet to providing supporting evidence for the claims of the writers cited earlier that popular music perpetuates traditional harmonic practice. But the final tonic harmony in these cases normally follows not the traditional V, but IV or iv. The Diamonds' "Little Darlin'" provides an example. (See example 5.17.)

5.17. Plagal cadence after common-practice patterns in the Diamond's "Little Darlin'."

I | I | vi | vi | ii7 | ii7 | V7 | V7   :| 3x

I | iv | I | I(add 6) |

The lack of periodic structure is not found solely in pieces with simple, traditional harmonic patterns. The Four Tops' "I Can't Help Myself (Sugar Pie, Honey Bunch)" is similar in its continuous repetition of a pattern ending on V. But in this case, the pattern uses a few more harmonies than do the previous examples and involves successions from the rock standard. (See example 5.18.) Slightly more complex examples in which all phrases end with V are John Lennon's "Woman" and the Beatles' "Michelle." (See also Chapter 3)

5.18. Antiperiodic structure with rock-standard root movement in the Four Tops' "I Can't Help Myself."

| I | | I | | V | | V | | ii | | ii | | IV | | V | :|

PREDOMINANCE OF THE SUBDOMINANT

The twelve-bar blues pattern is said to model the new standard of harmonic succession and possibly to have influenced its development. Another feature based on this pattern and adopted by many rock musicians is the emphasis on subdominant harmony—that is, the second most frequent chord in the pattern (second only to the tonic harmony), taking up three times as much time as the dominant. (In a frequently found variant of the blues pattern, the subdominant harmony fills the second measure of the pattern as well, thereby occupying *four* times as much time as the dominant.)

Many passages in rock involve only two harmonies, the I and the IV, a situation virtually unheard of in common-practice music except in codas (Schumann's "Ich grolle nicht," Handel's "Hallelujah!," etc.). The harmonic succession for the first two four-measure units of Carole King's "Tapestry," for instance, uses only I and IV. (See example 5.19.)

5.19. Chords I and IV alone in the first two units of Carole King's "Tapestry."

| I | | IV | | I | | IV | | I | | IV | | I | IV | | I | | |

The first two units of The Who's "Sally Simpson" employ a pattern similar to that of "Tapestry," although hypermetrically reversed, with the subdominant harmony in every strong measure. (See example 5.20. The structure of the melody, reaching G as both the peak and the cadential note of each phrase, as well as the music of both the ensuing passage and the introduction, shows clearly that these harmonies are indeed IV and I in G major, and not I and V in C major.)

5.20. Chords I and IV alone in the first two units of the Who's "Sally Simpson."

| IV | | I | | IV | | I | | IV | | I | | IV | | I | | |

Many other songs use IV and I exclusively, or almost so. Aretha Franklin's "Think" consists almost entirely of I and IV. Only once does another chord enter into play: the succession I-III-IV-I, strengthened by loud, sustained horn parts, appropriately accompanies a steadily rising vocal line carrying the single word "freedom." After an immediate repetition of the figure, the song never again uses a chord other than IV and I. "What's The Buzz," from Andrew Lloyd-Webber and Tim Rice's *Jesus Christ Superstar,* and Sly & the Family Stone's "Everyday People" use only I and IV, the first chord of each being a major-minor seventh.

The verse of Three Dog Night's "Family Of Man" uses the harmonic scheme shown in example 5.21. Besides containing a number of descending seconds and fourths, this pattern displays another common trait of rock in the duration of its subdominant harmony.

5.21. The durational predominance of IV in Three Dog Night's "Family Of Man."

IV   I | IV   I | iii   IV | IV | IV   iii | iii   IV | IV   I | V   IV I |

SECONDARY DOMINANTS

Chords traditionally thought of as secondary dominants are easily found in rock. That is, a piece in C major might incorporate a D major triad or a D dominant seventh. (Secondary dominants are rare in the minor mode. See Chapter 4 on harmonic palette.) But, as the reader might expect by now, these harmonies rarely function as secondary dominants. The following discussion will use symbols such as V/V, but as with all harmonies discussed in this chapter, the symbol is merely an indication of the pitch content.[15]

Although V/V is probably the most frequent secondary dominant in rock, it is in fact seldom followed by V. (The first bridge of the Police's "Every Breath You Take" contains a notable exception.) It is most often followed by an ascending third to IV, as in the first line of the Beatles' "Eight Days A Week." (See example 5.22.) Measure 12 of that song finds V/V ending a four-measure

5.22. Nontraditional successors to V/V in the Beatles' "Eight Days A Week."

I		V/V		IV		I		I		V/V		IV		I	
vi		ii		vi		V/V		I		V/V		IV		I	

114

5.23. Nontraditional successor to V/V in the Byrds' "I'll Feel A Whole Lot Better."

I		I		I		I		V		V		vi		V/V	
I		I		IV		ii		I		V		IV		VII	
I		I													

unit and preceding the opening tonic chord of the last phrase of the verse. (The resultant root movement is by descending second.) The Byrds' "I'll Feel A Whole Lot Better" uses the chord in a similar way. (See example 5.23.) The Barenaked Ladies' "Pinch Me" uses the chord several times, sometimes leading to IV, sometimes to I. V/V also is sometimes followed by ii, as in the second half of the chorus to "Lyin' Eyes" and in the chorus to Madonna's "Borderline." (See examples 5.13a and 5.24, respectively.) Note that in both "Lyin' Eyes" and "Borderline" other secondary dominants are followed by their respective traditional resolutions. The point is not that these traditional sequences are never found, but that they are far too infrequent to be called the standard in this music.

5.24. Nontraditional successor to V/V in the chorus of Madonna's "Borderline."

V⁶		V⁶/vi		vi	V		V⁶/V V/V		ii		I⁶		V		V	

Jim Croce's "Bad, Bad Leroy Brown" follows V/vi with IV, probably the most frequent choice in this music. (See example 5.25.) The succession is admittedly a common exception in the common practice, employing the ascending-second motion of the classic deceptive cadence. The difference is that in rock, V/vi-IV is the norm, not the exception. (Note: the V/vi in "Bad, Bad Leroy Brown" is itself a nontraditional successor to the preceding V/V.) Other choices for the successor to V/vi involving rock-standard root movement are possible, although less frequent. In the verse of the Beatles' "You're Gonna

5.25. The progression V/vi followed by IV in Jim Croce's "Bad, Bad Leroy Brown."

I		I		V/V		V/V		V/vi		IV		V	IV		I	V	:	

5.26. Nontraditional successors to V7/vi in (a) the Beatles' "You're Gonna Lose That Girl" and (b) the Cars' "Just What I Needed."

5.26 a.

I		V7/vi		ii		V		I		V7/vi		ii		V	

5.26 b.

I		V		vi		V/vi		I		V		vi		V/vi	

I		V		vi		V/vi		I		V		V/vi		IV	

Lose That Girl," V7/vi leads by descending second to ii, and in the Cars' "Just What I Needed," V/vi is followed by I. (See example 5.26.)

The V/ii is infrequent, and when used, it often resolves traditionally. Otis Redding's "(Sittin' On) The Dock Of The Bay," however, uses the chord nontraditionally and provides excellent examples of nontraditional use of other secondary dominants as well. (See example 5.27.) It should also be noted, however, that although the root movement in measures 2–4 is traditional, all instances of motion to the tonic harmony involve the rock-standard descending second or ascending third.

5.27. Nontraditional use of several secondary dominants in Otis Redding's "(Sittin' On) The Dock Of The Bay."

I		V/vi		IV		V/V	:	I		V/ii		I		V/ii	

I		V/V		I		V/ii	

In some music, identification of the V/IV presents a problem. First, V/IV is intervallically identical to I; any distinction must be made on the basis of function. (In the minor mode, V/IV, of course, differs intervallically from the tonic harmony and is therefore distinguishable from it. But secondary dominants are rare in minor-mode rock pieces and are not treated in this discussion.) Further, in certain rock pieces in which major-minor seventh chords on the tonic (and on other roots for that matter) are standard, V7/IV is structurally identical to Idom7 (see Chapter 4); again, any distinction made must be based on function. But if the theory allows the tonic harmony to precede any given chord, then a distinction on the basis of function cannot be made, and the label V7/IV represents a meaningless complication.

However, in pieces in which the triad is the standard harmonic structure,

5.28. Nontraditional choice after V7/IV in chorus of Elton John's "Don't Let The Sun Go Down On Me."

| I | | V$^4_2$/IV | | vi7 | | V$^6_5$/V | | I$^6_4$ | | V11 V | | I | | |

not the dominant-seventh chord, a case can be made for its presence, as in the chorus of Elton John's "Don't Let The Sun Go Down On Me." Because the seventh of the chord comes about as the result of a slow-moving linear descent in the bass, the traditional descending resolution of the pitch seems called for. This traditional melodic resolution in fact happens, but the resulting sixth scale degree supports not the traditional IV6 but the vi. (See example 5.28.)

Secondary vii° chords are infrequent in rock, as are all diminished chords, but when found, they often proceed contrary to the expectations prompted by their names. In Wings' "My Love," vii°7/V leads to I (this after the traditional resolution of a V7/ii). (See example 5.29.)

5.29. Nontraditional choice of chords after vii°7/V in Wings' "My Love."

| IV7 | | IV7 | | iii7 | | V7/ii | | ii7 | | iii7 IV | | vii°7/V | |
| I | | ii7 | | IV | | I | | | | | | |

Few rock pieces do not break the common practice in one of the ways described in this chapter. Where morphological units end on tonic harmony, the chord succession normally eschews traditional progressions. Where, on the other hand, the harmonies do follow traditional patterns, they normally do not lead to tonic harmony at the end of any given morphological unit—that is, they do not function in a way befitting the traditional name for such patterns: progression.

So, as with matters of phrase structure and cadences, we find rock composers rejecting the common practice. But regarding harmonic succession, the picture is so detailed that the question again arises whether this rejection is conscious and intentional. How can the unschooled musicians who are so often accused (either maliciously or endearingly) of perpetuating traditional three-chord patterns come up with something so revolutionary? I fear that many would respond by blaming the musicians' ignorance or the music's crude simplicity. "They know just enough to make mistakes," some might say. Or, "If they were familiar enough with the ramifications of traditional materials, they would use them correctly." Such answers smack not just of elitism, which could be correct for all the wrong reasons, but of unfounded elitism. To state that following ii with V requires sophistication but that following V with ii does not seems insupportable. The assumption that rock composers are entirely unsophisticated is insupportable as well. Leaving aside the indisputable fact that many rock composers have formal training, the consistency of the style demonstrates that composers learn patterns from their predecessors, if "only" by ear (the most suitable form of musical literacy, after all), and that these patterns could not in all cases be simply mistakes or misunderstandings by crude, ignorant musicians. The new style is the result, therefore, of creativity, not fallibility.

At lectures I am often asked if rock musicians are conscious of their creation; such a question, again, seems to assume the composers' ignorance as well as the notion that their ignorance could not be coupled with a consistent and at times complex system. I can only answer by pointing out that were we incapable of learning complex cultural systems without conscious effort, none of us would be talking about the question because we would not have learned a language. The question is highly intriguing, however, and should be pursued through personal contact with composers themselves.

To return to an earlier question, does music in which V follows ii have an effect different from music in which ii follows V? I can speak only for myself, but the answer is a resounding yes. The traditional scheme was not called progression meaninglessly. Common-practice progressions arose from the bed of the tendencies, resolutions, and goals of Western counterpoint. For instance, the V-I cadence and the vii°6-I alternative arose as the only consonant harmonizations of the standard intervallic cadence formula of the Renaissance: the major sixth moving in contrary motion to the octave.[16] The harmonic result is a pattern in which the root of the final chord is a note not present in the penultimate chord, a goal to be reached, a solution to be sought, a fresh look at the situation. Similarly, the chords that normally lead to V in common practice are the only two chords that contain the only two notes that can by step converge on (or expand to) the root of the V: ii and IV. Thus, ii moves to V, and the root of the new chord is a fresh note: scale degree five is not part of the ii chord. Then, V moves on to I, and the root of that new chord is a fresh note: scale degree one is not in the V chord.

The effect is, not surprisingly, almost completely reversed by the rock standard. (*Almost* completely: root movement by second in either direction provides a new note for the root of the second chord.) Several common-practice writers mention the importance of the root being a new note in progressive combinations, often pointing out that the lack of a new note for a root in ascending-third and descending-fourth root movement gives these combinations their special, nonprogressive effect.[17] And it is just this special flavor that the rock standard exploits: besides offering a fresh alternative to music that, after three hundred years, has become a cliché, the harmonic patterns common in the rock standard provide not so much a sense of progression toward a goal as they do stability and a subtly shifting point of view. As William H. Reynolds has noted, "Movement of a root up a third (to a strong note already present) may not sound like much of a change of chord."[18] In the succession IV-vi-I in Jonathan Cain's "Faithfully" (see example 5.7, above), the root of the vi chord does not resolve a structural dissonance in the previous chord: scale degree six is a part of the preceding IV chord as well. And the root of the final tonic does not appear on the scene as a fresh solution to the tendencies of the previous chord: scale degree one is a part of the preceding vi chord as well. The situation is the same in the motion from iii-V in the next line as well as in the final ii-IV-I.

I claimed to represent only my own views in describing the effect of rock successions. But in this case, the view is supported by the text of the song. The lyrics, concerning the traveling musician's constant separation from family, do not treat the situation as a problem that requires solution or as one that will get worse or better; it must be dealt with in the eternal present. The grammatically disconnected line "Wheels go round and round" from the first verse primarily suggests not only the wheels of the traveling band's bus but also cyclical nature of the circumstance. A straight line points somewhere and may reach an end that is out of sight; a circle, entirely present at a glance, reveals no end. The last portion of the lyrics, sung during the harmonic succession discussed just above, are these:

And being apart ain't easy on this love affair
Two strangers learn to fall in love again
I get the joy
Of rediscovering you
Oh, girl, you stand by me
I'm forever yours—faithfully.*

Now reconsider the harmonic scheme of Rod Stewart's "Forever Young." (See example 5.12, above.) In the ii-IV-vi of the second phrase, the ascending-third root movement provides no new notes for chord roots. Neither does the ii-IV-I of the last phrase. And what are the lyrics?

*FAITHFULLY, by Jonathan Cain. © 1982 Weedhigh-Nightmare Music. All Rights Reserved. Used by Permission. WARNER BROS. PUBLICATIONS U.S. INC., Miami, FL 33014

And no matter what you do
I'm right behind you—win or lose
forever young.*

Like the tonic note in a IV-I succession, the relationship between the persona of this lyric and the supposed recipient does not change with the circumstances.

Having examined the pitch practices of rock at a detailed, local level, we now proceed to the larger-scale issue of form.

form

The study of form deals primarily with the means of separation and contrast by which portions of a piece are made to sound distinct from one another, and with the order in which these portions are presented or repeated. In other words, theories of form seek to identify the features that prompt the perception of formal units (why does the first section seem to end here, and why does the following portion seem distinct enough to call it a second section?) and to recognize standard orders of those units (antecedent and consequent phrases in a period, for instance, or the ABA sequence of sections in ternary form). Chapter I dealt with some of these issues at the level of the phrase, a relatively small unit. This chapter builds on that foundation to examine standard formal structures of entire pieces and the methods used to create those forms.

Formal analysis of a piece includes the judgment that the piece has, say, an AB form, indicating that the piece has two sections, the second contrasting with the first, primarily with regard to melodic material. But we cannot begin the analysis of form by looking at patterns of contrast in order to determine where the sections begin and end. Melodic differences between sections are important and may be part of the reason for having different sections; that is, musical pieces could be said to have multiple sections to provide, for the sake of variety, an exposition of contrasting material in a systematic and easily accessible way. But it is difficult to base a formal analysis on melodic contrast in that it occurs all the time, even within sections. So noting features that define the special character of a given section is not the same as noting features that signal the beginning or end of a section as formally distinct from other sections. Sometimes the features themselves are the same; but the problems are not. Logically, the first problem in the analysis of form (and the fundamental problem for a book on general stylistic characteristics) is the discovery of features that delineate sections.

Consider as an analogy a speech. A speaker generally attempts to convey ideas; to help the audience comprehend the message in one hearing, he or she generally categorizes and presents related ideas in discrete sections. A campaign speech, for instance, might contain sections on the speaker's history and character, foreign policy, budgetary matters, and patriotic sentiment. The purpose of the separate sections is to clarify the exposition of ideas. But a good speaker will not make the listeners figure out on their own that the speech has moved on to a new category. Instead she will provide an introduction as the topics change and a summary at the end. The introduction and summary serve not only as reinforcements of what was said but also as formalized cues to alert the listener to the change of subject.

In a musical piece, we must look for formalized musical cues concerning form. Traditionally, the chief among these are cadence patterns and key schemes. But in rock, although these features may occasionally help delineate form, keys are not always distinct, and cadences don't usually fall into neat patterns. (See Chapters 2 and 3.) In rock, the relevant cues most often appear in the areas of text, instrumentation, rhythm, and harmony. In many cases, the patterns in these areas work together to create a clear form; in many others, changes in one or more areas work against a backdrop of stability in the other areas to create a subtler form. And in yet other cases, lack of alignment in the patterns of change of various areas makes for ambiguity.

Consider the case of REO Speedwagon's "Keep On Loving You." (See example 6.1.) The second phrase ("You should've known . . . didn't listen") is melodically identical to the first ("You should've seen . . . somethin' missin'").

6.1. The melody of the first seven phrases of REO Speedwagon's "Keep On Loving You."

"Keep On Loving You". Copyright © 1980 Kevin Cronin

However, the third phrase ("You played dead ... hissin'"), though it begins with the same three-note motive as do the first two phrases, differs from them melodically and rhythmically. Is this contrast high enough to justify saying that a substantial new section has begun? Or must we wait for the even more divergent seventh phrase ("And I'm gonna keep on lovin' you") before determining that a new section has arrived? Contrast of melodic material alone cannot determine the division into sections. Yet most people listening to the song would agree that it has two parts; they would probably call them verse and chorus, phrases 1–3 and 4–6 constituting verses 1 and 2, respectively, and phrases 7–9 constituting the chorus. What features contribute to this impression that phrase 7 marks the beginning of a new section? Traditionally, cadence patterns and key scheme would provide the significant information. But here the phrases all end on the V, and the song never leaves the key of C. Instead, the seventh phrase distinguishes itself in several ways more germane to rock style, including (1) the arrival of the title line, (2) the addition of background vocals and acoustic guitar, (3) the acoustic guitar's distinctive rhythm, providing the shortest notes heard in the song, and (4) the first appearance of tonic harmony, made even more prominent by occurring at the beginning of the phrase. The four areas represented here—text, instrumentation, rhythm, and harmony—prove to be the most common settings for formal cues in rock.

TEXT

Perhaps the surest way of distinguishing sections in rock is by textual repetition. Because textual patterns are easy to define and usually so clear-cut, we will deal with them first.

Text helps to define forms primarily in one way: the repetition or return of any text at least one line long highlights the accompanying musical passage.[1] When the text is only one line long and returns only after intervening material, we are likely to call the passage a "refrain," as in the Beatles' "I Saw Her Standing There":

Well, she was just seventeen
And you know what I mean
And the way she looked was way beyond compare.
So how could I dance with another
Oh, when I saw her standing there?
Well, she looked at me
And I, I could see
That before too long I'd fall in love with her.
She wouldn't dance with another
Oh, when I saw her standing there.

A text that is one line long and immediately repeated usually marks a chorus, as in Sam and Dave's "Soul Man" or Peter Frampton's "Show Me The Way." A text of several lines that returns after intervening material (although it may be immediately repeated first) also generally marks a chorus, as in Janis Joplin's "Me And Bobby McGee."

Although repetition of text consistently identifies the passage as a chorus

124

or refrain, it is an inefficient indicator of form for the listener. Were repetition of text our only criterion for identifying choruses and refrains, we would not be able to identify a chorus, for instance, until its second appearance. But, in fact, most listeners are able to identify choruses intuitively as they begin. Other clues to form will be discussed in subsequent sections, but a couple of textual clues, though seemingly trivial, provide significant help with real-time identification of formal delineations. When the title of a song is known (e.g., when the listener has the cover in hand or when a concert performer announces the name of a song), the words of the title usually signal the arrival of a refrain or chorus. Such is the case, for instance, with Gary Wright's "Dream Weaver" and Alannah Myles' "Black Velvet."

The distinction between refrain and chorus will be examined in more detail below. For now, suffice it to say that a refrain usually comprises a single line of recurring text at the end of each verse, whereas a chorus constitutes a separate section. Listeners can often tell immediately whether a key textual phrase signals the end of a verse or the beginning of a chorus. Why is this? In earlier tonal practice, strong cadences might provide clues; the presence of a perfect authentic cadence at the end of a phrase, for instance, prompts us to interpret that phrase as the end of the previous section, a section we would probably call a period; such a cadence, in fact, makes it difficult to hear the phrase as the first phrase of a new section. Rock does not normally employ cadences to create periodic forms, however (see Chapter 5). But we are not left without periods of any kind. After all, the linguistic fields of grammar and rhetoric deal with such notions as "phrase" and "period," and most rock pieces have a text.[2] Texts that do not poetically abandon normal sentence structure may offer clues. For instance, in the Everly Brothers' "All I Have To Do Is Dream," the grammatical status of the title line determines that its appearance marks the end of a verse and not the beginning of a chorus. (The harmonic succession, which simply provides another repetition of the I-vi-IV-V pattern that has pervaded the song to this point, provides no help.) The first verse begins with three dependent clauses:

> When I want you in my arms,
> When I want you and all your charms,
> Whenever I want you,*[3]

The arrival of the independent clause "All I have to do is dream" therefore provides the grammatical closure needed and, in addition to completing the rather long sentence, marks the end of the first section; in other words it functions as a refrain at the end of the first verse, not as the beginning of a chorus.

INSTRUMENTATION

By *instrumentation*, I mean the changing combinations of instruments, including voices, performing a piece. In songs (the better part of the repertoire), the arrival of the vocal line usually indicates the end of the introduction and the beginning of a verse. The arrival of a group of singers usually marks the beginning of (in fact provides the name for) the chorus. The entrance of other instruments (strings, for instance) can help delineate the form as well. Examples in which the entrance of a chorus marks the beginning of a section called a chorus include R. B. Greaves' "Take A Letter, Maria," Styx's "Babe," John Cougar Mellencamp's "Lonely Ol' Night," Blues Traveler's "Run-Around," and Peter Frampton's "Show Me The Way."

Janet Jackson's "Alright" demonstrates just how important instrumentation can be in the delineation of form. The song contains essentially just one chord, an F♯ with a B in the bass, although passing motion at the end of most phrases provides some brief and subtle variety. The song presents no major change of instrumental rhythm, either; once the full band enters, its rhythms remain consistent through five of the song's six and a half minutes. But the words "Friends come and friends may go," at the one-minute mark, distinctly indicate the beginning of a new section, what pop-music fans are inclined to call a chorus.* This impression cannot result from changes in harmony or rhythm, since the song contains no such changes. The perceived arrival of a new section is the result of the addition (partly by means of studio multitracking) of more voices, that is, a literal chorus. This interpretation is confirmed by the immediate repetition of these words and by their return after a second verse.

RHYTHM

Most people recognize rock as a genre that emphasizes rhythm, so it comes as no surprise that this device is used to distinguish sections or portions of sections. For instance, in many early songs of the period, instrumentalists distinguish verses through a method known as "stop time," a technique in which all

*ALRIGHT, by Janet Jackson, James Harris III, and Terry Lewis. © 1989 Flyte Tyme Tunes and Black Ice Publishing. All Rights Reserved. Used by Permission. WARNER BROS. PUBLICATIONS U.S. INC., Miami, FL 33014

the instruments play the same rhythm, usually consisting of short notes widely and unevenly separated. After the halting, unsteady effect of stop time, the arrival of a steady beat in which each measure is filled out with rhythmic activity appears as a great release of tension. Stop time usually appears during the first part of a verse, establishing a structural dissonance for which the latter part of the verse, with its steady beat, provides the resolution. Fats Domino's "Ain't That A Shame" provides an excellent example. (See example 6.2.) During the first part of each verse, all instruments play the same rhythm (6.2a); during the second half of each verse, the drums play a steady shuffle beat while several pitched instruments play the rhythm (6.2b).

6.2. Instrumental rhythms in Fats Domino's "Ain't That A Shame": (a) first half of verse and (b) second half.

Elvis Presley's "Jailhouse Rock" provides another example and hints at the way stop time is most commonly used later in the period. (See example 6.3.) During the introduction and again during the first part of each verse, the instruments play one rhythm (6.3a). In the second half of each verse, the instruments play a regular beat. What distinguishes this example and points toward the future is the ambiguity of the rhythm during the introduction (which at first can seem to be that found in example 6.3b).

6.3. Ambiguous instrumental rhythm in the introduction of Elvis Presley's "Jailhouse Rock": (a) as it proves to be and (b) as it might at first be interpreted.

The entrance of the vocal melody resolves the ambiguity; a single syncopation played by the instruments in quadruple time is a much more plausible interpretation than a bizarrely syncopated vocal line in triple meter. (See example 6.4, a and b, respectively). When offering this kind of ambiguity, an introduc-

6.4. Metrical interpretations of rhythms during the verse of Elvis Presley's "Jailhouse Rock": (a) the correct interpretation and (b)an implausibly syncopated interpretation.

Jailhouse Rock. Words and Music by Jerry Leiber and Mike Stoller. © 1957 (Renewed) JERRY LEIBER MUSIC and MIKE STOLLER MUSIC. All Rights Reserved

tion, rather than just coming first in the piece, fulfills an interesting function appropriate to its position: providing a chaos out of which the order of the song emerges. Van Halen's "Jump" provides a later example of the ambiguous use of syncopated rhythms in introductions. The principle is not unknown outside rock: many Bach fugues, for instance, begin with similar metrical ambiguity.

The Beatles' "While My Guitar Gently Weeps," although not using rigid stop time, employs similar rhythms in bass and drums to distinguish sections. (See example 6.5.) During each verse the rhythms haltingly emphasize the first

6.5. Representative instrumental rhythms in the Beatles' "While My Guitar Gently Weeps": (a) verse and (b) bridge.

6.5 a.

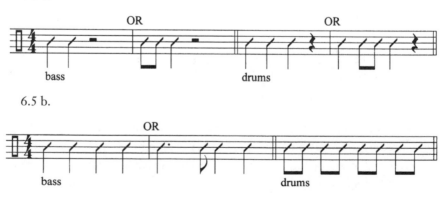

6.5 b.

part of each measure, reflecting the singer's disconnected train of thought as he looks in pain and despair around his room ("I look at the floor, and I see it needs sweeping"). During the bridges, the singer directs more focused thought toward the absent person who seems to be the cause of his anguish ("I don't know why nobody told you"); as his thoughts become more continuous, so do the rhythms of the bass and drums.*

Even when the instruments don't use stop time to make rhythmic differences quite so obvious, many songs use changes in rhythm to help delineate sections. For instance, in Men at Work's "Who Can It Be Now?" the drums play a steady beat and the bass plays continuous eighths throughout, but the rhythm guitars provide rhythmic contrast to help outline the form. (See example 6.6. Rhythm a occurs in the verse, b in the chorus.)

6.6. Instrumental rhythms in Men at Work's "Who Can It Be Now?"

In the Police's "Wrapped Around Your Finger," the instruments use complementary rhythms throughout but vary them from section to section. The bass, for instance, generally articulates beat 3, while keyboards and guitars play syncopated rhythms articulating the "and" of beat 2 rather than 3. But the rhythm of each of these instruments varies in a way consistent enough to distinguish sections. (See example 6.7.)

Vocal rhythms, like vocal melodic lines, will often show differences from section to section but do not always help the listener differentiate. Choruses in rock, however, have a tendency toward slower vocal rhythms than do verses. Peter Frampton's "Show Me The Way," which served as an example for textual and textural criteria of delineation, proves useful again in this context. (See example 6.8.) Other songs in which a slower vocal rhythm marks the beginning of the chorus include Danny & the Juniors' "At The Hop," the Who's "I Can See For Miles," Don McLean's "American Pie," Lionel Richie's "All Night Long (All Night)," and Blues Traveler's "The Hook." Although this relation-

---

*While My Guitar Gently Weeps. Words and Music by George Harrison. © 1968 HARRISONGS LTD. Copyright Renewed 1997. International Copyright Secured All Rights Reserved.

6.7. Instrumental rhythms in the Police's "Wrapped Around Your Finger":
(a) verse and (b) chorus.

6.7 a.

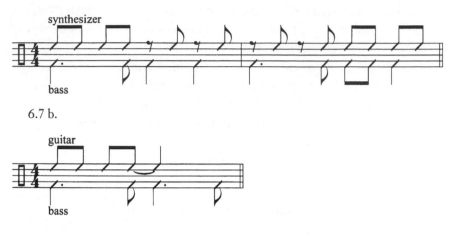

6.7 b.

HARMONY

ship will probably never form the primary criterion for determining the dividing point between sections, the information when valid can certainly be used to
corroborate the evidence provided by other areas.

In any style of Western music, differences of harmonic content and succession likely help define the character of distinct sections, sometimes even more

6.8. Vocal rhythms in (a) verse and (b) chorus of Peter Frampton's "Show Me
The Way."

6.8 a.

6.8 b.

than melodic differences do. But although melodic contrasts do not help much to delineate form in rock music, harmonic contrasts do. Of course in some songs the harmonies of sections differ to such a degree that the sections seem to be in different keys; such extreme differences are treated in Chapter 2. Much subtler variations, however, can at times provide just as much help in distinguishing sections. In rock, where repetition of harmonic patterns is so common, any break in the pattern will likely mark a significant moment in the form. For instance, since the Everly Brothers' "All I Have To Do Is Dream," as mentioned above, begins with several repetitions of I-vi-IV-V, any change in that pattern will be significant. The break at the end of the second verse by means of a I-IV-I pattern indicates a more significant formal articulation than that at the end of the first verse, suggesting that the song is about to proceed not to yet another verse but to a new section. The new harmonic pattern, IV-iii-ii-V-I and so on, provides one of the most obvious indications of the fulfillment of that hint.

Many rock songs use differences in chord successions to help distinguish sections. In many of these cases the different chord patterns differ even in the standard they follow. As explained in Chapter 5, rock chord successions often fall in a standard order contrary to that of earlier tonal music. Rock does use the older standard on occasion, however, many times to help define form. In Billy Joel's "Matter Of Trust," for example, after a verse that follows the rock standard (I-vi-I-vi-iii-V), the bridge uses a more traditional succession: IV-I6-ii-V-I-IV-V. In another example, the Beatles' "I Want To Hold Your Hand," while the first part of the verse suggests the rock standard with its descending-fourth root movement (I-V-vi-V/vi), the refrain reverts to the earlier standard: its pattern is IV-V-I-vi-IV-V-I. Here the difference in standards reflects the rhetorical construction of the verses; the rock standard, which normally leads away from tonic and tends not to resolve (see Chapter 1), accompanies the lines of the text in which the singer offers to tell a secret, makes requests, or the like, whereas the traditional standard, which tends toward resolution, repeats the textual refrain, "I want to hold your hand," thereby revealing the secret or emphasizing the request.

Normally we don't have to wait for the complete unfolding of a harmonic pattern to see that it differs significantly from what has come before. As explained in other chapters, rock makes much of the first measure of hypermetrical and formal units, placing harmonic and melodic resolutions there. Here, too, we see the significance of the first measure, in that new harmonic successions usually differ from their predecessors right from the beginning. We need hear only the first chord in the bridge of "All I Have To Do Is Dream," for instance, to know that the pattern is not that of the verse: the verses all begin on I, and the first chord here is a IV.

The principle found in this song can be generalized. In most rock pieces, verses start with tonic harmony. (Verses occasionally start with ii or some other chord; see chapter II.) In such cases, other sections (i.e., choruses and bridges) normally distinguish themselves by beginning on IV, V, or vi, the preference being IV.[4] Other choices such as III and VII are possible as well, although these may be just different enough to suggest key changes.

Songs in which the verse begins on I and the chorus on IV include James Taylor's "Fire And Rain," Loggins and Messina's "Danny's Song," Elton John's "Daniel," John Lennon's "Watching The Wheels," and Bruce Hornsby and the Range's "Mandolin Rain." Examples in which the verse starts on I and the bridge on IV include Buddy Holly's "Everyday"; Dan Fogelberg's "Hard To Say"; "I Don't Know How To Love Him," from *Jesus Christ Superstar*; the Eagles' "Love Will Keep Us Alive"; the Platters' "One In A Million"; and several well-known songs by the Beatles, such as "I Saw Her Standing There," "Please, Please Me," "Ticket To Ride," "Hey Jude," and "Back In The USSR." Songs in which the verse starts on I and the chorus starts on V include Billy Joel's "You May Be Right" and the Rolling Stones' "Brown Sugar." Examples of the verse beginning on I and the bridge on V include the Beach Boys' "Fun, Fun, Fun" and the Beatles' "Eight Days A Week."

The submediant (vi or VI) is used as the first chord of the bridge or chorus in Fleetwood Mac's "Say You Love Me" (chorus on vi), the Beatles' "Let It Be" (chorus on vi), the Doobie Brothers' "Listen To The Music" (chorus on vi), Jethro Tull's "Bungle in the Jungle" (chorus on VI), the Cure's "Love Song" (chorus on VI), and Carole King's "So Far Away" (bridge on vi). Once again, Peter Frampton's "Show Me The Way" serves us: the verse begins on I, the chorus on vi.

Of course, some exceptional songs use other relationships. In the Beach Boys' "Surfin' U.S.A.," both verse and chorus start on V. In Don Henley's "Heart Of The Matter," both verse and chorus begin on I and the bridge on VII. Songs in which the verse does not begin on I are unpredictable. Various relationships can be seen, for instance, in Cyndi Lauper's "Time After Time" (verse on ii and chorus on V), the Beatles' "All My Loving" (verse on ii and chorus on vi), and Gloria Estefan's "Can't Stay Away From You" (verse on iii and chorus on IV).

Harmony proves to be a decisive factor in the delineation of form in the somewhat ambiguous case of the Youngbloods' "Let's Get Together." The introduction essentially alternates two chords: A major with an added sixth, and

G major seventh. Because the A chord comes first, it is assumed to be the tonic harmony, so the succession is interpreted as I-VII. The vocal line enters over continued alternation of the same two chords (although the harmonic rhythm has changed). After a solo voice sings the first two phrases, a second voice joins in for the third phrase, still employing only the two chords of the introduction. In many rock songs, the entrance of additional voices marks the end of the verse and the beginning of the chorus, even where the harmonic pattern does not vary. (See "Instrumentation," above.) In "Let's Get Together," however, the harmonic contrasts accompanying the fourth phrase far supersede any contrast provided by the addition of a single voice for the third phrase, and these harmonic contrasts mark the beginning of the chorus. Starting at the fourth phrase, the harmonic succession is IV-V-I-IV-V-I. We notice a difference immediately with the entrance of a previously unheard chord, IV, at the beginning of the phrase. As the succession unfolds, we may note also that the succession involving VII, a chord almost completely absent in previous tonal styles, is replaced by a very normal succession by traditional standards, IV-V-I, thus marking a change in harmonic standards, as discussed above. Other features of the song—a change from arpeggios to strummed chords in the guitar, a change of drum beat, and a slight increase of tempo, as well as the addition of even more voices—confirm the division between verse and chorus at the beginning of the fourth phrase.

NAMES OF SECTIONS AND PASSAGES

It must be remembered that the point of formal analysis (i.e., morphological analysis) is not to identify passages with the proper labels, for the labels serve merely as points of perspective around which to organize our thoughts. The reader may not agree that what I have called the chorus of "Let's Get Together" should receive that label. Although it fits most of the criteria, it is in fact quite short. For some listeners, its brevity may be the salient feature and may prevent them from hearing the passage as a chorus. Perhaps other listeners would wish to call it a refrain. A problem arises with that label as well, however, since refrains normally consist of only one or at the most two lines of text, whereas this passage contains four. But the label is not the point. The point is that comparing the passage with passages called choruses or refrains in other songs helps focus our thinking on what makes this song different from others, what shapes the distinct experience of listening to this song in particular. Call it short chorus, call it long refrain. Either way, by paying attention to it long enough to name it we start to see that it somehow differs from other passages of its type. We start to notice that its purpose in this song is to provide the solution to the problem set out both musically and textually in the verses—that the faster tempo, the increased harmonic rhythm and harmonic variety, and the rising tessitura of the vocal melody point to a way out of the doldrums of the verse. We begin to notice that the entry of the chorus of voices demonstrates the enjoinment to "get together," and then we realize that the brevity of the passage serves to drive home the simplicity of the offered solution of love.

With this caution against rigid application of definitions in a fluid, creative, artistic context, we proceed to definitions of names of sections and passages.

In general, any instrumental music occurring before the entrance of the voice is called an introduction, even when the passage consists of only one chord, as in the Beatles' "A Hard Day's Night." In the so-called doo-wop style, introductions may incorporate voices, usually singing virtually nonsensical syllables, such as the "Sha-na-na" and "Dip-dip-dip" of the Silhouettes' "Get A Job." When the introduction, whether instrumental or vocal, features a distinct melodic idea, the passage often recurs later in the song; almost always, the recurring passage begins just as the voice finishes the last phrase of a section. Such is the case, for instance, in the Monkees' "Last Train To Clarksville" (see the discussion of the introduction of this song in Chapter 2), and Elton John's "Don't Let The Sun Go Down On Me." The passage could be called a "link" or "turnaround" when it reappears, but rock musicians generally speak simply of repeating the introduction.

Verse

The word *verse* comes from the Latin *vertere* or *revertere*, "to turn" or "to return." Saint Augustine spoke of verse being defined by a return to the beginning of a poetic metrical pattern with new text.[5] In current usage, the word refers to a return not of a poetic pattern but of a melodic pattern: verse refers to a section of a song that recurs a number of times, with a different text every (or nearly every) time. Verse may also refer to the text itself of one such statement of the musical verse. (This usage goes back as far as the responsorial chant of the early Middle Ages, in which a soloist sang successive lines of a biblical psalm or canticle, each with the same music and each followed by a response, a passage with a single, recurring text that was sung by the choir as a whole.) Although as a rule each verse presents a new text, a common exception occurs when the last verse repeats the lyric of the first verse. In rock songs, the verse, if present, usually occurs first; but many songs begin with a chorus before proceeding to the first verse. Examples include Chuck Berry's "Rock And Roll Music," the Hollies' "Bus Stop," and Eric Clapton's "I Shot The Sheriff."

Refrain

The word *refrain* comes from the Latin *refringere*, which means "to break again"; as its etymology implies, a refrain is a passage that breaks into the form (or onto the scene) repeatedly. Not a complete section, a refrain consists of one or two textual lines that recur periodically. A refrain normally ends a verse, as in "I Want To Hold Your Hand," or begins a chorus, as in the Lovin' Spoonful's "Do You Believe In Magic." In some cases the refrain ends the verse *and* begins the chorus, as in Bob Seger and the Silver Bullet Band's "Old Time Rock And Roll." Occasionally, a refrain begins a bridge, as in Dan Fogelberg's "Hard To Say." Again, the refrain is not a complete section but rather a specially designated part of the verse, bridge, or chorus in which it appears.

Chorus

This word can have two meanings. In its current usage, *chorus* refers to a musical section that recurs numerous times with a fixed text of several lines. In this usage it is distinct from a verse in that the same text occurs with each chorus, whereas the text normally changes for each verse. It is distinct from a refrain in that a refrain consists usually of only one line of text, and at most two lines. The name chorus derives from the typical practice of using multiple singers to perform the section after the presentation of a verse by a soloist, a practice stemming directly back to popular-song practice in the nineteenth century and coincidentally foreshadowed by the responsorial chant described above. The entrance of a chorus of singers marks the beginning of the section called chorus in, for instance, the Beach Boys' "Help Me, Rhonda." Some other examples are listed above under "Instrumentation."

An understanding of the second meaning of the word *chorus* requires some background in the history of popular song.[6] In the 1840s and 1950s, verse-chorus form became predominant in American popular song. At that time, the chorus was typically half as long as each of the many verses and presented material similar or identical to that of the verse. By the turn of the century, the importance of the verse and the number of them had decreased. At the same time, the chorus had assumed more musical and textual importance and independence, as well as greater length. Generally as long as the verse by this time, the chorus in such songs as Charles K. Harris' "After the Ball" (1892) and "A Good Cigar Is a Smoke" (1905), by Harry B. Smith and Victor Herbert, went on for thirty-two bars.

By the 1930s, this trend having continued, the chorus of most popular songs far outweighed the verse; many songs had only one verse, which was rarely performed and often unknown by the public. For instance, if someone today was asked to sing "Over The Rainbow" (1938), by E. Y. Harburg and Harold Arlen, she would almost certainly start with the words "Somewhere over the rainbow, Way up high." The portion starting with these words, however, is actually only the chorus of the song; the verse, not sung by Judy Garland in *The Wizard of Oz*, and thus largely ignored or forgotten, begins with the words "When all the world is a hopeless jumble."* Similarly, few of the millions who know Irving Berlin's "White Christmas" (1940) remember—or have ever heard—the verse, which begins with descriptions of the sunny weather and green grass of Southern California in December. Some songs from the period in fact consist of a chorus alone, without verse; as the lyric to Frank Loesser's "On A Slow Boat To China" (1948) reveals, "There is no verse to this song."† Other examples of verseless songs include "Smoke Gets In Your Eyes," by Otto Harbach and Jerome Kern (1933; recorded in the rock era by the Platters, in 1958, and others). Now, a chorus intended to be independent of a verse must have not only length but formal complexity as well; the double-period form of "After The Ball" won't do. In many songs from this period, "Over The Rainbow" and "Smoke Gets In Your Eyes" included, the chorus has taken on a multisectional form itself, usually a rounded-binary form. The most common format is AABA, the second and third statements of A achieving tonal closure.[7] In some cases, "Smoke Gets In Your Eyes," for instance, the first A does not reach a closed cadence, while in others, such as "Over The Rainbow," it does.

Occasionally in early rock 'n' roll history, this common song form from the previous era—a vestigial verse, followed by a long chorus in rounded-binary form constituting the bulk of the song—crops up. Lenny Welch's "Since I Fell For You" (a remake of a 1947 Paul Gaylen hit) and Neil Sedaka's "Breakin' Up Is Hard To Do" (1975 version) provide excellent examples. Recognizing this connection with the standards of the previous era of popular song and recalling the earlier practice of eliminating verses in performance or, more important, in composition ("On A Slow Boat To China," etc.), we may justly say that some songs from the rock period represent the chorus of a song without a verse; the song is the chorus. This interpretation seems especially valid when the song begins with a refrain consisting of the title words, and when the song is in rounded-binary form.

6.9. The evolution of common song forms through the 1950s.

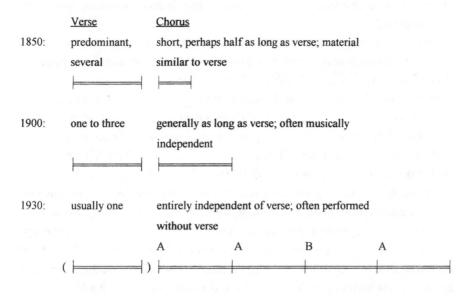

	Verse	Chorus
1850:	predominant, several	short, perhaps half as long as verse; material similar to verse
1900:	one to three	generally as long as verse; often musically independent
1930:	usually one	entirely independent of verse; often performed without verse

In such a case, since the verse is absent and the chorus, in the old sense of the word, constitutes the whole song, it may be better to use the word *chorus* to refer only to the most repeated musical passage (the A passage in the scheme outlined above) and the word *bridge* to refer to the contrasting material (the B section). (See example 6.9.) If this usage is accepted, when a song begins with the title words, especially when the song is in rounded-binary form, the first passage may be called a chorus, even if the text after the refrain changes with each subsequent repeat of the passage. Examples include Fats Domino's "I'm Walkin'." (Other examples are listed below, under "Rounded Binary.")

Bridge

As its name implies, the bridge connects two other sections. A bridge, therefore, never begins a song and usually leads to another section. It usually appears only once or twice in a given song and, if twice, generally carries the same text. New sections are rarely introduced after the first appearance of the bridge; songs in which the bridge follows a verse normally do not contain choruses, and songs in which the bridge follows two consecutive statements of a chorus normally do not contain verses. The bridge is sometimes called the "middle 8," perhaps because it is often eight measures long.

Any passage of music heard first only after the second statement of the chorus can be called a bridge. This is true whether the pattern preceding the passage in question is chorus-chorus, as in the retrospective forms described just above, or verse-chorus-verse-chorus, as in Elton John's "Someone Saved My Life Tonight."

In a song starting with a verse, bridge may refer to the song's second section if the passage leads only to another statement of the verse, and the passage either (1) is shorter than the verse or (2) doesn't end on tonic harmony, though the verse does. Del Amitri's "Roll To Me" provides an excellent example of the latter possibility. The song begins with two verses. At the end of each verse, tonic harmony arrives at the same time as the completion of a textual sentence with the words "Roll to me." The second section ends with a V chord at the end of the question "Guess who will be there?"* The harmonic cadences line up perfectly with the textual punctuation: tonic harmony helps define the end of the section ending with a statement, while dominant harmony works with the grammatical question to produce a sense of need for a response at the end of the second section. Because the verses establish the relevance in this song of cadences on tonic harmony (not a given in rock music), the leading nature of the dominant harmony at the end of the second section takes on added significance and gives that section the sense of being a bridge.

Rock songs tend to have instrumental bridges. Examples include Styx's "Babe," the Moody Blues' "Nights In White Satin," Eric Clapton's "Let It Grow," and Alanis Morissette's "You Learn" (the bridge includes textless vocals).

The instrumental bridge is particularly associated with the early hits of the group Chicago. Top 40 examples include "Make Me Smile," "Questions 67 and 68," "Call On Me." In less familiar songs such as "Introduction" and "All Is Well," these instrumental bridges are extended into multisectional passages sometimes even longer than the vocal portions of the song. A hybrid form in which the bridge begins as a more or less typical vocal bridge and subsequently moves on into further, instrumental sections appears in the Top 40 hits "Just You 'n' Me" and "No Tell Lover."

COMPLETE FORMS

Now that the methods of delineating sections and the definitions of the main types of section have been established, we can examine the ways these sections work together to constitute completed forms. Forms fall into four categories: strophic, rounded binary, verse-chorus-bridge, and compound binary. Exceptions exist, of course, but they do not have enough similarities to form a distinct category.

Strophic

A strophic song can, by definition, be divided into two or more exact (or essentially exact) repetitions of the same musical material. Short passages of material falling outside the repeat scheme frequently occur as introductions and codas; Bill Haley and the Comets' "Rock Around The Clock" provides a classic example. The repeated portion of music may be called the strophe (although rock musicians generally do not use this term themselves).

In the simplest form, a single, undivided harmonic pattern (usually of eight, twelve, or sixteen measures) is repeated several times; in this situation the strophe consists of only one section, usually a verse. Good examples include Chuck Berry's "No Particular Place To Go," Bryan Hyland's "Sealed With A Kiss," and Simon and Garfunkel's "The Sounds Of Silence." In most cases, each verse ends with a refrain. A repeated harmonic pattern may sometimes represent verses, and sometimes the chorus. For instance, in Jim Croce's "Bad, Bad Leroy Brown" the entrance of the chorus of singers and of the title line distinguishes the beginning of each chorus, even though the harmonic pattern is identical to that of the verse, and the melody is similar. Occasionally, as in Eric Clapton's "After Midnight," the strophe consists of chorus only (in the second sense of the word *chorus*, as defined above).

The single-section strophic form was especially common in the 1950s, when so many of the songs followed a blues or blues-based progression; the building of melodic, rhythmic, and textual variations on a consistently repeated harmonic succession and phrase pattern is a major part of the blues tradition, so it is quite natural that these songs would avoid even the minor formal complexity of a contrasting section. (Elvis Presley's "Stuck On You" provides the exceptional example of a blues song with a bridge.) Examples of strophic songs using the blues progression include Little Richard's "Long Tall Sally," the Del Vikings' "Cool Shake," the Diamonds' "The Stroll," and Joey Dee and the Starlighters' "Peppermint Twist." Examples of strophic songs using harmonic patterns similar to the blues include Elvis Presley's "Heartbreak Hotel," and the Beach Boys' "Surfin' U.S.A."

In the 1960s, strophic songs began to move toward the binary form, although blues and blues-based songs such as Michael Jackson's "Black And White" continue to be written. (Other examples are given in Chapter 5.) The two-part strophe usually consists of verse and chorus, but occasionally the order is reversed. Countless rock songs employ the verse-chorus strophic form. Representatives include Mark Dinning's "Teen Angel," Bad Company's "Can't Get Enough," the Police's "Wrapped Around Your Finger," Collective Soul's "The World I Know," and George Harrison's "What Is Life?" In many cases, like Cat Stevens' "Wild World," part or all of one verse (usually the third) is played instrumentally, usually to showcase an improvised instrumental solo.

Rounded Binary

As its name implies, a rounded-binary form consists of a pattern involving two sections: in rock these two sections are either chorus and bridge or verse and bridge. It is called rounded because the bridge, acting as the connector, cannot end the song but instead must always lead back *around* to the other section.[8] In these rounded-binary pieces, the distinction between verse and chorus as a label for the first section—at times a debatable distinction—generally depends on the placement of a refrain; if the refrain comes at the end of the first section or is not present at all, the first section may be called a verse, and if it comes at the beginning, the section may be called a chorus. In the first ten years or so of the rock period, the chorus-bridge type dominated; from the late 1960s on, the situation was reversed. Examples involving a verse and bridge include Ritchie Valens' "Donna" (1958), the Miracles' "Shop Around" (1960), Blood, Sweat and Tears' "You've Made Me So Very Happy" (1969; the bridge is quite long and complex in this example), and Billy Joel's "Just The Way You Are" (1977). Examples involving a chorus and bridge include the Poni-Tails' "Born Too Late" (1958), Bobby Vee's "Devil Or Angel" (1960), George Harrison's "Give Me Love (Give Me Peace On Earth)" (1973), and the Pretenders' "Don't Get Me Wrong" (1986).

Verse-Chorus-Bridge

The tendency to make the third verse in a strophic song an instrumental for the sake of variety was noted above. The textural variety created by dropping the voices does not change the essential form, however, since in these cases the harmonies follow the same pattern as in the other verses. But in numerous cases, the desire for variety after the second chorus results in a completely new section: a bridge. The resulting form is something of a hybrid of the other two forms. It resembles verse-chorus strophic form in that a verse and chorus come one after the other two or three times, but it differs in that it has in the middle of the song a third section that doesn't fit into the otherwise consistent scheme of repetition. It resembles rounded-binary form with its bridge, but it differs in that the bridge is preceded by two distinct sections, not just one. Not exactly

6.10. The evolution of common song forms through 1970.

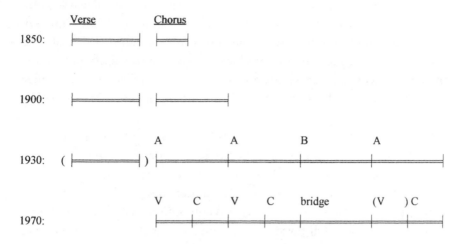

like any other musical form, the verse-chorus-bridge form nevertheless finds a link with tradition. If the verse and chorus together can represent an expansion of the A passage of the rounded-binary pattern (described above, under "Chorus") the verse-chorus-bridge form can be seen as the latest step in the 150-year-old process of elaborating the chorus. (See example 6.10.)

Two varieties exist. In the most numerous type, the bridge leads to a return of the chorus only, and the chorus is usually repeated a number of times to end the song. Examples include the Righteous Brothers' "You've Lost That Lovin' Feelin'," Elton John's "Someone Saved My Life Tonight," Amy Grant's "Every Heartbeat," and Tina Turner's "What's Love Got To Do With It?"

In the second variety, the bridge leads to a third verse-and-chorus pair. Examples include the Beatles' "You're Gonna Lose That Girl," Seals and Crofts' "Summer Breeze," and Billy Joel's "Innocent Man." "You're Gonna Lose That Girl" differs slightly from the norm in that the chorus begins the song. Other songs with a verse, chorus, and bridge deviate even more significantly from the norms outlined here but not consistently enough to form a pattern. For instance, Peter Cetera's "One Good Woman" follows the pattern VCVCB-VBCC.[9] Carly Simon's "Haven't Got Time For The Pain" follows the even more unusual pattern VCBCVBC.

Compound Binary

A song in compound-binary form, heard mainly in the 1960s and 1970s, can be divided into two principal parts. In many songs, the two parts are even labeled separately, as in Chicago's "Dialogue (Parts I & II)." In a compound-binary song, the first part, itself as long as or longer than a normal song, usually follows one of the forms outlined above. As a result it may be dubbed a "super-section": although a principal division of a piece, it in turn is divided into several sections. The second part is generally structured around several repetitions of a single melodic line or chord progression or both. This second division or part as a rule presents previously unheard material; were it otherwise, the passage would not be distinguished as transcendent to the form of the first part.

One of the earliest examples, the Beatles' "Hey Jude," forms the model. The first part of the song is in rounded-binary form, following the pattern CCBCBC. (The first section is labeled here a chorus, since the text, while differing on the whole with each return of the section, begins with the title words, "Hey Jude," every time.) This part of the composition could have stood as the entire song; it lasts a full three minutes and six seconds. But instead of concluding with a simple tag or a fade-out after a few repetitions of the last line, it proceeds to the famous "na-na" section, which lasts another three minutes and fifty-four seconds.

Each example, though following this model to some extent, seems to have its own idiosyncrasy. For instance, in Derek and the Dominoes' "Layla," the second part, which begins with several repetitions of the same harmonic and melodic pattern, proves to be in rounded-binary form. In this case, both parts can be called supersections since they each constitute a primary division that itself divides into several sections. (Incidentally, the piece known as "Layla" came about as a simple concatenation of two pieces: a song by Eric Clapton and an instrumental by the drummer Jim Gordon.) In Grand Funk Railroad's "Closer to Home/I'm Your Captain," the second part repeats its pattern several times at a fairly slow tempo and then accelerates for several more repeats. In Led Zeppelin's "Stairway To Heaven," the second part is much shorter than the first but serves as much more than a simple tag or coda because of its unique tempo, its important text, and its presentation of the highest melodic pitches of the piece.

As we have seen, with respect to form, rock reveals an ambivalent relationship with the past. In its strophic form, it carries on a tradition found in popular song of the nineteenth century but also links the music to the traditions of hymns and ballads. Ostensibly, America's "Horse With No Name" differs little from the famous cowboy ballads "I'm A-Ridin' Old Paint" and "The Old Chisolm Trail" in purpose, form, and even subject matter.[10] In its rounded-binary form, rock forges a direct link with the previous era of popular music.

But it is also connected through this form to the dance suites and minuet movements of the eighteenth century; it seems that people have danced to rounded-binary forms for at least three hundred years.

On the other hand, verse-chorus-bridge form and compound-binary form, while preserving links with the past, represent new trends. The former, the most complex standard song form since the *rondeau* of the fourteenth century, resembles that form only in its complexity, not in its details. And compound-binary form, while simple in conception, is nevertheless unlike any predecessor. So once again, this time in the area of form, we realize that rock is greatly indebted to the past, even though tradition has been altered to create something new and distinct.

7
analyzing a hit

In the first chapter of *Explaining Music*, Leonard Meyer distinguishes between two approaches to musical analysis: "style analysis," a process that "discloses and defines those probabilities—those rhythmic, melodic, harmonic, and textural relationships—which are characteristic of the music of a particular period, a form, or a genre"; and "critical analysis," a process that "seeks to understand and explain what is idiosyncratic about a particular composition."[1] The second is the most naturally beneficial; since we are almost all interested in music because of particular compositions, understanding Music without understanding individual pieces seems to miss the point. As Meyer points out, however, style analysis must come first, both because "particulars are invariably understood in the light of classes and norms" and because "our under-standing of what the composer *actually* did is significantly dependent upon our understanding of what he *might* have done."[2]

The first six chapters of this book present a stylistic analysis of rock. That is, they lay out in some detail the textures, rhythms, melodic and harmonic pat-terns, and forms that are statistically normal in rock music. This foundation, now established, makes possible the construction of legitimate, reasonable critical analyses of particular pieces. In this chapter, rather than focusing on common features and presenting pieces merely as examples I make the first move toward critical analysis of specific rock pieces.

In the context of rock style, though, these analyses should achieve two goals: they should not only demonstrate by example the possibility of critical analysis of rock songs but also legitimize the observations made in previous portions of the book. These dual-purpose analyses come in three pairs. First comes a demonstration that songs from nearly opposite ends of the rock era in fact fol-low principles outlined in each chapter of this book. Next come two herme-neutic analyses of songs that demonstrate the usefulness of the formal models described in this book: usefulness to the composer in making a philosophical statement and usefulness to the analyst in explicating that statement. Last come analyses of two songs usually thought of as beyond the structural norms of rock, demonstrating that the musical complexity and sophistication of such pieces rests firmly on a foundation of standards shared by other, simpler songs.

"HELP ME, RHONDA"

"Help Me, Rhonda" (1965), by Brian Wilson of the Beach Boys, provides an excellent example of many of the features discussed in this book. The song uses the major palette, follows a V/V with the tonic harmony, uses its first appear-ance of the V chord to help signal the arrival of the chorus, features an eleventh chord prominently, and ends the verse with a ii-I cadence, all common patterns in the rock idiom. Perhaps most interestingly, we find in this song that Brian Wilson as composer, arranger, and producer uses clever instrumental lines and the distinctive voices of his group to determine not just the textural arrange-ment but primary compositional aspects as well.

The song is in verse-chorus-bridge form, with the instrumental bridge com-ing in the place of a third verse, according to the common pattern. The chorus announces its arrival by emphasizing the title lyric and by using the chorus of singers to present the main melodic material, as opposed to the verse's use of the chorus as a response to the lead singer. The key of D♭ is established by the first chord and confirmed by the harmonic use of the major palette for D♭ and by the melodic use of first the [024579] hexachord with [0] as tonic ([0] = D♭) and then the [013568T] set with [1] as tonic ([1] = D♭).

In harmonic language, the piece draws on a variety of ideas, presenting a different standard feature with almost every phrase. The first and second phrases present the same simple succession, I-V11-I, $\hat{3}$ being the most prominent melodic pitch during the V11 chord. The third phrase offers the pattern vi-IV-V/V. The root movement is down by a third in both cases, opposite to the more common pattern in rock, but in ending with a V/V chord, as opposed to one of a more limited number of traditional choices, the phrase reveals loyalty to a new standard. When the fourth phrase begins on I, we see another way in which this secondary dominant follows the rock standard: in rock, V/V precedes IV or I more often than it precedes the V suggested by its name. The fourth phrase continues with a ii-I cadence, representing the variety of penultimate chords used at closed cadences and demonstrating the descending-second root movement typical of rock. The first, second, and fourth phrases all begin their final chord on the downbeat of their respective third measures.

The first four-measure unit of the chorus contains only two chords, V and I. The first of these chords, as the first appearance of the basic V chord (not V11) helps signal the arrival of the chorus by the use of a fresh harmony at the beginning of a hypermeasure. The second chord of the chorus, I, arrives on the third downbeat, again showing the song's preference for harmonic cadences on strong downbeats. After a second four-bar unit identical to the first, the harmonic pattern of the chorus's third phrase, IV-vi-I, serves as a reflection of the *verse's* third phrase, bringing back two of its three chords but reversing their sequence in order to resolve the anomaly of the nonstandard root motion of the earlier phrase: now the thirds in the root succession appear in ascending form. Although the basic harmonic pattern of the fourth phrase of the chorus follows a traditional succession, ii-V-I, two features place it firmly in the rock tradition: (1) the placement of the last chord on the third downbeat and (2) the melodic emphasis during the V chord of the first and, to a lesser extent, third and sixth scale degrees. Rhythmically and formally the cadence is very strong, and harmonically a sense of resolution is provided by motion toward the tonic chord, but melodically the phrase provides little suspense; the tonic begins the phrase, receives emphasis by embellishment in the first measure, receives emphasis by repetition in the second measure, and then ends the phrase. (See example 7.1.) This final melodic phrase can be viewed as simply a prolongation of the tonic pitch, an enlarged and embellished version of the cadences associated with English folk song found in Chapter 3.

The instrumental bridge offers a wry comment on the history of rock har-

146

7.1. The final vocal phrase of the chorus (plus guitar riff) of "Help Me, Rhonda," showing emphasis on tonic pitch throughout.

HELP ME RHONDA, by Brian Wilson and Mike Love. © 1965 (Renewed) Irving Music, Inc. All Rights Reserved. Used by Permission. WARNER BROS. PUBLICATIONS U.S. INC., Miami, FL 33014

monic successions. The blues progression has been described as a precursor to rock harmonic practice, influential both in the nontraditional root movement outlined in its cadential formula, V-IV-I, and in its emphasis on the subdominant, IV. The instrumental bridge presents what is essentially a blues harmonic pattern (its twelve bars, as compared to the sixteen measures of all other sections help identify it as such), but with one change: the cadential pattern here is ii-IV-I. Two significant effects result from this change. First, the connection between the blues pattern and the standards of rock root movement is confirmed by the replacement of one pattern from the rock standard, a descending second (V-IV), with another, the ascending third (ii-IV). Second, the similarity of the ii chord and the IV (they have two notes in common) makes the emphasis on the subdominant seem even stronger in this version. Thus, the V at the beginning of the subsequent chorus appears fresher and seemingly inevitable.

The most important features of rock standards in "Help Me, Rhonda" have to do with phrase rhythm. For most of the piece, the phrase rhythm follows the 2 + 2 model, two measures in each group devoted to the solo vocal line and two devoted to instrumental lines and choral effects. (See, e.g., the phrase shown in example 7.1) It is tempting to dismiss them as instrumental filler and background vocals, but how can we relegate these parts to secondary roles? Anyone who has ever heard this song on the car radio and sung along with friends knows that the triplet guitar riff and the "bow bow" vocals form just as integral a part of the composition as the texted vocal melody and are sung with just as much, if not more, gusto.[3]

Twice in the song the 2 + 2 pattern gives way to a different structure. The third line of the verse changes to a 1 + 1 model. In rock this pattern almost always represents a structural dissonance that must be resolved by the subsequent arrival of a cadence on a strong downbeat, and it does so here; the fourth, concluding line of each verse brings back the 2 + 2 model with its more metrically solid cadence. (The timing of the beginning of the "bow bow" bass line—simultaneously with the harmonic and vocal cadence—keeps the cadence from sounding too solid.) Again in the chorus the normal pattern of two measures of melody plus two measures of instrumental lines or choral response gives way; this time the 2 + 2 division of the four-measure hypermeasure remains, but each half is filled with the chorus of voices, singing repetitively, "Help me, Rhonda! help, help me, Rhonda!" Here we come across a situation arising often throughout the period, that of a chorus singing lyrics of love about a specific person. In this regard, the group vocals can be regarded as secondary to the lead singer, for it is the lead who finishes up the sentence and the formal section with the words "get her out of my heart." Again the unusual phrase structure is treated as an aberration that must be rectified, a dissonance that must be resolved, in light of this last line's close on the third downbeat of the fourth hypermeasure of the chorus. The Beach Boys' vocal harmony therefore operates here not just as a favorite, distinctive sound used to improve recognition of the song but as a compositional determinant.

"BARELY BREATHING"

In the years since "Help Me, Rhonda," rock has undergone many changes of style: the British invasion, Motown, psychedelic rock, acid rock, country rock, jazz rock, MOR, progressive rock, heavy metal, funk rock, disco, punk rock, New Wave, techno-pop, rap, hip-hop, alternative rock, and grunge have all made their marks on the vistas of rock history, each affecting the genre as a whole. But do any threads of consistency run through the whole fabric, or is the history of rock a crazy quilt of disparate swatches? Does a Rock Music exist in a structural, musical sense, or is it only a list of styles connected by virtue of features of their social context—popularity, commercialism, electronic dissemination, and the like? This book makes the case, convincingly I hope, that formal stylistic trends do indeed unify the four decades of music we know as rock. A look at Duncan Sheik's "Barely Breathing" (1996) shows that, thirty-one years later, many of the same kinds of structural patterns found in "Help Me, Rhonda" still appear. The phrase structure, key relationships, harmonic content and successions, and form of "Barely Breathing" all follow models outlined in earlier chapters, although in creative ways that contribute to our understanding of the character of the song's persona.

The song is in verse-chorus-bridge form (VCVCBC pattern), the sections being distinguished by key, harmonic succession, harmonic palette, melodic structure, and lyrical content. Each section consists essentially of repetitions of a four-measure, four-chord harmonic succession—a different pattern and initiating harmony for each section. Although added tones (fourths and seconds mostly) color each harmony, the basic patterns are these: Em7-A7-C-D on the verse, Cmaj7-G-Am7-F on the chorus, and D-Am7-C-Gm7 on the bridge.

This harmonic plan results in at least one long-range pattern of development: each section presents, when it is introduced, more idiomatic rock root movement than any of the previous sections. The first succession heard, that of the verse (the introduction uses the harmonic succession of the verse as well), results in the following pattern of root movement: up by fourth (E to A), up by third (A to C), up by second (C to D), and—in returning to the beginning of the pattern—up by second (D to E). Only the motion up by third fits the idiomatic rock standard, which includes motion down by second, up by third, and down by fourth.

The chorus appears next in the song. Its succession employs the following pattern of root movement: down by fourth (C to G), up by second (G to A), down by third (A to F), and—when the pattern repeats—down by fourth (F to C). Half the harmonic motion in this second section, then, conforms to the rock standard, that is, the two instances of motion down by fourth, whereas in the verse only one case out of four fits.

The last section introduced, the bridge, uses this pattern of root movement: down by fourth (D to A), up by third (A to C), down by fourth (C to G), and—on the repeat—down by fourth (G to D). Thus, in this section, all of the root motion corresponds to the standard rock pattern. Because each of the other sections uses root motion outside the standard, the bridge completes the plan of presenting more idiomatic rock successions with each new section. We have seen other pieces in which the degree of conformity to the rock standard of root motion helps delineate form. But in no other piece have we seen such a systematic use of the standard in establishing a progressive plan covering almost the entire song.

Because of the identity of the first harmony as well as the melodic importance of E, G, and B, the verse is best analyzed in E minor. The minor mode seems appropriate for the serious, judgmental nature of lines such as "I know what you're doing" and "You really can't be serious." In the context of this key, the chords prove to act as i7, IV7, VI, and VII, all from the chromatic-minor system. Interpreted in E minor, the harmonic pattern appears more idiomatically rock oriented than it did when its root movement was analyzed out of the context of key. Both the chromatic-minor harmonic system and the specific chord succession VI-VII-i place the pattern within rock's harmonic tradition.

The E-minor chord disappears in the chorus, as does the E in the melody; the melody now moves in short waves (as if barely breathing!) between G and B, moving up as far as D only once, near the end. As a result, the chorus represents a change of key to the relative major, G. Without the context of other information, the harmonies might appear to represent I-V-vi-IV in the key of C, but the melodic structure together with the rarity in rock of diatonic-third key relationships (such as Em and C) rule this interpretation out. The harmonies in relation to G major act as IV7, I, ii7, and VII, all from the diatonic portion of the major system.[4] The inclusion of the major VII in a major key identifies the succession as an idiomatic rock pattern even more than the observation, made earlier, of the root movement alone. The change to what might be called the "kinder, gentler" major mode, together with a softer beat and more sustained tones, corresponds with a change in text. The lyrics now focus more on the persona's self than on the character being sung to:

> I am barely breathing
> And I can't find the air
> I don't know who I'm kidding.*

The change in key, far from being simply a technical feature, helps us into the persona's psyche in order to see that he is less harsh in his judgment of himself than in his judgment of the woman, although he does not remove himself entirely from blame. We need not admire the persona for his stance, and we may ponder whether he sees the situation and his part in it clearly. But that we have a character of dimension to ponder at all is due partly to the succession of keys in the piece.

A change in the phrase rhythm highlights another subtle change in the lyrics at the end of the chorus. Throughout the verse and most of the chorus, the vocal melody consists of short phrases, each acting as a large pickup to a downbeat. The end of the chorus offers the first change in that structure, the

---

*"Barely Breathing". © 1996 Careers-BMG Music Publishing, Inc. (BMI)/Duncan Sheik Songs (BMI)/Happ-Dog. Music (BMI). All rights reserved. Used by permission.

short phrases having been abandoned in favor of a relatively extended line carrying the melody all the way from one strong downbeat to the next:

I don't suppose it's worth the price,
It's worth the price,
The price that I would pay.

The change of phrase structure coincides with the lowering of determination suggested in the text. The potential for a change of heart hinted at in these words (he's at least speculating about paying the price) is made more explicit at the end of the second entry of the chorus with the added line "But I'm thinking it over anyway."

Determination of the key of the bridge presents some problems. The first three harmonies (D, Am7, and C) act as V, ii7, and IV in G major. But what do we do with the following chord: a Gm7? Assuming G still functions as the tonic pitch, the chords represent a mixed harmonic system: ii fits the major system but not the chromatic-minor or natural-minor system, V fits the major and chromatic-minor systems, not the natural-minor system, and III and i fit the chromatic-minor and natural-minor systems but not the major system. The contrasts presented in the lyrics in this section suit the surprising sensation of the juxtaposition of contrasting harmonic systems. The bridge begins on the bright V chord with the words "I've come to find," a hint of some degree of optimism or at least stability. What has this song's persona come to find, though? The words accompanying the next chord—a darker, minor chord—tell us: "I may never know." He has learned only that he may never learn anything else; the only stability is instability. The darkest chord of the piece, the G-minor chord, is reserved for the most consequential contrast: "Is it friend or foe?" The question is not "Is it friend or former friend?" At this point, previous hints about the character of the person being sung to (e.g., "I know what you're doing," "You really had me going," "There's . . . only you to blame") become clear: this woman is not just unsure of her own heart, but culpably ambivalent. Mr. Sheik appropriately reserves the dark chord for this important revelation. As the harmonic pattern of the bridge repeats, the bright D-major chord, even brighter in the context of the G-minor chord just heard, provides the emotionally right setting for the next phrase of the text: "I rise above." The next line of the lyric, "Or sink below," provides the contrast. The word "sink" corresponds figuratively with the drop in the emotional content of the text and corresponds literally with the sinking harmonic motion as the D-major chord moves down to the A-minor chord.

As I explained elsewhere, rock does not necessarily work toward closure. "Barely Breathing" in fact works to avoid closure, especially harmonic closure. It is not enough to say that none of the sections ends with closure. In fact, each section reserves its most unstable chord for its end. The harmonic pattern of the verse ends with the highly unstable VII chord. After repeating this harmonic pattern, each verse ends with two measures of an F-major chord, the Neapolitan (or flat-II) in the key of E minor, a chord even more unstable (because of its chromaticism) than the VII. Each chorus also ends with an F major chord, VII in the context of the G-major tonality of the chorus. As noted in chapter IV, while VII is sometimes found with the diatonic chords of the major system, it actually represents a degree of chromaticism. The harmonic pattern of the bridge ends, as we have seen, with the surprising minor i chord, made more unstable by the emphasis on the seventh scale degree in the melody. The song eventually ends (it does not fade out) on the VII. Although the melody ends on the tonic pitch, it actually contributes to the unstable sound of the ending since the tonic pitch is dissonant with relation to the VII chord. The last words heard are

I know what you're doing
I see it all too clear.

In light of the doubts expressed earlier in the lyrics, and especially in light of the open-ended conclusion, we may wish to ask if the persona of "Barely Breathing" truly does know what he's doing. If he really sees the situation all too clearly, why is he not more determined to act upon a solution? The formal structure of the song works with the lyrics—sometimes confirming them, sometimes clarifying them—to render a sympathetic picture of the anguish of the human certainty of uncertainty.

"DOES ANYBODY REALLY KNOW WHAT TIME IT IS?"

Chicago's first album, *Chicago Transit Authority*, appealed to the psychedelic tastes of the record-buying public of 1969 through a new eclectic sound whose sources included not only hard rock, blues, cool jazz, free jazz, soul, and Latin dance music but also classical music of the early twentieth century, such as Stravinsky, Bartók, and Schoenberg. Keyboardist Robert Lamm's "Does Anybody Really Know What Time It Is?"—their earliest recorded hit, although it was not released until 1970, after the success of their second album—draws upon several of these sources while packaging them nicely in an overall structure lying within the ideas outlined in this book.

The song as it appears on the album is in compound-binary form; that is, it consists of two extended sections (supersections) of equal status, at least one of which divides into subsections. The first supersection consists of an improvised piano solo, the second of the song proper (the portion played on the radio), performed by the full band. In between is a transitional passage played by the band that serves as an unusually long introduction in the radio version. The first supersection on the album version (it was played quite differently in concert, as evidenced by Chicago's live fourth album) contains constantly shifting meters and tempos and a nonstop string of dissonant chords, all containing a tritone above the bass, and outlines no clear pitch center. The second supersection, by contrast, clearly establishes G as tonic, stays in one meter and tempo, and uses only chords with one or more perfect fifths and no tritones. The transitional passage strikes a middle line, centering around G but only loosely, occasionally changing meters but maintaining a steady pulse, emphasizing chords with perfect fifths but using in the climactic sonority a tritone above the bass for the last time in the piece.

The song proper includes a short introduction, a verse and chorus (this pair played three times), and a short coda. The introduction consists mostly of alternations of G and C major-seventh chords, each one measure long. The Gmaj7 chords come on the hypermetrically strong measures, establishing the key. Both the verse and chorus begin with G or G major-seventh harmonies as well, confirming the key. Also confirming the key is the clear outline of a G major triad in the first vocal phrase, even where the skips to and from chord tones outline local dissonances in the context of the current chords. (See example 7.2.)

The chord content of the song follows a distinctive pattern common in early works by Chicago: the roots all come from the natural-minor scale (the

7.2. Tonic triad outlined in the first vocal phrase of "Does Anybody Really Know What Time It Is?" Circled notes indicate nonchord tones; arrows indicate members of tonic triad.

"Does Anybody Really Know What Time It Is?". Written by Robert Lamm. © 1969 Lamminations Music/Aurelius Music (ASCAP). All Rights Reserved. Used By Permission.

7.3. Pseudo-boogie pattern from "Does Anybody Really Know What Time It Is?"

"Does Anybody Really Know What Time It Is?". Written by Robert Lamm. © 1969 Lamminations Music/Aurelius Music (ASCAP). All Rights Reserved. Used By Permission.

song uses G, B♭, C, D, E♭, and F as roots), but the chord quality is often that of the major seventh. The result is clearly a version of the chromatic-minor system, although seventh chords in that system are usually dominant sevenths. The only exception comes with a pseudo-boogie pattern used to prolong the D major harmony at each of its appearances: D-Em-F-Em coupled with a D pedal in the trumpet. (See example 7.3.)

Both verse and chorus end with open cadences. The text of each verse presents a narrative of encounters between the song's persona and people he meets on the street, and each ends with the words "And I said." Thus, the anticipation of the upcoming quotation (what did "I" say?) perfectly matches the open-endedness of the harmony's close on the embellished V chord. But the persona's response to these encounters, as given in the chorus, is not a definitive statement either, consisting of two direct questions and one implied question:

Does anybody really know what time it is?
Does anybody really care?
If so I can't imagine why
We've all got time enough to cry [in the third chorus: die].

Again, the text suggests an open ending, provided in this case by the chorus's harmonic cadence on IV.

The most interesting connections between text and music, however, are in the details of the verse. (See example 7.4.) Each verse begins with the line "As I was walking down the street one day," continues with a description of another person or a crowd of people accosting the singer, and ends with the words "And I said." In other words, each verse follows a tripartite scheme in which the

7.4. The lead sheet of verse of "Does Anybody Really Know What Time It Is?," showing changes in melodic pitch source, the variety of phrase rhythms, and diminishing melodic motive.

singer speaks of himself, others, and then again himself. These changes in subject correspond exactly to important changes in the harmony. Although all the chords of the verse fit the chromatic-minor palette for G, the emphasis on B♭ and E♭ in measures 3–10 might be heard as a change of key to B♭ (the B♭ chords come in the strong measures). At the very least, these chords present eight measures of the flat side of the chromatic palette, corroborated by the use of B♭ and, once near the end of each verse, E♭ in the melody. This passage, whether it be taken as tonicization or simply emphasis of the chromatic portions of the tone system, corresponds almost exactly to the change of subject in the verse. At the mention of the street, just before the downbeat of measure 3, the first chromatic note enters: while melody and harmony both present B♮s in measure 1, the chord in the third measure contains B♭. The flat chords continue all through the passage describing the other people's behavior. One beat after the return of the first-person pronoun, however, the embellished D major chord enters and the flats disappear. After this, the chords and melody remain within the confines of the G major scale throughout the chorus for the rest of the singer's response. Thus, the presence of the G major scale (with occasional F♮) corresponds with the persona's references to himself while the natural-minor scale, with its B♭s and E♭s, corresponds to depictions of others.

The meaning of the text is also reflected in the phrase rhythm and motivic structure of the verse. The verse is twelve measures long and is easily heard in three four-bar hypermeasures, each of the three vocal phrases lying within a hypermeasure in a different way: the first phrase follows a modified 2 + 2 model, the second the extension-overlap model, and the third the first-down-beat model (although it is actually centered on the third downbeat). Although the phrase rhythm of the chorus is much more regular and predictable (often a prerequisite to success on Top 40 radio), the conditions in the verse provide a fluid, meaningful, and dynamic shape, especially in connection with motivic development in the melody. The first vocal phrase follows an inverted-S curve, reaching its peak, D, on the fourth note, descending to D an octave lower on the eighth note, and rising again to G for the last two notes. The brass instruments answer the vocal phrase with a shortened and modified version of its melody: in imitation of the middle portion of the vocal line, the trumpet plays a five-note descending figure beginning on D (an octave higher than in the voice).[5] The line uses B♭s instead of B♮, as indicated above, but the syncopated rhythm, the P4 leading to the lowest note, and above all the basic contour—a descent from D—make the connection to the vocal phrase clear; the ten-note figure has been reduced to one of only five notes. In the second vocal phrase, D is again quite prominent, four times initiating a syncopated descending figure. Now the melody has been reduced to just four notes: D, D, C, and B♭. So while the length of the vocal phrase has become longer (two and a half measures in phrase 1, five measures in phrase 2), the melodic material has become shorter. The contrast beautifully represents the difference between the two views of time represented in the song; the persona takes the time to watch others hurrying endlessly while ultimately achieving nothing, just as the elongated phrase reflects the melodic material rushing and repeating itself only to end eventually where it started—on D.

The reduction of the melodic motive has not reached an end, though. After the longest-sounding chord of the piece, an E♭ major seventh, enters at the end of the second vocal phrase (the timing of this long chord suits the words of the second verse: "Her diamond watch had stopped cold dead"), the D major chord with the pseudo-boogie embellishment returns. Here the trumpet's repeating Ds appear as the ultimate reduction of the opening material, to a single note, clicking with watchlike precision twice every second.

It is here we begin to understand that the contrasts of the two supersections of the composition represent the contrasting views of life and time on a grander scale. The arrival of the G major seventh chord and of the steady beat at what I have called the introduction to the song proper appears as a great release to the tensions of the first supersection, with its dissonant chords and constantly changing meters and tempos. By following the admittedly beautiful and fascinating first half with the better-known second half, Mr. Lamm seems to be telling us that the frustrations resulting from attempts to bend time to our purposes can be superseded by a carefree attitude (the background vocalists sing during the chorus, "I don't care about time") that allows us to find a distinctive voice within the framework of inexorable time.

"BRAIN DAMAGE" AND "ECLIPSE"

Pink Floyd's classic *Dark Side of the Moon* album (1973) displays several of the earmarks of the concept album. The nonstop connections between pieces, the musical reprise of the song "Breathe," and the return in the last song of the words "all you touch and all you see" from the first song—all suggest we are to take the album as a single artistic endeavor, to be interpreted as a whole rather than as a series of discrete pieces. The existence of a tradition of writing songs whose apparent profundity is ultimately empty, dating back at least to John Lennon's "I Am The Walrus," leaves one to wonder how seriously we should take *Dark Side of the Moon,* or any rock concept album. Did composers like Lennon want to fool the critics or did their immaturity and the narrowness of their personal philosophy leave them with nothing substantial to say? To the extent that this album means anything, any one part must be interpreted in relation to the others. An analysis of the last two numbers on the album, "Brain Damage" and "Eclipse," must be preceded by a foundational understanding of the work as a whole.

The ten songs on the album were all written by various subsets of the group's membership: David Gilmour, Nick Mason, Richard Wright, and Roger Waters. Mr. Waters collaborated on or wrote by himself every piece with lyrics, and it is widely acknowledged that he was the band's primary guiding force during their most successful years. The lyrics, the first basis of our interpretation, appear to be about strategies for survival in an insane world. The philosophy has elements of existentialism; in "Breathe," we are told that

> Long you live and high you fly
> But only if you ride the tide

and that in a world where

> All you touch and all you see
> Is all your life will ever be©*

*BREATHE. Words by Roger Waters; Music by Roger Waters, David Gilmour, and Rick Wright. TRO—© Copyright 1973 (Renewed) Hampshire House Publishing Corp., New York, NY. Used by Permission

we should "Look around and choose [our] own ground." The last line of "Breathe" tells us that the need for the existentialist series of acts of self-definition is the imminence of death. The next piece with lyrics, "Time," elaborates, pointing out that the urgency of life is realized only when it is too late. To the young, the song says,

You are young and life is long and there is time to kill today
And then one day you find ten years have got behind you.©*

But those who have reached the time of life when time has become a reality are told:

You're older
And shorter of breath and one day closer to death
Every year is getting shorter, never seem to find the time.

At this point in the album, critiques of the normal ways of the world come to the fore, reflecting many of the leftist, antiestablishment views so pervasive in rock through the early 1970s: there is a stance against dehumanization caused by greed, war, and organized religion, and a stance for acceptance and fraternity. The need for community and love was already briefly referred to in the first song:

Don't be afraid to care
Leave but don't leave me.

Stoic acquiescence is quickly dismissed near the end of "Time": "Hanging on in quiet desperation is the English way." A gentle but sure rejection of organized religion is expressed in the reprise of "Breathe"; although the singer seems to accept the sound of a distant church bell as an element of his comfortable experience at home by the fire, he is not present with "the faithfull." This song can also be taken, however, as ironically assuming the persona of one of the people the album is criticizing, thus denouncing the casual acceptance of religion without any personal commitment.

Certainly the first song of side 2, "Money," facetiously assumes a persona, this time of the person for whom material wealth is the sole criterion of happiness yet who nevertheless must spend words trying to rationalize this position:

*TIME. Words and Music by Roger Waters, Nicholas Mason, David Gilmour and Rick Wright. TRO—© Copyright 1973 (Renewed) Hampshire House Publishing Corp., New York, NY. Used by Permission

> Money it's a crime
> Share it fairly but don't take a slice of my pie.©*

The next song, "Us And Them," describes the military as a cold institution that cares nothing for the humanity of the people it controls:

> And the General sat, and the lines on the map
> Moved from side to side
> . . . .
> And who knows which is which and who is who

and whose efforts cannot ultimately be justified:

> And in the end it's only round and round and round
> Haven't you heard it's a battle of words.©†

I'm not saying that the philosophy is consistent, well thought out, or even meant to be taken seriously, and I do not necessarily agree with any part of it, although I find it all interesting. But insomuch as the album means anything, that meaning is clearly reflected in the music for the last two numbers, "Brain Damage" and "Eclipse," both by Roger Waters alone. The lyrics of "Brain Damage" make clear that alienation in the world results in lunacy. This lunacy takes several forms reminiscent of themes from earlier songs; they range from retention of (or reversion to) childhood ways ("Remembering games and daisy chains and laughs") to simple nonconformity ("And if the band you're in starts playing different tunes") to paranoia ("And if your head explodes with dark forebodings").©‡

The most powerful form, however, is a type of schizophrenia; that the singer suffers from this malady becomes apparent only gradually: after the early lines "The lunatic is on the grass" and "The lunatic is in the hall" and a subtle shift of focus with "The lunatics are in my hall," the third verse begins "The lunatic is in my head." The duality of personalities is neatly reflected in the presence of two versions of the third scale degree in the verse. (See exam-

*MONEY. Words and Music by Roger Waters. TRO—© Copyright 1973 (Renewed) Hampshire House Publishing Corp., New York, NY. Used by Permission
†US AND THEM. Words and Music by Roger Waters and Rick Wright. TRO— © Copyright 1973 (Renewed) Hampshire House Publishing Corp., New York, NY. Used by Permission
‡BRAIN DAMAGE. Words and Music by Roger Waters. TRO—© Copyright 1973 (Renewed) Hampshire House Publishing Corp., New York, NY. Used by Permission

7.5. Lunacy and sanity as represented by two forms of the third scale degree in the melody of "Brain Damage," by Pink Floyd.

BRAIN DAMAGE. Words and Music by Roger Waters. TRO—© Copyright 1973 (Renewed) Hampshire House Publishing Corp., New York, NY. Used by Permission

ple 7.5.) Each verse, in fact, appears as a struggle between the two forms, the normal form (F♯) beginning the melody, the lowered form (F♮) intruding twice, each time with no immediate resolution, and the verse finally resolving from above on the normal form. (F♯ appears in the final chord and as a passing tone near the end of the melody in each verse; in some verses, the melody ends on F♯ rather than D.) Since the song is in the major mode, it is natural that the major third scale degree should represent the normal and the lowered third the pathological, a correspondence clearly borne out twice in the song. In the first verse, the lowered third accompanies the word "grass," the arena for childhood games and other nonconformist behavior. The verse ends with the normal third in the last harmony, appearing simultaneously with the last word of the line "Got to keep the loonies on the path," the path representing conventional, or at least tolerable, behavior. In the third verse, the lowered form comes on the last word of the line "The lunatic is in my head," the very word that tells us the singer himself is suffering. The return of the normal form comes with the word "sane."

Another musical duality in this song involves the use of two keys. If the distinction between the keys were clear, the situation would not deserve more than a passing remark. But while the verses are clearly in D major, the identity

7.6. Two tonal interpretations of the chorus of "Brain Damage."

	G		A		C		G	
D:	IV		V		VII		IV	
G:	I		V/V		IV		I	

of the key in the chorus is somewhat cloudy. (See example 7.6.) Like the personalities in the singer's head, there seem to be two keys going on at once. All the chords of the chorus fit the chromatic-minor palette for D major, so the mere harmonic content of the passage suggests no reason for shifting interpretive paradigms. But the passage both begins and ends on G major, and the melody centers around B instead of a pitch more stable in the context of D. The chords all work in G major as well (either major or chromatic-minor palette), and in fact the passage contains no D major harmony; so the passage taken by itself clearly suggests a G major interpretation. The emphasis of the harmony on the G major chord and of the melody on B does not become apparent, however, until the fourth measure of the section; recognition of the second key is as gradual as the singer's realization of the lunatic's presence in his head. The singer's prescription for his now recognized malady is to seek communal refuge in the commiseration of lunatics, whom he offers to meet on the dark side of the moon, the moon being the etymologically appropriate place for lunatics (the English "moon" equates to the Latin *luna*), and the reference to the dark side suggesting that lunatics do not enjoy the salubrious effects of the sun.

Beginning with a textual reference to "Breathe" ("All that you touch / All that you see"), "Eclipse" consists of a litany of life's activities, a litany whose seemingly relentless length refers back to another line of "Breathe":

And when at last the work is done
Don't sit down it's time to dig another one.[©*6]

The harmonic pattern, which seamlessly prolongs the key of D, portends to go on forever, also; the repetition of the open-ended succession I-V$^4_2$/IV-VI-Vsus is just the kind of pattern that rock songs fade out with.

The rhythmic pattern of the voice is simple and repetitive as well, but herein lies a feature suggesting that a change might be forthcoming. Within a

*ECLIPSE. Words and Music by Roger Waters. TRO—© Copyright 1973 (Renewed) Hampshire House Publishing Corp., New York, NY. Used by Permission

triple-meter framework, each short vocal phrase comes to rest on an even-numbered downbeat. (If the piece is heard in 6, these melodic cadences come halfway through their respective measures, an even more nonstandard situation.) This nonstandard pattern usually constitutes a kind of structural dissonance that eventually must resolve with a standard cadence on an odd-numbered downbeat (In Chapter 1 I describe a similar situation in Elton John's "Goodbye Yellow Brick Road."

Change in fact eventually occurs. The truly wonderful passage begins at the end of the sixth repetition of the harmonic pattern, that is, with the twenty-fourth vocal phrase. The masterly extension of this line works subtly, beat by beat. Each of the preceding twenty-three lines, most being four syllables long, reaches its final note on (or around) the fourth beat, that is, the first downbeat of the second three-beat measure. In this twenty-fourth line, however, the fourth syllable, the beat corresponding to the end of each of the twenty-three previous lines, is the syllable "un." This is clearly the first syllable of an as yet uncompleted word; more text, and therefore a longer melody, are required and expected. But the completion of the word reveals it to be a preposition, the word "under." Again, at least one more word, a noun, is required. But the next we word we hear is "the," an article again requiring a subsequent noun. When "sun," the resolution of the preceding preposition and article, arrives, we realize that we have been brought step-by-step to a partial melodic resolution in a standard metrical placement for the first time in the song: "sun" appears with the return of the I chord at the beginning of what promises to be the seventh repetition of the harmonic pattern. The association of sun and the tonic chord, with its major third, comes as no surprise; the sun here contrasts with the moon, which was associated in "Brain Damage" with lunacy and the lowered third scale degree.

The I chord coming at the beginning of a hypermeasure, we expect a continuation—and a continuation we get. The next beat shows us that the long string of noun phrases was actually a compound subject in search of a verb; we are presented with the copula "is." "Is what?" we ask. The next two beats tell us that everything under the sun is "in tune." The arrival of these words is important, in that they are the first affirmation in the album that health and order exist; the implication is that the existentialist life of continuous self-defining action encouraged in "Breathe" and lived out in "Eclipse" will provide meaning.

The triumph of health and order lasts only two beats, however; the next word is "but." (The barrage of twists and changes is worthy of a Hollywood thriller from the 1940s.) The word "sun" returns on the next downbeat, with the arrival of the V^4_2/IV; the sunny major third is still present in the chord, but its light is obscured by the dissonant seventh in the bass, a musical phenomenon perfectly suited to the next few words, which tell us that the sun "is eclipsed by the moon." Order may exist, but we are doomed to know about it yet never enjoy it. It is no accident that the word "moon" arrives with the VI chord and its lowered third scale degree.

With the word "moon," we get the first long note of the piece, and it comes at the end of a sentence, on the downbeat of an odd-numbered measure; everything suggests that the melody has reached its final cadence. According to rock standards, we therefore believe that we have heard the final philosophical statement; the piece could go on instrumentally repeating the harmonic pattern and then fade out and still be something special. But what ensues ironically supersedes this resolution. The V chord is left out of the pattern this time, and the chord succession proceeds directly to a sustained tonic harmony. The early arrival of the I chord, not on the downbeat of the large hypermeasure defined by the previous repetitions of the harmonic pattern, allows the rhythm simply to stop. The chord does not coincide with the inception of a new pattern, as it has previously and as it does generally in rock, but clearly at the end of a pattern, at the rare (for rock) moment of total harmonic resolution. The succession directly from VI to I means that we hear for the first and only time in these two pieces the immediate resolution of the lowered third scale degree to the normal third scale degree, as the chorus sustains the word "moon." The status of the moon has been lifted with the third scale degree from the deviant to the standard; the distinction between lunacy and normalcy is dissolved. Over a fading heartbeat, a distant voice (the lunatic in my head?) says, "There is no dark side in the moon really. As a matter of fact it's all dark." The abnormal is normal. Like Solomon, whom he alludes to, Mr. Waters has learned that existential action, and indeed everything under the sun, is vanity.

"WHAT A FOOL BELIEVES"

"What A Fool Believes" (1978), written by Michael McDonald of the Doobie Brothers, is far more complex and sophisticated than the typical rock composition, although this hit stayed in the Top 40 for fourteen weeks and topped the charts for a time. Despite its distinct features, however, this complexity—which touches phrase structure, rhythm, harmonies, and form—is based on principles found in most rock and described in this book.

The form is essentially binary, although the boundary between the verse and chorus is blurred (as outlined below). The verse of the song is primarily in D♭ major, with characteristic excursions to the relative key, B♭ minor. The chorus, in E, provides a chromatic-third relationship with the main key of the

7.7. Keyboard part in the introduction to "What A Fool Believes."

WHAT A FOOL BELIEVES, by Michael McDonald and Kenny Loggins.
© 1978 Milk Money Music and Snug Music. All Rights Reserved. Used by
Permission. WARNER BROS. PUBLICATIONS U.S. INC., Miami, FL
33014.

verse, another of the most common key relationships in rock.[7] Although the
chorus repeats a very straightforward harmonic pattern, ii7-V11-I-vi7, the verse
provides plenty of harmonic interest and ambiguity. The very first sonority
sets the tone. (See example 7.7.)

A number of interpretations are possible: the chord is an A♭13(sus); the
chord is a G♭ major seventh, with an added tone in the bass; the chord is really
A♭7, D♭ and F being embellishments; and so on. The problem is not that we
have no way to interpret the sonority but that we must interpret it without
knowing which is right. Because most rock songs begin with a stable structure
that proves to be the tonic harmony, there are few examples of opening unstable harmonies that can be compared. On the other hand, each interpretation
above is complex given the usual harmonic straightforwardness of rock—triads and seventh chords in root position, with occasional suspensions and added
tones. The second half of the first measure is no clearer; whether this harmony
is to be interpreted as G♭(2) with subsequent passing tones or A♭7 with the seventh in the bass depends partly on how the first ambiguous cluster is interpreted. The second measure offers the first pure triad, D♭, and therefore sug-

gests the key. The chord is not allowed much stability, however; besides coming in the second measure of four as opposed to the first or fourth (usual places for tonic harmonies), it is in inversion. On the other hand, the five-flat pitch content of the passage confirms the notion of D♭ as tonic. The sonority on the downbeat of the third measure, identical to the first sonority except for the bass, presents further complexities; the top line, for instance, moves from F to E♭ at the same time the bass moves from E♭ to F. If the essential harmony is thought to be E♭, G♭, and B♭, the motion from F to E♭ may be viewed as a resolution of a nonchord tone. But because F is so prevalent, perhaps it should be viewed as a proper part of the chord—the ninth. The fourth measure adds two twists to the harmonic succession. First, the apparent resolution on B♭ minor seventh weakens the sense of key (although beginning a phrase on a major chord and ending it on the relative minor occurs commonly in rock (see Chapter 2, under "Multiple Keys"). Even more interesting is the chromatic harmony at the end of the measure, a harmony based on the seldom used whole-tone scale (passages in Stevie Wonder's "You Are The Sunshine Of My Life" and Deodato's "Also Sprach Zarathustra (2001)" come to mind as two such rare instances in rock).

Another level of complexity plays out in the rhythmic interaction between the accompanimental pattern from example 7.7 and the melody. The unifying thread of the complex pattern, the simultaneous use of syncopated and unsyncopated figures, can be seen in the second half of the introduction, when a synthesizer melody is added to the texture.[8] The pattern becomes more interesting, however, with the entrance of the voice and the addition of textual accents. (See example 7.8.) The first line in fact presents a type of textual syncopation: the accented syllables "long" and "-go" (of "ago") begin on the weak half of their respective beats, while the unaccented syllable "a-" comes on the metrically strong downbeat. Although the rhythm of this passage taken without words is not syncopated (the string of even eighth notes promotes no beat or part of a beat over any others), the textual accents are.

The accent on "long" in the first line coincides with the syncopation of the harmonic pattern. The beginning of the next line, however, places all the accented syllables in appropriate metrical positions, thereby conflicting with the syncopation of the piano part: the accented syllables "sen-," "-men-," and "fool" all come directly on their respective beats, while the unaccented syllables "-ti-" and "-tal" come on the second half of the beat. The irony here is that while the last, unaccented syllable of "sentimental" arrives in a straightforward, unsyncopated fashion on the weak part of the beat, the piano part simultaneously plays an accented, syncopated chord. Similar examples occur later in

7.8. Rhythmic intricacy in the verse to "What A Fool Believes."

the verse; note, for instance, the conflict with the piano part in the unsyncopated setting of the words "for his nostalgic tale," "never coming near," and "it never really was."

Further conflict arises when a syncopated vocal line clashes with an unsyncopated portion of the piano part. Consider the figure with the words "tryin' hard": its last syllable, an accented syllable, comes on the second part of the

7.8. Continued

WHAT A FOOL BELIEVES, by Michael McDonald and Kenny Loggins. © 1978 Milk Money Music and Snug Music. All Rights Reserved. Used by Permission. WARNER BROS. PUBLICATIONS U.S. INC., Miami, FL 33014.

fourth beat, an extremely weak metrical position, while the unaccented syllable "-in'" precedes it on the fourth beat, and no word appears on the following downbeat. Yet the piano part does not support the rhythm of the line with its own syncopation: beat 4 of the measure in question and the downbeat of the following measure each present basic quarter notes. So the rhythms of the vocal line and piano are out of synch, often in the verse: syncopated vocal lines appear against square piano rhythms, and square vocal lines appear against syncopated piano rhythms.

Just often enough to keep the pattern unpredictable, however, the vocal and accompanimental parts align. The syncopated syllable "long" in the first line coincides with a syncopated accent in the piano part, and the downbeat placement of the last word of the line "She musters a smile" coincides with a chord played squarely on the downbeat. Most rock vocal lines incorporate syncopated rhythms, but the interesting, unpredictable sequence of conflicts—and occasional alignment—between syncopated and unsyncopated figures in this song lends it an unusual level of rhythmic complexity.

On a larger scale, the rhythm of the vocal line presents equal complexity, again based on common rock patterns. Because some vocal lines are separated by extensive rests (as between "long ago" and "The sentimental") and others by none at all (as between "don't see" and "Tryin' hard"), the phrase structure of the verse as a whole is varied and unpredictable. The rock pattern of lines ending on odd-numbered downbeats, however, serves as a unifying factor. Note, for instance, the metrical placement of the end of the line "For once in his life she musters a smile." The line "Never coming near what she wanted to say," not notated in example 7.8, is similar.

On an even larger scale, the form of the piece as a whole exhibits an unusual level of subtlety and ambiguity. "What a Fool Believes" clearly has two main parts: a verse and a chorus. The problem concerns where to place the line "But what a fool believes he sees, no wise man has the power." Rock conventions suggest that the entrance of a second vocal track and of the title line marks the beginning of the chorus. The appearance of an F♯ minor seventh chord at the beginning of the line confirms this notion by suggesting a key change. In addition, two other features normally associated with beginning gestures occur at the end of that line. First, the tonic chord of the new key, E major, doesn't appear until the end of the line. Just as it appears, the high, sustained string line that distinguishes the second part of the verse disappears. Because of the combination of the arrival of harmonic stability and the change in instrumentation, the moment in question seems a significant formal delineator. If the chorus is seen to begin at this later point, the title line could be considered either part of the verse or a transitional line.

In the end, the original interpretation proves to be correct. Of obvious importance in this determination is the repetition of the harmonic pattern of the line in question; its ii7 and V11 consistently return in the repeating ii7-V11-I-vi7 pattern of the chorus. The interpreter, however, must not overlook the significance of the words. Although the verse tells the story of a rather awkward meeting between a man and a woman he mistakenly believes is still in love with him, the line in question begins a series of explanations and rationalizations for the man's actions. The marked distinction between the rhetoric of the verse and that of the chorus clearly places the line in the latter section. Although the ambiguity of boundaries may not seem appropriate for a passage whose purpose is clarification, the revelation in the fade-out that the persona of the song is the man in the story shows retrospectively that the text of the chorus is an admission of suppressed truth, a glimmer of reality revealed by the singer only long enough to explain why he can't allow its presence in his conscious thought. The persona's thinking isn't as clear as he would wish, and therefore the ambiguity is fitting.

Common patterns of rock are the foundation of every aspect of this song and its complex structures. The tight packing of accepted methods of chordal embellishment creates a complex and ambiguous harmonic framework for the verse. The rapid succession of a variety of small- and medium-scale rhythms in the vocal line creates a complex, unpredictable configuration. And the number of features generally used to establish formal demarcations in rock is so great and their character so disparate that although they usually align for the purposes of formal clarity, they are arranged here to create ambiguity. The implication of this analysis is that while most songs of the pop era are simple, the common traits of the style and their possible combinations are rich enough to allow for moderately complex compositions. And remember that this analysis deals with only traditional features: phrase structure, rhythm, keys, harmonic types and successions, instrumentation, and form. Were pitch inflection, rhythmic inflection, and timbre to be considered—parameters easy to judge in general terms but difficult to analyze in detail—the complexity would increase. This rock song, though based on standard rock patterns, is not simple or crude, is not repetitious, and certainly uses more than "just the same three chords."

"THE ENDLESS ENIGMA"

"What A Fool Believes" offers a moderate level of sophistication, but to get a truer view of the complexity possible in rock, one must look to the progressive-rock bands of the 1970s. The music of this genre often incorporates extended length, detailed polyphony, unusual harmonies, and complex forms. But even these grow out of rock's stylistic standards. "The Endless Enigma," by Keith Emerson and Greg Lake of Emerson, Lake & Palmer (also known as ELP)—in some minds the most successful of the progressive-rock bands—demonstrates that all the above characteristics act as embellishments of common structures of rock style.[9]

We begin with the form of this lengthy piece, which will prove useful to other parts of the analysis (See example 7.9.) Overall the piece is in compound-ternary form, as suggested by the track division on the recording (visible on the original LP) and by the three separately named segments: "The Endless Enigma (Part I)," "Fugue," and "The Endless Enigma (Part II)."

Determining where the division between "Part I" and "Fugue" lies, however, creates an interesting trilemma. After an ametrical introduction, "Part I" clearly centers around a set of verses, mostly in F♯, played by the full band (organ, bass, and drums in this case—the organ and drums both electronically distorted through means of pre-amp overdrive) and sung by Greg Lake. At one point the band stops, and a rhapsodic, metrically free piano solo begins, starting in D-minor. (See example 7.10 for a transcription of this passage and the

7.9. Form of "The Endless Enigma," by Emerson, Lake, & Palmer.

Passage	Instrumentation	Meter	Key	Time
a	Synthesizer, piano, bongos	free	none	0' 00"
b	Piano, organ, drums, bass	6/8	C♯ minor?	1' 37"
c	Organ, bass, drums	6/8	C minor	1' 59"
d	Organ, bass, drums	6/8	C♯?	2' 27"
verse 1	Organ, bass, voice, drums	4/4	F♯	2' 34"
verse 2	Organ, bass, voice, drums	4/4	F♯	3' 12"
verse 3	Organ, bass, voice, drums	4/4	E♭-F♯	3' 47"
verse 4	Organ, bass, voice, drums	4/4	E♭-F♯	4' 47"
e	Organ, bass, drums	6/8	C♯m-F♯	5' 46"
f	Piano	free	Dm et al.	6' 04"
g	Piano, bass, percussion	var.	C	6' 44"
fugue	Piano, bass, percussion	4/4	C et al.	7' 31"
h	Piano, bass, drums	4/4	C-F♯	8' 39"
i	Organ, synth, bass, chimes	4/4	F♯	8' 57"
verse 5	Organ, synth, bass, voice, drums	4/4	F♯	9' 27"
verse 6	Organ, synth, bass, voice, drums	4/4	F♯	10' 09"
coda	Organ, synth, bass, drums	6/8	?	10' 20"
end	—	—	—	10' 36"

next, the passages labeled "f" and "g" in example 7.9.) The dramatic changes in instrumentation, metrical organization, and key suggest a division at this point. The physical division on the LP, however, comes about forty seconds later, just as the piano begins a new passage with a fairly steady pulse (although the meter changes often) and new, distinctive melodic material in C (passage "g" in the chart). Neither of these divisions marks the beginning of a fugue, however, which the name of the middle part promises. An actual fugue, based on the melodic material just introduced, begins about forty-five seconds into the track marked on the LP. We are left with three possible interpretations. Does "Fugue" begin with the entrance of the piano, with the introduction of the new melodic material, or with the beginning of the actual fugue?

The second dividing point is almost as difficult to locate. After the fugue, the division on the LP marks the beginning of a homophonic passage played by piano, bass, and drums (passage "h" in example 7.9). Although the texture of the passage contrasts with the preceding fugue, it is otherwise similar to the middle portion of the composition. For instance, the passage begins in C, the key of most of the middle portion (although it ends in F♯, the key of the verses

7.10. Passages "f" (marked "Freely") and "g" (marked "In strict tempo") from "The Endless Enigma."

(*continued*)

7.10. Continued

7.10. Continued

(*continued*)

7.10. Continued

THE ENDLESS ENIGMA. Words and Music by Keith Emerson and Greg Lake. © Copyright 1971 (Renewed) by Leadchoice Ltd. Administered Worldwide by Campbell Connelly & CO., Ltd. International Copyright Secured. All Rights Reserved. Reprinted by Permission.

of "Part II"); its harmonies and melody are similar to those of passage "g," just before the actual fugue; and its instrumentation is essentially the same as that at the end of the fugue (bass and percussion enter partway through the fugue). But even though these features suggest that the passage is still part of the middle, finding a place between the beginning of this passage and the return of the sung verses is difficult because of the absence of any appreciable pause in the rhythmic flow.

Wherever one chooses to make the divisions, the overall impression is one of three major passages, each with several subsections. The extended length of "The Endless Enigma" and its formal complexity express the classical training of the composer and keyboardist, Keith Emerson; few rock pieces last more than ten minutes, and ternary form is rare in rock. Because of the emotive power of the human voice, however, this complex form seems to revolve around the two sets of sung verses, in much the same way that the first three, instrumental movements of Beethoven's Symphony no. 9 seem to act as a prelude to the fourth, choral movement. Each verse ends on the dominant harmony, a common feature of verses in rock songs. (See Chapter 1, under "V-I Motion Between Units.") So although the form of the composition as a whole displays external stylistic influences, its core, a modified strophic song, is very much in the mainstream of rock practice.

Almost every metrical passage in the piece divides into groups of two or four measures, the only notable exception being the end of the first verse. In other words, a typical, regular hypermeter predominates; there is little complexity in this regard. The entrance of the vocal line, however, allows for some interesting interaction between vocal phrases and this fairly regular hypermetrical structure. (Most of the instrumental passages continuously repeat rhythmic motives rather than dividing into phrases.) For example, although two-fifths of the song's twenty-five vocal phrases follow a traditional 3 + 1 model, the structures common to rock nonetheless prevail. (See Chapter 1 for a description of the standard models.) Each verse, for instance, ends with a short phrase leading to an odd-numbered downbeat.

The rhythm of the single phrase of verse 6, an extension-overlap structure, is especially important. (See example 7.11.) The voice and harmony both resolve on the tonic at the end of the line, "Now that it's done I've begun to see the reason why I'm here." The moment marks the first and only time in the piece when the high tonic pitch and the tonic harmony are heard together. As a result, text, melody, and harmony all seem to work together to achieve a sense of resolution.

But as the title suggests, the piece will not end with a sense of resolution.

7.11. Verse 6 and the coda of "The Endless Enigma."

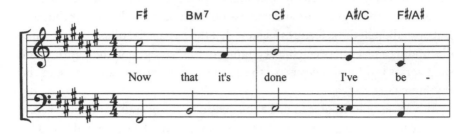

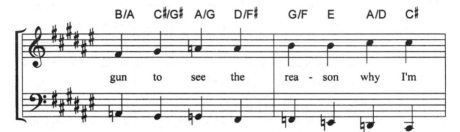

The tonic harmony is not the last harmony of the piece. Its arrival, together with the tonic pitch, comes on a strong, odd-numbered downbeat, which, as Chapter 1 explains, is a point of inception, not of resolution. Lake holds the high F♯, and a new passage begins that explores tritone relationships, then chromatic-third relationships, building in pitch level and dynamic intensity, and eventually ending by sustaining the most dissonant sonority of the piece.

7.11. Continued

THE ENDLESS ENIGMA. Words and Music by Keith Emerson and Greg Lake. © Copyright 1971 (Renewed) by Leadchoice Ltd. Administered Worldwide by Campbell Connelly & CO., Ltd. International Copyright Secured. All Rights Reserved. Reprinted by Permission.

Had the final vocal phrase concluded on a traditional, even-numbered downbeat, the piece would have ended with resolution, but the use of the rock standard propelled the music past the point of resolution into the meaning-laden coda.

Phrase rhythms not common to either standard, however, also add interest to the piece. The second-to-last phrase of each verse, for example, features an unusual cadence. (See example 7.12.) The vocal line ends, unresolved, on the seventh scale degree, on the third beat of the phrase's fourth measure. The harmony continues to a resolution but arrives at the tonic early, on the fourth beat of the measure. The chord is sustained for two beats; the downbeat of the next measure is completely unarticulated. The lack of coordination between melody and harmony, the unusual metrical placement of the chord of resolution, the deemphasis of the downbeat, and the lack of resolution in the vocal line

7.12. An unusual cadence in "The Endless Enigma."

THE ENDLESS ENIGMA. Words and Music by Keith Emerson and Greg Lake. © Copyright 1971 (Renewed) by Leadchoice Ltd. Administered Worldwide by Campbell Connelly & CO., Ltd. International Copyright Secured. All Rights Reserved. Reprinted by Permission.

work together to produce a distorted, disorienting effect. The text speaks of a modernist conflict between the apparent lack of truth, justice, and beauty in the world and the inability to quit believing that such ideals exist. These rhythmically awkward cadences, as well as the mixture in the rest of the phrases of old and new forms, suits the subject well.

The piece uses primarily major and minor triads but contains many sonorities that are unusual for rock, harmonies that can be interpreted as major triads with some other note in the bass—for instance, a C major triad with an F or D in the bass. Edward Macan, in his book on English progressive rock, cites the description of these chords by three influential keyboard players of the progressive-rock movement.[10] Gary Brooker of Procol Harum is quoted as saying, "I've always been quite a lover of playing the wrong note in the bass to alter the sound of a chord"; Tony Banks of Genesis remarked that "you come up with interesting changes when you change chords simply by changing the bass notes"; and Keith Emerson describes the resulting sonorities as "major chords played off against the root next door." Because the bass notes in these chords are not always "next door" to the root, Brooker's terminology seems preferable to Emerson's, and the chords will therefore be called "wrong-bass chords" in the discussions that follow. These harmonies, while uncommon outside progressive rock, are nevertheless suggested by the typical practice of holding the notes of a chord as pedal points while moving the bass line, as in the phrase from the Goo Goo Dolls' "Name." (See example 4.7.) So even these somewhat unusual chords arise as an extension of basic rock style. The distinctiveness of their use here consists merely in their variety. In "Name" for instance, we hear a D major triad with D in the bass, then D major with B in the bass, and then D major with G in the bass. But in "The Endless Enigma," an A major triad with G in the bass is followed by D with F♯ in the bass and then G with F in the bass, and so on.

On the other hand, a few harmonies in the piece cannot be so readily traced to basic rock practice. Quite unusual for rock are the chords with an added raised fourth that appear in the introductory passages and coda. (See, e.g., the chords in m. 11 of example 7.11.)

As Chapter 3 explains, rock only rarely makes use of the traditional V-I cadence with the tonic chord on the fourth downbeat of a phrase. In "The Endless Enigma," the avoidance of the traditional cadence is almost palpable. The phrases ending on the fourth downbeat employ either IV-I or VII-I cadences. The distorted cadences described above and shown in example 7.11 do employ a V-I harmonic pattern, but the tonic harmony comes on the fourth beat of fourth measure, and the melody is left unresolved. In the last phrase of verses 1 through 5, the melody ends on the tonic note, but the harmony underneath is VI. In the third and fourth verses, which are longer and more complex with regard to form than the others, the first two phrases each end with the tonic pitch in the melody, but here the harmony is vi. Verse 6 ends with a V-I cadence, but, as described above, the tonic chord comes on the fifth downbeat of the phrase.

The pitch content of the vocal melodies supports the key of the various passages of the verses in ways outlined in Chapter 2; the unusual complexity comes not in the scales themselves but in the use of so many in a single piece. Diatonic sets appear in the first two verses: the major scale ([013568T] with [1] as tonic) for the bulk of each of these verses with Mixolydian flavoring (a "lowered" seventh suggests [013568T] with [8] as tonic) near the end. Verses 3 and 4 begin with a melody similar to that of verses 1 and 2 but employ only the notes of a pentatonic scale ([02479] with [0] as tonic). The lowered third occurs on the line "Please open their eyes" in each of these verses and in the very short sixth verse, suggesting either a blues transformation of the major scale or a shift to the natural-minor scale ([013568T] with [T] as tonic). The instrumental melodies make use of the standard pitch-source sets as well, but some Lydian-influenced passages and the virtually atonal, chromatic passages near the beginning go beyond typical rock practice.

The keys of "The Endless Enigma" also verge on the slightly unusual. The main keys found in the verses are F♯ and E♭; the chromatic-third relationship between them is common to rock. The main key of "Fugue," C, forms another chromatic-third relationship with E♭, the secondary key of the verses, but it shares a tritone relationship with F♯, one of the main keys of the verses, a relationship that is strange for rock (except in some heavy-metal styles largely outside the scope of this book).

These two key relationships are echoed at a local level in chord relationships in some of the instrumental passages of the introduction and the coda. These harmonic relationships form combinations of chords not found in any of the standard rock harmonic palettes. The coda, for instance, begins with F♯ and C triads, a tritone apart. Although this pair of harmonies technically forms a part of both the E and B♭ chromatic-minor palettes (think C and G♭ for the second possibility), the chords forming a tritone relationship in that palette (II and VI) rarely occur in the same piece. (The lack of either E or B♭ as tonic anywhere in the piece also discourages this interpretation.) The coda goes on with a succession of major triads based on chromatic-third relationships: B, D, F, and G♯. Although the idea of keeping the chord quality consistent is reminiscent of the generating principle of the chromatic-minor system, this particular combination of roots doesn't form a part of any rock palette in any key.

179

Most portions of the piece, however, follow the harmonic palettes outlined in Chapter 4. The first part of verses 1 through 4 uses the diatonic portion of the major system, and the last part the chromatic-minor palette (A, B, C♯, D, and E harmonies, all major triads, in the key of F♯). The passage marked "In strict tempo" in example 7.10 employs the major system with chromatic chords (V/ii, V/V, and V/vi all appear, usually with "wrong bass notes"; see above.) The portion after the repeat sign uses the chromatic-minor system for C major: major triads on C, D, E♭, F, G, A♭, and B♭ represent the complete palette. Verse 6 (see example 7.11) presents a mixture of systems. All the chords are major triads (most with wrong basses), and most come from the chromatic-minor palette for F♯ (F♯, A, B, C♯, D, and E all appear in this passage); but the passage also incorporates V/vi (the A♯ triad in m. 2) and N (the G triad in m. 4). Chapter 4 presented examples of songs using mixed systems, but rarely does a piece of rock use eight different chords in a single phrase.

The harmonic successions of "The Endless Enigma" follow the rock standards of root movement occasionally, as in the descending second in the I-vi-V pattern at the beginning of verses 1 and 2. But most passages actually follow traditional standards of root movement. (See Chapter 5.) The root motion of verse 6, interestingly, can be viewed in two ways. If we accept the typical analysis of the complex harmonies as a basic triad supplemented by a dissonant bass note, we view the passage as proceeding almost entirely by the traditional ascending second, descending third, and ascending fourth (F♯, B, C♯, A♯, F♯, B, C♯, A, D, G, E, A, C♯, F♯). The only exception comes with the penultimate chord: the motion from A to C♯ is an ascending third. The complexity of the passage depends more on the high number of chords used and the inclusion of wrong basses. If, on the other hand, we reject in a sense Gary Brooker's terminology in favor of Keith Emerson's and view the bass notes not as wrong but as the actual roots, we interpret the passage as proceeding entirely by descending step, in accordance with the standard more common to rock.

Progressive rock is sometimes called "art rock" or "classical rock," a reference to the notion that bands who play this genre have infused stylistic traits from older, classical styles into the rock idiom. "The Endless Enigma" seems especially rich with contrasting elements from different eras, contrasts suitable to the philosophical confusion of its lyrics: the polyphony of the fugue versus the homophony of the verses, the acoustic instrumentation of the middle portion versus the electronic sounds (including even distorted drums) of the outer portions, the hymnlike quality of the beginning of verses 1 through 4 versus the brash self-declarations of the ends of those verses. We've seen, however, that the borrowings from the past have little to do with bringing this piece closer to a traditional sense of tonality. In some of ELP's other recordings—such as their renditions of Mussorgsky's *Pictures at an Exhibition* (originally composed in 1874), the march from Tschaikovsky's *Nutcracker* (after B. Bumble and the Stingers' "Nutrocker" from 1962; Tchaikovsky's original composition was written in 1892), Bartók's *Allegro Barbaro* (1911), and Copland's "Fanfare for the Common Man" (1942)—the product admittedly consists essentially of playing a classical piece with rock instruments. But it is important to note that none of the pieces listed dates from earlier than the 1870s. All the pieces were written by composers whose historical timeframe or Eastern European roots (or both) led them to push the boundaries of traditional, mainly Germanic tonality or to seek alternatives in other pitch-centric folk musics. Mozart won't be found on a progressive-rock album. So the result of this direct borrowing on the rest of ELP's repertoire was not a conformity to the rhythmic, harmonic, or melodic practice of traditional tonality. Much of that practice survived through the Tin Pan Alley era into the popular song of the early 1950s and beyond (although it ceased being the dominant style after the advent of rock 'n' roll), and so was available to rock composers without their having to draw upon classical influences. Progressive-rock bands instead borrowed from classical composers ideas about extended length, motivic unity, texture, instrumentation, and expression. But progressive rock is still rock; the language of harmony, melody, and phrase structure remain largely founded on the principles outlined in this book. In these respects, Emerson, Lake & Palmer are still closer to the Beach Boys than to Bach, to Motown than to Mozart.

exercises

When asked to cite a song, indicate the title, performers, composers, and year of recording or release. Choose examples that have not been mentioned in the text.

CHAPTER 1: PHRASE RHYTHM

A. Structures and Patterns

1. Using metrical charts like those found in this chapter, chart a hypothetical example of each of the phrase-rhythm models described in this chapter:
   a. 2 + 2 model
   b. extension-overlap model
   c. first-downbeat model
   d. elision model
   e. 1 + 1 model
2. Make a phrase-rhythm chart of the Beatles' "Fixing A Hole" (1967).

B. Examples

1. Find at least one rock song in which most phrases follow the 2 + 2 model. Make a phrase-rhythm chart of at least one section of the song, showing measure numbers and beat numbers and indicating the vocal phrases through means of brackets and lyrics.

2. Find at least one rock song in which a phrase following the extension-overlap model ends the chorus and overlaps with the return of the material from the introduction. Make a phrase-rhythm chart of the chorus.

3. Find at least one rock song in which the vocal line of the verse begins after the first beat of the first hypermeasure. Does the song later use extension-overlap phrase rhythm? Is the vocal gap at the beginning of the verse filled in later verses by the end of the last phrase of the preceding section? Make a phrase-rhythm chart of the verses in question.

4. Find at least one rock song in which most phrases follow the first-downbeat model. Identify the song, and make a phrase-rhythm chart of at least one section.

5. Find at least one rock song in which a cadence on (or near) the fourth downbeat is followed by two measures of vocal rest. Make a phrase-rhythm chart of the section in which this elision occurs.

6. Find at least one rock song in which every section ends with the V chord.

7. Find at least one rock song in which the lyrics deal, through images of wheels or turning, with a cyclical or unresolved (unresolvable?) situation.

C. Composition

1. Write one verse of a song using the blues progression (or a modification of it) in which the vocal phrases all follow the first-downbeat model.

2. Write a short song in which the first verse begins with a rhythmically and grammatically isolated word (such as the word "time" at the beginning of "It Might Be You"). Construct the song so that the word standing in the same place in the second verse is actually the last word of the last phrase of the preceding section (such as, in the same song, the word "life" at the beginning of the second verse but at the end of the line "It might be you all of my life").

D. Discussion

The models of rock phrase rhythm described in this chapter contribute, by emphasizing strong downbeats, to the primacy of the beat rather than of the vocal melody. On the basis of this interpretation, we might expect to see these phrase rhythms less prevalent in slow songs. Do you think the models described here are as common in slow songs since 1955? Use specific examples to defend your argument. Would you call the slow songs you use as examples "rock songs"?

CHAPTER 2: KEY AND MODE

A. Structures and Patterns

1. The following scales, as given in PC-set notation, represent Ionian (major), Mixolydian, and Aeolian (natural-minor) scales. Which is which?
   a. [023578T]
   b. [024579T]
   c. [024579E]
2. Assume [0] is C. Write the following scales, as given in PC-set form, on a staff. Be sure to repeat the first note (C) an octave higher as the last note of each scale.
   a. [02479]
   b. [0357T]
   c. [023578T]
   d. [024579T]
   e. [024579E]
   f. [024579]
   g. [02357T]
3. Write the scales from question 2 with [0] = E.
4. Given a standard pentatonic set ([02479]) where [0] = G, what note is likely the tonic if the tonic chord is minor? And if the tonic chord is major?
5. If the tonic chord of a passage is E major and the melody uses a pentatonic set according to the standard pattern, what notes does the melody employ?
6. If the tonic chord of a passage is F minor and the melody uses a pentatonic set according to the standard pattern, what notes does the melody employ?
7. Write the following scales on a staff.
   a. B Ionian
   b. F Ionian
   c. A Mixolydian
   d. E♭ Mixolydian
   e. D Aeolian
   f. F♯ Aeolian

8. Given a standard diatonic set ([013568T]) where [0] = A, what note is tonic if the set is arranged as an Ionian scale? As an Aeolian scale? As a Mixolydian scale?

9. Suppose that a given song uses A, B, C♯, D, E, F♯, and G as its pitch source. What key is the piece in if these pitches represent an Aeolian scale? An Ionian scale? A Mixolydian scale?

10. Given the most common six-note subset of the diatonic set ([024579]) where [0] = D, what chord is likely the tonic if the tonic chord is minor? If the tonic chord is major?

11. If the tonic chord of a passage is B♭ major and the melody uses a hexatonic (six-note) set according to the standard pattern, what notes does the melody include?

12. If the tonic chord of a passage is E minor and the melody uses a hexatonic (six-note) set according to the standard pattern, what notes does the melody include?

13. For each of the following keys, identify the relative key: D major, F♯ minor, E♭ major, B major.

14. For each of the following keys, identify the parallel key: E major, G minor, A major, F♯ minor.

15. Identify the four major keys that share a chromatic-third relationship with D major.

16. Identify the four major keys that share a chromatic-second relationship with F major.

17. Listen to Mark Morrison's "Return of the Mack" (1997). Determine the chords of the verse. What is the most likely key given these two chords? Do other features of the song support that interpretation?

18. Listen to Backstreet Boys' "Quit Playing Games (with My Heart)" (1997). The song uses only a few chords: F♯ minor, F♯ major, G, A, and B minor. These chords could represent two different keys, one using the major palette and one using the natural-minor palette (with the optional variations of quality for iv (IV) and v (V). What chord do the verse and chorus promote as tonic? How? What chord does the bridge promote as tonic? How?

B. Examples

1. Find one rock piece in which the first chord does not prove to be the tonic chord. Explain the situation completely. In other words, tell what the key is, explain how you know it to be the key, and give a roman numeral analysis of the first chord as well as any other pertinent chords.

2. Find one passage in a rock piece that is tonally ambiguous. In a paragraph, describe and explain the problem. Be sure to tell what keys the passage might be in and give the case for each possible key.

3. Find a rock piece that employs a persistently initiating harmony, that is, a piece in which a single chord begins every hypermetrical unit in the whole piece.

4. Find a rock song in which a seventh chord is used as a tonic harmony.

5. For each of three of the scales listed in question A(2), find a rock song that uses the scale as a melodic pitch source.

6. Find a rock song whose melodic pitches cannot be reduced to any of the scales listed in question A(2).

7. One song from Tom Petty & the Heartbreakers' *Greatest Hits* album presents a problem in key determination very much like the one involved in Fleetwood Mac's "Dreams." Find the song and write a paragraph explaining the problem and what you perceive to be its solution.

8. For each of the following key relationships, find a rock song in which the keys of two sections exhibit that relationship. In each case, give the key for each section and the name of the key relationship.
   a. relative major and minor
   b. parallel major and minor
   c. fourth relationship
   d. chromatic third relationship
   e. chromatic second relationship

C. Composition

1. Write a short song in which the key of the verse and the key of the chorus share a chromatic-third relationship. Identify the scales you used in the melody for each section.

D. Discussion

Why do most rock pieces have a tonal center? Why haven't rock musicians more often abandoned keys altogether?

CHAPTER 3: CADENCES

A. Structures and Patterns

1. Imagine a V-I harmonic cadence in combination with each of the following, typical melodic cadences. Assume the first note sounds with

the first chord and the second note with the second chord. Identify each note that doesn't fit the harmony it is heard with.

    a. $\hat{2}$-$\hat{1}$

    b. $\hat{3}$-$\hat{1}$

    c. $\hat{6}$-$\hat{1}$

2. Imagine a IV-I harmonic cadence in combination with each of the following, typical melodic cadences. Assume the first note sounds with the first chord and the second note with the second chord. Identify each note that doesn't fit the harmony it is heard with.

    a. $\hat{1}$-$\hat{1}$

    b. $\hat{5}$-$\hat{1}$

    c. $\hat{6}$-$\hat{1}$

    d. $\hat{1}$-$\hat{3}$

    e. b$\hat{3}$-b$\hat{3}$

    f. b$\hat{7}$-$\hat{1}$

B. Examples

1. For three of the following chords, find a rock song in which a fourth-downbeat cadence occurs on that chord: I, ii, iii, iv, IV, v, V, vi, VI. Identify the songs and locate the cadences within them by the lyrics being sung at the appropriate moment.

2. Find rock songs that contain a ii-I cadence, a IV-I (or IV-i or iv-i or iv-I) cadence, a V-I (or V-i or v-i or v-I) cadence, and a vi-I (or VI-i) cadence. Identify the songs and locate the cadences within them by means of the lyrics sung at the times in question.

3. Find a rock song in which every hypermeasure ends with the V chord.

4. Pick a number one song from the past forty years and write a list of all the cadence formulas it uses, noting the last two chords and the last two scale degrees of each cadence as well as the lyrics sung at the first instance of each cadence type.

5. Find a rock piece that uses a V11-I cadence. Identify the location of the cadence by the lyrics being sung at the time in question.

6. Find a rock song in which the studio recording fades out while a live recording does not. Describe the band's strategy for ending the performance of the song.

C. Composition

1. Write a short song using at least four different cadences.

2. Write a song in which no section ends with closure. Decide how

you would end a performance of the song, and perform it for the class.

D. Discussion

Is rock music's predilection for fade-outs an indication of rock musicians' disregard for the future? In other words, does the fade-out suggest that rock musicians don't think much or care about how nonmusical things end?

CHAPTER 4: CHORD TYPE AND HARMONIC PALETTE

A. Structures and Patterns

1. Write the following chords on a staff:
   a. D7(#9)
   b. F7(#9)
   c. Am(add2)
   d. B♭(add2)
   e. G(add4)
   f. E♭(add4)
   g. C6
   h. E6
   i. Fm(maj7)
   j. Bm(maj7)
   k. Cm7/F
   l. G#m7/C#
   m. Fsus
   n. C#sus

2. On a staff, write the chords of the major palette for the keys of D, F, B, and A♭. Write sheet-music-style chord symbols above each chord and roman numerals below each.

3. On a staff, write the chords of the natural-minor palette for the keys of D minor, E minor, B♭ minor, and F# minor. Write sheet-music-style chord symbols above each chord and roman numerals below each.

4. On a staff, write the chords of the chromatic-minor palette for the keys of A, F minor, E♭, and B minor. Write sheet-music-style chord symbols above each chord and roman numerals below each.

5. Suppose that the chorus of a given song uses the following chords (but not necessarily in the following order): A, Bm, D, and G. Given that one of these chord is the tonic harmony, what key or keys might these

chords represent (there may be as many as four)? For each key you named, identify the palette (or palettes) these four chords might have come from.

6. Suppose a song in C uses the following chords: C, D, E♭, G, and B♭. Which palette is being used?

7. Suppose a song in A uses the following chords: A, B, D, E, F♯, and G. Which palette is being used?

8. Suppose a song in D minor uses the following chords: Dm, G, B♭, and C. Which palette is being used?

9. Suppose a song in B minor uses the following chords: Bm, D, Em, F#m, and A. Which palette is being used?

10. Listen to Sister Hazel's "All for You" (1997). What chords do the bass and guitar play in the chorus? Listen to the chorus that uses just voices and drums. Notate the voice parts. Assuming these voice parts are the same as those sung during other choruses (are they in fact?), how do they change or add to the harmonies?

11. Listen to Foreigner's "Feels like the First Time" (1977). The introduction and the first part of the verse use the same basic pitch pattern over a tonic pedal in the bass. Notate the passage. If the guitar and organ pitches are interpreted as partial chords, what chords might they be? What does the rapid, high-pitched synthesizer part in the chorus add to these chords? To the vocals in the chorus? Which palette do these chords come from? What are the chords in the second part of the verse? (Don't forget to check the bass line for harmonic inversions.) Can one palette account for all the chords in the song?

12. Listen to Janet Jackson's "Together Again" (1998). The verse incorporates a half-diminished seventh chord. Notate the chords to the verse using sheet-music-style chord symbols. Does the half-diminished seventh work in the typical fashion outlined in this chapter?

B. Examples

1. Find at least one rock piece that uses the major palette. Find one piece that uses the natural-minor palette. Find a piece that uses the chromatic-minor palette. Using sheet-music-style chord symbols and carefully indicating measures, make a chord chart of these pieces that could be read by a keyboard player or guitar player.

2. Find a rock piece whose chords do not fit neatly into any one of the three palettes described in this chapter.

C. Composition

Using one of the three palettes, write a piece for guitar, piano, or synthesizer.

D. Discussion

How many sources might a rock musician have for learning chords? How might rock musicians in the 1960s or 1970s have learned the palettes described in this chapter? What influences do you think led rock musicians to use these three palettes as opposed to other hypothetically possible systems? (Note: these questions ask the sources or causes of both the musicians' knowledge of the harmonic idioms of the styles and of the idioms themselves.)

CHAPTER 5: CHORD SUCCESSION

A. Structures and Patterns

1. Imagine a song in a major key using the diatonic portion of the major palette. After the flat-VII chord, what three chords (in roman numerals) might occur next if rock-standard root motion follows? If the song is in D, what chords (root and quality) would these be?
2. Imagine a song in a minor key using the natural-minor palette. After the VI chord, what three chords (in roman numerals) might occur next if rock-standard root motion follows? If the song is in C minor, what chords (root and quality) would these be?
3. Imagine a song in a major key using the chromatic-minor palette. After the IV chord, what three chords (in roman numerals) might occur next if rock-standard root motion follows? If the song is in E major, what chords (root and quality) would these be?
4. What common pattern described in this chapter does Michael Jackson's "Billie Jean" (1982) exemplify?
5. Which part of the Beatles' "Hey Jude" (1968) follows traditional standards of root movement, and which part follows the newer, rock standard?
6. Listen to Shawn Colvin's "Sunny Came Home" (1997). Notate the chords in both sheet music style (root, quality, and bass) and roman numerals. (You may decide that the key changes during the song.) What palette or palettes does each section use? Make a list of all the root motions in the song: in the middle of each pair of chords, indicate which way the root moves and by how far. How often does the song follow the rock standard of root movement outlined in this chapter?

Hypothetical example:

Major palette

C		D	F	G	F	C	F		Am	G	F	C
C: I		V/V	IV	V	IV	I	IV		vi	V	IV	I
	↑2		↑3	↑2	↓2	↓4	↑4	↑3		↓2	↓2	↓4

Seven times out of ten, the song follows the rock standard. If motion from I is not counted (motion from I doesn't necessarily follow a standard), the rock standard is seen as even more prevalent: seven out of eight pairs follow the standard.

7. Listen to 98 Degrees' "Invisible Man" (1997). Notate the chords in both sheet music style (root, quality, and bass) and roman numerals. What palette or palettes does the song use? Make a list of all the root motions in the song: in the middle of each pair of chords, indicate which way the root moves and by how far. How often does the song follow the rock standard of root movement outlined in this chapter? What slightly unusual chords are used, and where?

B. Examples

1. Find two instances of rock songs with root motion down by a second, two instances of root motion up by a third, and two instances of root motion down by a fourth. Identify the locations of these successions by citing the lyrics sung at that moment.

2. Find a rock piece in which a secondary dominant is left by root motion down by second, up by third, or down by fourth.

C. Composition

1. Write a short song using only the I and IV chords.

2. Write a short song in which one section uses predominantly rock-standard root movement and another section uses predominantly traditional root movement.

D. Discussion

Rock music continues to draw on older music for ideas, even as it continues to develop its own standards. Does the popular music of the past forty years suggest reasons for a continuing conservative streak? Do songs that stress the new standard of root motion appeal to a particular audience? Does conservatism have anything to do with chart success one way or another?

CHAPTER 6: FORM

A. Structures and Patterns

1. Watch a television show, and write down the clues that help you divide the show into sections and subsections. Draw an analogy between your observations and the way music is divided into sections.
2. Listen to Jewel's "Foolish Games" (1995). List the features of the song that should indicate the beginning of the chorus even to a first-time listener—one acquainted with rock style, that is.

B. Examples

1. Find a rock song that uses stop time. Notate the rhythm that the instruments use during the stop time.
2. Find a rock song in which either a guitar or keyboard instrument plays one distinct rhythmic pattern in one section and another distinct rhythmic pattern in another. Identify the sections both by name (verse, chorus, etc.) and by the first lyrics of the section; notate the rhythm used in each section.
3. For each of the forms below, find one rock piece that follows that form. Identify the song and the form, indicate the first harmony (in sheet music style as well as by key and roman numeral) of each section, and provide the first lyrics of the first instance of each section.
   a. Strophic
   b. Rounded binary
   c. Verse-chorus-bridge
   d. Compound binary

C. Composition

Write a song in one of the forms discussed in this chapter. Perform it for the class. Ask the class to identify the form they perceive. Explain your conception of the form and how you delineated the sections. Discuss whether your formal plan was successful.

D. Discussion

Do any cultural patterns suggest connections between the individual rock forms and particular ideas, categories of ideas, or expressive ideals? That is, do pieces in some given form tend to be serious? Lighthearted? Sentimental? Political? Spiritual? Funny? Fast? Slow? Complex? In minor keys? Sung by women? Fun to dance to? Popular? Cult classics? For any trend that you have found, speculate on the reason for the connection. If you didn't find any trends, speculate on why trends have not developed (as far as you are aware).

ANSWERS TO SELECTED EXERCISES
Chapter 1

A.1.a

1 2 3 4 | 2 2 3 4 | 3 2 3 4 | 4 2 3 4 |

Chapter 2

A.1.a. Aeolian
A.2.a. C D E G A C
A.3.b. E G A B D E
A.7.c. A B C♯ D E F♯ G
A.12. E F♯ G A B D (E)
A.16. E♭ major, E major, G♭ major, G major

Chapter 3

A.2.a. Both notes fit the chords.
A.2.b. 5̂ does not fit the IV chord. 1̂ fits the I chord.

Chapter 4

A.1.a. D F-sharp A C E♯
A.1.c. A B C E
A.1.i. F A♭ C E
A.1.m. F B♭ C
A.2. (D major)

D	E	Em	F♯	F♯m	G	Gm	A	Am	B	Bm	C
I	V/V	ii	V/vi	iii	IV	iv	V	v	V/ii	vi	VII

Chapter 5

A.1. vi ii IV. In the key of D, these are Bm, Em, and G.

select
discography

The following albums should prove useful in locating recordings of the examples cited in this book. Many of the pieces can be found on a performer's latest compilation album. A long list of albums entitled *Greatest Hits* or *Favorites* would get tedious, however, and risk being out of date, in that record publishers seem to release a classic band's *Golden Hits* one year and *Number One Hits* the next. As a result, only significant titles are included here.

American Graffiti soundtrack
Atlantic Rhythm and Blues, vol. 6
The Beatles, *Please Please Me, A Hard Day's Night, Help!, Revolver,*
    Sgt Pepper's Lonely Hearts Club Band, The Beatles
Boston, *Boston*
Chicago, *Chicago Transit Authority*
Emerson, Lake & Palmer, *Trilogy*
Fleetwood Mac, *Fleetwood Mac, Rumours*
Dan Fogelberg, *Phoenix*
Forrest Gump soundtrack
Peter Frampton, *Frampton Comes Alive*
Goo Goo Dolls, *A Boy Named Goo*
The Jimi Hendrix Experience, *Are You Experienced?*

Hootie and the Blowfish, *Cracked Rear View*
Jefferson Airplane, *Surrealistic Pillow*
Billy Joel, *The Bridge, The Stranger*
Carole King, *Tapestry*
Paul McCartney and Wings, *Band On The Run*
Men At Work, *Business As Usual*
The Moody Blues, *Days Of Future Passed*
Alanis Morissette, *Jagged Little Pill*
Motown's Biggest Pop Hits
Oasis, *(What's The Story) Morning Glory?*
Pink Floyd, *Dark Side Of The Moon*
R.E.M., *Automatic For The People*
Duncan Sheik, *Duncan Sheik*
Carly Simon, *Anticipation*
Soul Asylum, *Grave Dancers Union*
Sting, *Ten Summoner's Tales*
James Taylor, *Flag, JT*
10,000 Maniacs, *Our Time In Eden*
Tootsie soundtrack
Totally '80s, from Razor & Tie Music
The Who, *Tommy* soundtrack

musical
references

All pieces analyzed or mentioned in the text are listed below. Only the most pertinent recordings have been included. Numbers following the composers' names indicate the chapters in which the songs are cited.

TITLE	PRIMARY RECORDING(S)	COMPOSER(S)
"After Midnight"	Eric Clapton, 1970	J. J. Cale, 4, 6
"After the Ball"	N/A; pub. 1892	Charles K. Harris, 6
"Against All Odds (Take a Look At Me Now)"	Phil Collins, 1984	Phil Collins, 4
"Ain't No Mountain High Enough"	Diana Ross, 1970	Nickolas Ashford and Valerie Simpson, 2
"Ain't No Sunshine"	Bill Withers, 1971	Bill Withers, 4
"Ain't That A Shame"	Fats Domino, 1955	Antoine "Fats" Domino and Dave Bartholomew, 6
"Air That I Breathe"	The Hollies, 1973	Michael Hazelwood and Albert Hammond, 3
"All Along The Watchtower"	The Jimi Hendrix Experience, 1968; U2, 1987	Bob Dylan, 1, 4
"All By Myself"	Eric Carmen, 1975	Eric Carmen (after Rachmaninoff), 4
"All I Have To Do Is Dream"	The Everly Brothers, 1958	Boudleaux Bryant, 6

TITLE	PRIMARY RECORDING(S)	COMPOSER(S)
"All Is Well"	Chicago, 1972	Robert Lamm, 6
"All My Loving"	The Beatles, 1963	John Lennon and Paul McCartney, 4, 6
"All Night Long (All Night)"	Lionel Richie, 1983	Lionel Richie, 4, 6
"Already Gone"	The Eagles, 1974	Jack Tempchin and Bernie Leadon, 1
"Alright"	Janet Jackson, 1989	Janet Jackson, James Harris III, and Terry Lewis, 6
"Also Sprach Zarathustra (2001)"	Deodato, 1972	Arranged from Richard Strauss, 7
"American Pie"	Don McLean, 1971	Don McLean, 4, 6
"And I Love Her"	The Beatles, 1964	John Lennon and Paul McCartney, 2
"Angel"	Aerosmith, 1987	Steven Tallarico and Desmond Child, 4
"Angie"	The Rolling Stones, 1973	Mick Jagger and Keith Richards, 4
"Anticipation"	Carly Simon, 1971	Carly Simon, 1
"Ask Me Why"	The Beatles, 1963	John Lennon and Paul McCartney, 4
"At The Hop"	Danny & the Juniors, 1957	Singer, Medora, and White, 6
"B.S.U.R. (S.U.C.S.I.M.I.M.)."	James Taylor, 1979	James Taylor, 1
"Baba O'Riley"	The Who, 1971	Pete Townshend, 4, 5
"Babe"	Styx, 1979	Dennis DeYoung, 6
"Back In The High Life Again"	Steve Winwood, 1986	Steve Winwood and Will Jennings, 2
"Back In The U.S.A."	Chuck Berry, 1959	Chuck Berry, 4
"Back In The USSR"	The Beatles, 1968	John Lennon and Paul McCartney, 6
"Bad, Bad Leroy Brown"	Jim Croce, 1973	Jim Croce, 2, 4, 5, 6
"Bad Moon Rising"	Credence Clearwater Revival, 1969	John Fogerty, 1, 5
"Band On The Run"	Paul McCartney and Wings, 1973	Paul McCartney, 4
"Banks of the New-foundland"	N/A	Traditional, 3
"Barbara Ann"	The Beach Boys, 1965	Fred Fassert, 2
"Barely Breathing"	Duncan Sheik, 1996	Duncan Sheik, 7

TITLE	PRIMARY RECORDING(S)	COMPOSER(S)
"Because Of You"	98°, 1998	Anders Bagge, Arntor Birgisson, Christian Karlsson, Patrick Tucker, 1
"Being For The Benefit Of Mr. Kite"	The Beatles, 1967	John Lennon and Paul McCartney, 1
"The Best"	Tina Turner, 1989	H. Knight and M. Chapman, 1
"Billie Jean"	Michael Jackson, 1982	Michael Jackson, 1, 3
"Black And White"	Michael Jackson, 1991	Michael Jackson, 5, 6
"Black Velvet"	Alannah Myles, 1989	Christopher Ward and David Tyson, 6
"Blue Collar Man (Long Nights)"	Styx, 1978	Tommy Shaw, 4
"Boogie Nights"	Heatwave, 1977	Rodney Temperton, 4
"Borderline"	Madonna, 1983	Reggie Lucas, 3, 5
"Born To Run"	Bruce Springsteen, 1975	Bruce Springsteen, 1
"Born Too Late"	The Poni-Tails, 1958	Tobias and Strouse, 6
"Brain Damage"	Pink Floyd, 1973	Roger Waters, 7
"Breakdown"	Tom Petty and the Heartbreakers, 1976	Tom Petty, 4
"Breakin' Up Is Hard To Do"	Neil Sedaka, 1962, 1975	Neil Sedaka and Howard Greenfield, 6
"Breakup Song (They Don't Write 'Em)"	The Greg Kihn Band, 1981	Greg Kihn, 2
"Breathe"	Pink Floyd, 1973	Roger Waters, David Gilmour, Richard Wright, 7
"Breathless"	The Corrs, 2000	R. J. Lange and the Corrs, 2
"Broken Wings"	Mr. Mister, 1984	Richard Page, Steve George, and John Lang, 4
"Brown Sugar"	The Rolling Stones, 1971	Mick Jagger and Keith Richards, 4, 6
"Bungle In The Jungle"	Jethro Tull, 1974	Ian Anderson, 6
"Bus Stop"	The Hollies, 1966	G. Gouldman and B. Fahey, 6
"Call Me" (theme from American Gigolo)	Blondie, 1980	Giorgio Moroder and Debbie Harry, 1, 2
"Call On Me"	Chicago, 1974	Lee Loughnane, 6
"Can't Get Enough"	Bad Company, 1974	Mick Ralphs, 4, 6
"Can't Stay Away From You"	Gloria Estefan, 1987	Gloria Estefan, 6

TITLE	PRIMARY RECORDING(S)	COMPOSER(S)
"Carefree Highway"	Gordon Lightfoot, 1974	Gordon Lightfoot, 2
"Caribbean Queen"	Billy Ocean, 1984	Diamond and Ocean, 4
"Carry On Wayward Son"	Kansas, 1976	Kerry Livgren, 4
"Cat's In The Cradle"	Harry Chapin, 1974	Harry Chapin, 4
"China Grove"	The Doobie Brothers, 1973	Tom Johnston, 1, 4
"Cindy"	N/A	Anonymous, 1
"Closer To Home/ I'm Your Captain"	Grand Funk Railroad, 1970	Mark Farner, 6
"Cocaine"	Eric Clapton, 1977	J. J. Cale, 2, 4
"Coco Jamboo"	Mr. President, 1997	Ken Matthiesen, Delroy Rennalls, and Rainer Gaffrey, 2
"Coconut"	Nilsson, 1971	Harry Nilsson, 4
"Colour My World"	Chicago, 1970	James Pankow, 4
"Come Go With Me"	Dell-Vikings, 1957	C. E. Quick, 5
"Come To My Window"	Melissa Etheridge, 1993	Melissa Etheridge, 2
"Coming Around Again"	Carly Simon, 1986	Carly Simon, 1
"Cool Shake"	The Del Vikings, 1957	Alex Kramer and Joan Whitney, 6
"Crocodile Rock"	Elton John, 1972	Elton John and Bernie Taupin, 3
"Crying"	Roy Orbison, 1961	Roy Orbison and Joe Melson, 4
"Daisy"	N/A	Harry Dacre, 1
"Daniel"	Elton John, 1972	Elton John, 6
"Danny's Song"	Loggins and Messina, 1971	Kenny Loggins, 6
"Day Tripper"	The Beatles, 1965	John Lennon and Paul McCartney, 4
"Dear Prudence"	The Beatles, 1968	John Lennon and Paul McCartney, 3
"Desperado"	The Eagles, 1973	Don Henley and Glenn Frey, 3
"Devil Or Angel"	Bobby Vee, 1960	Blanche Carter, 6
"Dialogue (parts 1 & 2)"	Chicago, 1972	Robert Lamm, 6
"Do Right Woman"	Aretha Franklin, 1967	Dan Penn and Chips Moman, 1
"Do You Believe In Magic"	The Lovin' Spoonful, 1965	John Sebastian, 2, 6

TITLE	PRIMARY RECORDING(S)	COMPOSER(S)
"Does Anybody Really Know What Time It Is?"	Chicago, 1969	Robert Lamm, 7
"Donna"	Ritchie Valens, 1958	Ritchie Valens, 6
"Don't Get Me Wrong"	The Pretenders, 1986	Chrissie Hynde, 6
"Don't Let Me Be Misunderstood"	The Animals, 1965	Benjamin, Marcus, and Caldwell, 2, 4
"Don't Let The Sun Go Down On Me"	Elton John, 1974	Elton John and Bernie Taupin, 3, 5
"Don't Look Back In Anger"	Oasis, 1995	Noel Gallagher, 3, 4
"Don't Look Down"	Lindsey Buckingham, 1992	Lindsey Buckingham, 1
"Don't Worry, Baby"	The Beach Boys, 1964	Brian Wilson and R. Christian, 2
"Don't Worry Be Happy"	Bobby McFerrin, 1988	Bobby McFerrin, 4
"Down Under"	Men At Work, 1982	Colin Hay and Ron Strykert, 4
"Dream Weaver"	Gary Wright, 1975	Gary Wright, 2, 3, 6
"Dreams"	Fleetwood Mac, 1977	Stevie Nicks, 2
"Dust In The Wind"	Kansas, 1977	Kerry Livgren, 4
"The Eagle And The Hawk"	John Denver, 1971	John Denver and Mike Taylor, 4
"Ebony And Ivory"	Paul McCartney and Stevie Wonder, 1982	Paul McCartney, 4
"Eclipse"	Pink Floyd, 1973	Roger Waters, 7
"Eight Days A Week"	The Beatles, 1964	John Lennon and Paul McCartney, 2, 5, 6
"The End Of The Innocence"	Don Henley, 1987	Don Henley and B. R. Hornsby, 4
"The Endless Enigma"	Emerson, Lake & Palmer, 1972	Keith Emerson and Greg Lake, 7
"Every Breath You Take"	The Police, 1983	Sting, 4, 5
"Every Heartbeat"	Amy Grant, 1991	Amy Grant, Wayne Kirkpatrick, and Charlie Peacock, 6
"Everyday"	Buddy Holly, 1957	Charles Hardin (a.k.a. Buddy Holly) and Norman Pettis, 6
"Everyday I Write The Book"	Elvis Costello and the Attractions, 1983	Elvis Costello, 4
"Everyday People"	Sly & the Family Stone, 1968	Sly Stone, 5

TITLE	PRIMARY RECORDING(S)	COMPOSER(S)
"(Everything I Do) I Do It For You"	Bryan Adams, 1991	Michael Kamen, Bryan Adams, and Robert John Lange, 4
"Everything I Own"	Bread, 1972	David Gates, 4
"Everytime You Go Away"	Paul Young, 1985	Daryl Hall, 4
"Evil Woman"	Electric Light Orchestra, 1975	Jeff Lynne, 2
"Face The Fire"	Dan Fogelberg, 1979	Dan Fogelberg, 2
"Faithfully"	Journey, 1983	Jonathan Cain, 3, 5
"Family Of Man"	Three Dog Night, 1971	P. Williams and J. Conrad, 5
"Fanny Mae"	Buster Brown, 1960	Clarence L. Lewis, Morris Levy, and Waymon Glasco, 4
"Fire And Rain"	James Taylor, 1969	James Taylor, 6
"The Flame"	Cheap Trick, 1988	Bobby Mitchell and Nick Graham, 4
"Follow You Down"	The Gin Blossoms, 1996	Scott Johnson, Bell Leen, Phillip Rhodes, Jesse Valenzuela, and Robin Wilson, 2
"Fooling Yourself (Angry Young Man)"	Styx, 1977	Tommy Shaw, 3
"For What It's Worth"	Buffalo Springfield, 1966	Stephen Stills, 3
"Forever Young"	Rod Stewart, 1988	Rod Stewart, J. Cregan, and K. Savigar, 1, 5
"Fortunate Son"	Credence Clearwater Revival, 1969	J. C. Fogerty, 3, 4
"Le Freak"	Chic, 1978	Bernard Edwards and Nile Rodgers, 4
"Free Bird"	Lynyrd Skynyrd, 1973	Allen Collins and Ron Van Zant, 4
"Free Falling"	Tom Petty, 1989	Tom Petty and Jeff Lynne, 4
"The Freshmen"	The Verve Pipe, 1996	Brian Vander Ark, 3
"Fun, Fun, Fun"	The Beach Boys, 1963	Brian Wilson and Mike Love, 6
"Funkytown"	Lipps Inc, 1980	Steven Greenberg, 2
"Get A Job"	The Silhouettes, 1957	Earl Beal, Raymond Edwards, William Horton, and Richard Lewis, 6
"Get Down Tonight"	K. C. and the Sunshine Band, 1975	Harry "KC" Casey and Richard Finch, 4

TITLE	PRIMARY RECORDING(S)	COMPOSER(S)
"Girl"	The Beatles, 1965	John Lennon and Paul McCartney, 1
"Give A Little Bit"	Supertramp, 1977	Rick Davies and Roger Hodgson, 1
"Give Me Love (Give Me Peace On Earth)"	George Harrison, 1973	George Harrison, 6
"Glory Of Love"	Peter Cetera, 1986	Peter Cetera, David Foster, and Diane Nini, 4
"A Good Cigar Is a Smoke"	N/A; pub. 1905	Harry B. Smith and Victor Herbert, 6
"Good For Me"	Amy Grant, 1991	Tom Snow, Jay Gruska, Amy Grant, and Wayne Kirkpatrick, 4
"Goodbye Yellow Brick Road"	Elton John, 1973	Elton John and Bernie Taupin, 1, 4, 7
"Got A Hold On Me"	Christine McVie, 1984	Christine McVie and Todd Sharp, 1
"Green Onions"	Booker T. and the MG's, 1962	Booker T. Jones, Steve Cropper, Al Jackson, and Lewie Steinberg, 4
"Hallelujah!"	N/A	George Frederick Handel, 5
"Hand In My Pocket"	Alanis Morissette, 1995	Alanis Morissette and Glen Ballard, 3
"Hand Me Down World"	The Guess Who, 1970	Kurt Winter, 2
"Handy Man"	Jimmy Jones, 1959; James Taylor, 1977	Jimmy Jones and O. Blackwell, 3
"Happy Together"	The Turtles, 1967	Gary Bonner and Alan Gordon, 3, 4
"A Hard Day's Night"	The Beatles, 1964	John Lennon and Paul McCartney, 4, 6
"Hard To Say"	Dan Fogelberg, 1981	Dan Fogelberg, 6
"Harvest Moon"	Neil Young, 1992	Neil Young, 1
"Haven't Got Time For The Pain"	Carly Simon, 1974	Carly Simon, 6
"Heart Of The Matter"	Don Henley, 1989	Mike Campbell, Don Henley, and J. D. Souther, 1, 6
"Heartache Tonight"	The Eagles, 1979	Don Henley, Glenn Frey, Bob Seger, and J. D. Souther, 1
"Heartbreak Hotel"	Elvis Presley, 1956	Mae Boren Axton, Tommy Durden, and Elvis Presley, 6
"Help Is On Its Way"	Little River Band, 1977	Glenn Shorrock, 3

TITLE	PRIMARY RECORDING(S)	COMPOSER(S)
"Help Me"	Joni Mitchell, 1973	Joni Mitchell, 4
"Help Me, Rhonda"	The Beach Boys, 1965	Brian Wilson, 1, 6, 7
"Here Comes The Sun"	The Beatles, 1969	George Harrison, 4
"Here, There, And Everywhere"	The Beatles, 1966	John Lennon and Paul McCartney, 1
"Hey Joe"	Jimi Hendrix Experience, 1967	Billy Roberts, 2
"Hey Jude"	The Beatles, 1968	John Lennon and Paul McCartney, 3, 4, 6
"Hip To Be Square"	Huey Lewis and the News, 1986	Bill Gibson, Sean Hopper, and Huey Lewis, 4
"Hold My Hand"	Hootie and the Blowfish, 1994	Mark Felber, Bryan Felber, Dean Felber, Darius Rucker, and Jim "Soni" Sonefeld, 2
"Home Again"	Carole King, 1971	Carole King, 3
"The Hook"	Blues Traveler, 1994	John Popper, 6
"Horse With No Name"	America, 1971	Dewey Bunnell, 6
"Hotel California"	The Eagles, 1976	Don Felder, Don Henley, and Glenn Frey, 1
"Hound Dog"	Elvis Presley, 1956	Jerry Leiber and Mike Stoller, 2
"House Of The Rising Sun"	The Animals, 1964	Traditional, arranged by Alan Price, 4, 5
"Hungry Like The Wolf"	Duran Duran, 1982	Andy Taylor, John Taylor, Roger Taylor, Nick Rhodes, and Simon LeBon, 2
"I Am The Walrus"	The Beatles, 1967	John Lennon and Paul McCartney, 7
"I Can See For Miles"	The Who, 1967	Pete Townshend, 4, 6
"I Can't Get Next To You"	The Temptations, 1969	Norman Whitfield and Barrett Strong, 2
"I Can't Help Myself (Sugar Pie, Honey Bunch)"	The Four Tops, 1965	Brian Holland, Lamont Dozier, and Edward Holland, Jr., 5
"I Don't Know How To Love Him"	Yvonne Elliman, 1970	Andrew Lloyd-Webber and Tim Rice, 6
"I Feel The Earth Move"	Carole King, 1971	Carole King, 4
"I Get Around"	The Beach Boys, 1964	Brian Wilson, 1
"I Heard It Through The Grapevine"	Marvin Gaye, 1968	Norman Whitfield and Barrett Strong, 2

TITLE	PRIMARY RECORDING(S)	COMPOSER(S)
"I Just Called To Say I Love You"	Stevie Wonder, 1984	Stevie Wonder, 3
"I Know What I Like"	Huey Lewis and the News, 1986	Chris Hayes and Huey Lewis, 4
"I Saw Her Standing There"	The Beatles, 1963	John Lennon and Paul McCartney, 4, 6
"I Shot The Sheriff"	Eric Clapton, 1974	Bob Marley, 4, 6
"I Started a Joke"	The Bee Gees, 1968	Barry, Robin, and Maurice Gibb, 1
"I Still Haven't Found What I'm Looking For"	U2, 1987	U2, 5
"I Want To Hold Your Hand"	The Beatles, 1963	John Lennon and Paul McCartney, 6
"I Want To Know What Love Is"	Foreigner, 1984	Mick Jones, 1
"I Was Only Joking"	Rod Stewart, 1978	Rod Stewart and Gary Grainger, 3
"I Woke Up In Love This Morning"	The Partridge Family, 1971	Irwin Levine and L. Russell Brown, 4
"I Won't Hold You Back"	Toto, 1982	Steve Lukather, 1
"I Wouldn't Want To Be Like You"	The Alan Parsons Project, 1977	Eric Woolfson and Alan Parsons, 2
"I'd Really Love To See You Tonight"	England Dan and John Ford Coley, 1976	Parker McGee, 3
"I'll Feel A Whole Lot Better"	The Byrds, 1965	G. Clark, 5
"I'm A-Ridin' Old Paint"	N/A	Traditional, 6
"I'm So Afraid"	Fleetwood Mac, 1975	Lindsey Buckingham, 3, 4
"I'm The Only One"	Melissa Etheridge, 1993	Melissa Etheridge, 4
"I'm Walkin'"	Fats Domino, 1957	Antoine "Fats" Domino and Dave Bartholomew, 6
"(I've Been) Searchin' So Long"	Chicago, 1974	James Pankow, 1, 2
"I've Got To Get A Message To You"	The Bee Gees, 1968	Barry, Robin, and Maurice Gibb, 2
"Ich grolle nicht"	N/A	Robert Schumann, 5
"If"	Bread, 1971	David Gates, 3
"If I Ever Lose My Faith In You"	Sting, 1993	Sting, 1
"If I Fell"	The Beatles, 1964	John Lennon and Paul McCartney, 1

TITLE	PRIMARY RECORDING(S)	COMPOSER(S)
"If You Could Read My Mind"	Gordon Lightfoot, 1970	Gordon Lightfoot, 4
"Innocent Man"	Billy Joel, 1983	Billy Joel, 3, 6
"Into The Great Wide Open"	Tom Petty, 1991	Tom Petty and Jeff Lynne, 1
"Introduction"	Chicago, 1969	Terry Kath, 6
"Invisible Touch"	Genesis, 1986	Tony Banks, Phil Collins, and Mike Rutherford, 3
"It Don't Matter To Me"	Bread, 1970	David Gates, 2
"It Might Be You" (theme from Tootsie)	Stephen Bishop, 1982	Dave Grusin and Alan and Marilyn Bergman, 1
"It's A Mistake"	Men At Work, 1983	Colin Hay, 4
"It's My Party"	Lesley Gore, 1963	John Gluck, Wally Gold, Seymour Gottlieb, and Herbert Wiener, 4
"It's Only Rock 'N Roll (But I Like It)"	The Rolling Stones, 1974	Mick Jagger and Keith Richards, 3
"Jailhouse Rock"	Elvis Presley, 1957	Jerry Leiber and Mike Stoller, 6
"Jet"	Paul McCartney, 1973	Paul McCartney, 1
"Joy To The World"	Three Dog Night, 1970	Hoyt Axton, 4
"Juke Box Hero"	Foreigner, 1981	Lou Gramm and Mick Jones, 3
"Jump"	Van Halen, 1983	Edward Van Halen, Alex Van Halen, Michael Anthony, and David Lee Roth, 4, 6
"Jumping Jack Flash"	The Rolling Stones, 1968	Mick Jagger and Keith Richards, 1, 5
"(Just Like) Starting Over"	John Lennon, 1980	John Lennon, 3, 4
"Just The Way You Are"	Billy Joel, 1977	Billy Joel, 4, 6
"Just What I Needed"	The Cars, 1978	Ric Ocasek, 5
"Just You 'N' Me"	Chicago, 1973	James Pankow, 6
"Karma Chameleon"	Culture Club, 1983	Roy Hay, Philip Pickett, George "Boy George" O'Dowd, Michael Craig, and Jonathan Moss, 3
"Karn Evil 9"	Emerson, Lake & Palmer, 1973	Keith Emerson, Greg Lake, and Peter Sinfield, 1
"Keep On Loving You"	REO Speedwagon, 1980	Kevin Cronin, 6
"Kind Of A Drag"	The Buckinghams, 1966	James Holvay and Gary Beisber, 2

TITLE	PRIMARY RECORDING(S)	COMPOSER(S)
"Knock on Wood"	Eddie Floyd, 1966	Eddie Floyd and Steve Cropper, 4
"Kodachrome"	Paul Simon, 1973	Paul Simon, 2
"Lady Marmalade"	LaBelle, 1974	Bob Crewe and Kenny Nolan, 4
"Last Train To Clarksville"	The Monkees, 1966	Neil Diamond, 2, 5, 6
"Layla"	Derek and the Dominoes, 1970	Eric Clapton and Jim Gordon, 6
"Lead Me On"	Amy Grant, 1988	Amy Grant, Michael W. Smith, and Wayne Kirkpatrick, 4
"Let It Be"	The Beatles, 1970	John Lennon and Paul McCartney, 6
"Let It Grow"	Eric Clapton, 1974	Eric Clapton, 4, 6
"Let's Get Together"	The Youngbloods, 1967	Chet Powers, 6
"Let's Hear It For The Boy"	Deniece Williams, 1984	Thomas Snow and Dean Pitchford, 4
"Light My Fire"	The Doors, 1967	Robbie Krieger and Ray Manzarek, 1
"Like A Rolling Stone"	Bob Dylan, 1964	Bob Dylan, 5
"The Lion Sleeps Tonight"	The Tokens, 1961	Traditional, 3, 5
"Listen To The Music"	The Doobie Brothers, 1972	Tom Johnstone, 6
"Little Darlin'"	"The Diamonds, 1957	Maurice Williams, 5
"Little Jeannie"	Elton John, 1980	Elton John and Gary Osbourne, 3
"Loco-Motion"	Little Eva, 1962; Grand Funk, 1973	Gerry Goffin and Carole King, 2
"The Logical Song"	Supertramp, 1979	Rick Davies and Roger Hodgson, 2, 3
"Lonely Ol' Night"	John Cougar Mellencamp, 1985	John Cougar Mellencamp, 6
"Lonely People"	America, 1974	Dan and Cassie Peek, 2
"Lonely Too Long"	The Young Rascals, 1967	Felix Cavaliere, 4
"Long Tall Sally"	Little Richard, 1956; Pat Boone 1956	Enotris Johnson, "Little Richard" Penniman, and Robert Blackwell, 5, 6
"Long Time"	Boston, 1976	Tom Scholz, 4
"Look Away"	Chicago, 1988	Diane Warren, 1
"Losing My Religion"	REM, 1991	Bill Berry, Peter Buck, Mike Mills, and Michael Stipe, 4

TITLE	PRIMARY RECORDING(S)	COMPOSER(S)
"Louie Louie"	The Kingsmen, 1963	Richard Berry, 4
"Love Lies Bleeding"	Elton John, 1973	Elton John and Bernie Taupin, 1
"Love Potion No. 9"	The Clovers, 1959	Jerry Leiber and Mike Stoller, 4
"Love Song"	The Cure, 1989	Robert Smith, Simon Gallup, Boris Williams, Porl Thompson, Roger O'Donnell, and Laurence Tolhurst, 6
"Love Takes Time"	Mariah Carey, 1990	Mariah Carey and Ben Margulies, 4
"Love Will Keep Us Alive"	The Eagles, 1994	James Capaldi, Paul Carrack, and Peter Vale, 6
"Love Will Keep Us Together"	Captain & Tennille, 1975	Neil Sedaka and Howard Greenfield, 4
"Luanne"	Foreigner, 1981	Lou Gramm and Mick Jones, 1
"Lucille"	Little Richard, 1957; Everly Brothers, 1960	"Little" Richard Penniman and Albert Collins, 1, 4
"Lyin' Eyes"	The Eagles, 1975	Don Henley and Glenn Frey, 3, 5
"Maggie May"	Rod Stewart, 1971	Rod Stewart and Martin Quittenton, 2, 3
"Magic Man"	Heart, 1976	Ann and Nancy Wilson, 1
"Magical Mystery Tour"	The Beatles, 1967	John Lennon and Paul McCartney, 4
"Main Street"	Bob Seger, 1977	Bob Seger, 2
"Make It With You"	Bread, 1970	David Gates, 4
"Make Me Smile"	Chicago, 1969	James Pankow, 4, 6
"Mandolin Rain"	Bruce Hornsby and the Range, 1986	B. R. Hornsby and John Hornsby, 6
"Mary Had a Little Lamb"	N/A	Sarah Hale, 3
"A Matter of Trust"	Billy Joel, 1986	Billy Joel, 1, 5, 6
"Maybe I'm Amazed"	Paul McCartney, 1970	Paul McCartney, 4
"Me And Bobby McGee"	Janis Joplin, 1970	Kris Kristofferson and F. Foster, 6
"Michelle"	The Beatles, 1966	John Lennon and Paul McCartney , 1, 5
"Midnight Special"	Credence Clearwater Revival, 1970	Traditional, arr. J. C. Fogerty, 2

TITLE	PRIMARY RECORDING(S)	COMPOSER(S)
"Missing You"	John Waite, 1984	John Waite, Charles Sanford, and Mark Leonard, 3
"Monday, Monday"	The Mamas and the Papas, 1966	John Phillips, 4
"Money"	Pink Floyd, 1973	Roger Waters, 5, 7
"More Than A Feeling"	Boston, 1976	Tom Scholz, 4
"Mother's Little Helper"	The Rolling Stones, 1966	Mick Jagger and Keith Richards, 4
"Mr. Tambourine Man"	The Byrds, 1965	Bob Dylan, 3
"Mrs. Robinson"	Simon and Garfunkel, 1968	Paul Simon, 1
"Mrs. Vanderbilt"	Paul McCartney and Wings, 1973	Paul McCartney, 4
"My Favorite Mistake"	Cheryl Crow, 1998	Cheryl Crow and Jeff Trott, 2
"My Girl"	The Temptations, 1965	Smokey Robinson, 2
"My Love"	Paul McCartney and Wings, 1973	Paul McCartney, 3, 5
"My Prerogative"	Bobby Brown, 1988	Gene Griffin and Bobby Brown, 4
"Name"	The Goo Goo Dolls, 1995	The Goo Goo Dolls, 4, 7
"Never Been To Spain"	Three Dog Night, 1971	Hoyt Axton, 1
"Never Knew Love Like This Before"	Stephanie Mills, 1980	Reginald Lucas and James Mtume, 4
"The Night Before"	The Beatles, 1965	John Lennon and Paul McCartney, 1
"The Night They Drove Old Dixie Down"	The Band, 1971; Joan Baez, 1971	Robbie Robertson, 4
"Nights in White Satin"	The Moody Blues, 1967	Justin Hayward, 2, 4, 5, 6
"No Particular Place To Go"	Chuck Berry, 1964	Chuck Berry, 1, 6
"No Reply"	The Beatles, 1964	John Lennon and Paul McCartney, 1
"No Tell Lover"	Chicago, 1978	Lee Loughnane, Danny Seraphine, and Peter Cetera, 6
"Noah's Dove"	10,000 Maniacs, 1992	Natalie Merchant, 2, 5
"Norwegian Wood"	The Beatles, 1965	John Lennon and Paul McCartney, 2
"Not Alone Any More"	The Traveling Wilburys, 1988	The Traveling Wilburys, 4

TITLE	PRIMARY RECORDING(S)	COMPOSER(S)
"Nutrocker"	B. Bumble and the Stingers, 1962	Arranged from P. I. Tchaikovsky, 7
"Oh, Susanna!"	N/A	Stephen Foster, 1
"The Old Chisolm Trail"	N/A	Traditional, 6
"Old Time Rock And Roll"	Bob Seger and the Silver Bullet Band, 1978	George Jackson and Tom Jones III; 2, 6
"On a Slow Boat to China"	N/A; pub. 1948	Frank Loesser, 6
"On Broadway"	The Drifters, 1963; George Benson, 1978	Barry Mann, Cynthia Weil, Jerry Leiber, and Mike Stoller, 4
"On The Western Skyline"	Bruce Hornsby and the Range, 1986	B. R. Hornsby and John Hornsby, 2
"One Fine Day"	The Chiffons, 1963	Gerry Goffin and Carole King, 4
"One Good Woman"	Peter Cetera, 1988	Peter Cetera and Patrick Leonard, 3, 6
"One In A Million"	The Platters, 1956	Jean Miles and Tony Williams, 6
"One Of These Nights"	The Eagles, 1975	Don Henley and Glenn Frey, 4
"One Of Us"	Joan Osborne, 1995	Eric Bazilian, 3
"One Thing Leads To Another"	The Fixx, 1983	Cy Curnin, Adam Woods, Alfred Agius, Jamie West-Oram, and Rupert Greenall, 4
"Only Wanna Be With You"	Hootie and the Blowfish, 1994	Mark Bryan, Dean Falber, Darius Rucker, and Jim "Soni" Sonefeld, 3
"Over My Head"	Fleetwood Mac, 1975	Christine McVie, 1
"Over the Rainbow"	N/A; pub. 1938	E. Y. Harburg and Harold Arlen, 1, 6
"Paint It, Black"	The Rolling Stones, 1966	Mick Jagger and Keith Richards, 4
"Peggy Sue Got Married"	Buddy Holly, 1958	Buddy Holly, 5
"Peppermint Twist"	Joey Dee and the Starlighters, 1961	Joey Henry and Dee Glover, 6
"Piano Man"	Billy Joel, 1973	Billy Joel, 3
"Pinball Wizard"	The Who, 1969	Pete Townshend, 4
"Pinch Me"	The Barenaked Ladies, 2000	Steven Page and Ed Robertson, 5
"Play That Funky Music"	White Cherry, 1976	Robert Parissi, 4
"Please, Please Me"	The Beatles, 1963	John Lennon and Paul McCartney, 3, 6

TITLE	PRIMARY RECORDING(S)	COMPOSER(S)
"Praise You"	Fatboy Slim, 1998	Norman Cook and Camille Yarbrough, 3
"Proud Mary"	Credence Clearwater Revival, 1969	J. C. Fogerty, 4
"Purple Haze"	Jimi Hendrix Experience, 1966	Jimi Hendrix, 4
"Questions 67 and 68"	Chicago, 1969	Robert Lamm, 6
"Ramblin' Man"	The Allman Brothers Band, 1973	Forrest Richard Betts, 2
"Rapture"	Blondie, 1980	Chris Stein and Debbie Harry, 5
"Refugee"	Tom Petty and the Heartbreakers, 1979	Tom Petty and Mike Campbell, 1, 4, 5
"Relax"	Frankie Goes to Hollywood, 1985	William Johnson, Mark O'Toole, and Peter Gill, 4
"Rhiannon"	Fleetwood Mac, 1975	Stevie Nicks, 2
"Rhythm Of The Night"	DeBarge, 1985	Diane Warren, 4
"Ridin' The Storm Out"	REO Speedwagon, 1973	Gary Richrath, 4
"The Right Thing To Do"	Carly Simon, 1972	Carly Simon, 4
"Rikki, Don't Lose That Number"	Steely Dan, 1974	Walter Becker and Donald Fagen, 1
"Rock And Roll Music"	Chuck Berry, 1957	Chuck Berry, 4, 6
"Rock Around The Clock"	Bill Haley and the Comets, 1954	M. C. Freedman and J. DeKnight, 4, 6
"Rock Show"	Paul McCartney and Wings, 1975	Paul McCartney, 4
"Rocket Man"	Elton John, 1972	Elton John and Bernie Taupin, 3, 4
"Rock'n Me"	Steve Miller, 1976	Steve Miller, 2
"Roll On Down The Highway"	Bachman-Turner Overdrive, 1974	C. F. Turner and Randy Bachman, 4
"Roll Over Beethoven"	Chuck Berry, 1956	Chuck Berry, 1
"Roll To Me"	Del Amitri, 1995	Justin Currie, 6
"Roll With It"	Oasis, 1995	Noel Gallagher, 4
"Rosalinda's Eyes"	Billy Joel, 1978	Billy Joel, 1
"Run to Me"	The Bee Gees, 1972	Barry, Robin, and Maurice Gibb, 1
"Run-Around"	Blues Traveler, 1994	John Popper, 6
"Runaway"	Del Shannon, 1961	Charles Westover (alias Del Shannon) and Max Crook, 5
"Runaway Train"	Soul Asylum, 1992	David Pirner, 4

TITLE	PRIMARY RECORDING(S)	COMPOSER(S)
"Sally Simpson"	The Who, 1969	Pete Townshend and Roger Daltrey, 5
"Saturday Night's Alright For Fighting"	Elton John, 1973	Elton John and Bernie Taupin, 3
"Save Me"	Fleetwood Mac, 1990	Christine McVie and Eddy Quintela, 4
"Say You Love Me"	Fleetwood Mac, 1975	Christine McVie, 6
"Sealed With A Kiss"	Brian Hyland, 1962; Gary Lewis & the Playboys, 1968; Bobby Vinton, 1972	Udell and Geld, 6
"Second Hand News"	Fleetwood Mac, 1977	Lindsey Buckingham, 2
"Sgt. Pepper's Lonely Hearts Club Band"	The Beatles, 1967	John Lennon and Paul McCartney, 4
"Shake It Up"	Cars, 1981	Ric Ocasek, 1
"Shake, Rattle, & Roll"	Bill Haley and the Comets, 1954	C. Calhoun, 2, 5
"She Loves You"	The Beatles, 1963	John Lennon and Paul McCartney, 4
"She's A Woman"	The Beatles, 1964	John Lennon and Paul McCartney, 1
"She's Always A Woman"	Billy Joel, 1977	Billy Joel, 1
"Sherry"	The 4 Seasons, 1962	Bob Gaudio and Bob Crewe, 1
"Shop Around"	The Miracles, 1960; Captain & Tennille, 1976	William "Smokey" Robinson and Berry Gordy, 6
"Show Me The Way"	Peter Frampton, 1975	Peter Frampton, 6
"Since I Fell For You"	Lenny Welch, 1963	Woodrow Johnson, 6
"Sister Golden Hair"	America, 1975	Gerry Beckley, 3
"(Sittin' On) The Dock Of The Bay"	Otis Redding, 1969	Otis Redding and Steve Cropper, 1, 5
"Smoke Gets In Your Eyes"	The Platters, 1958	Otto Harbach and Jerome Kern, 6
"Smoke Of A Distant Fire"	The Sanford/Townsend Band, 1977	Gary and Bethie Kennedy, 2
"Smoke On The Water"	Deep Purple, 1972	Ritchie Blackmore, Ian Gillan, Roger Glover, Jon Lord, and Ian Paice, 2, 4
"So Far Away"	Carole King, 1971	Carole King, 6
"Somebody To Love"	Jefferson Airplane, 1967	Grace Slick, 2, 4, 5
"Someone Saved My Life Tonight"	Elton John, 1975	Elton John and Bernie Taupin, 4, 6

TITLE	PRIMARY RECORDING(S)	COMPOSER(S)
"Something"	The Beatles, 1969	George Harrison, 2
"Sorry Seems To Be The Hardest Word"	Elton John, 1976	Elton John and Bernie Taupin, 2
"Soul Man"	Sam and Dave, 1967	Isaac Hayes and David Porter, 6
"The Sounds Of Silence"	Simon and Garfunkel, 1965	Paul Simon, 6
"Space Oddity"	David Bowie, 1969	David Bowie, 4
"Squeeze Box"	The Who, 1975	Pete Townshend, 2
"St. Anne"	N/A	William Croft, 3
"Stairway To Heaven"	Led Zeppelin, 1971	Jimmy Page and Robert Plant, 2, 6
"Stand By Me"	Ben E. King, 1961	Ben E. King, Jerry Leiber, and Mike Stoller, 2
"Still . . . You Turn Me On"	Emerson, Lake & Palmer, 1973	Greg Lake, 1
"The Story In Your Eyes"	The Moody Blues, 1971	Justin Hayward, 2
"Strange Brew"	Cream, 1967	Eric Clapton, Felix Pappalardi, and Gail Collins, 5
"The Stroll"	The Diamonds, 1958	Otis and Lee, 6
"Stuck On You"	Elvis Presley, 1960	Aaron Schroeder and J. Leslie McFarland, 6
"Stuck With You"	Huey Lewis and the News, 1986	Chris Hayes and Huey Lewis, 2
"Summer Breeze"	Seals and Crofts, 1971	James Seals and Dash Crofts, 4, 6
"Summer, Highland Falls"	Billy Joel, 1976	Billy Joel, 1
"Sundown"	Gordon Lightfoot, 1974	Gordon Lightfoot, 4
"Superstar"	Murray Head, 1970	Tim Rice and Andrew Lloyd-Webber, 3
"Surfin' U.S.A."	The Beach Boys, 1963	Chuck Berry, 6
"Sweet Baby James"	James Taylor, 1970	James Taylor, 3
"Sweet Home Alabama"	Lynyrd Skynyrd, 1974	Ronnie Van Zant, Ed King, and Gary Rossington, 2, 5
"Take A Letter, Maria"	R. B. Greaves, 1969	R. B. Greaves, 6
"Take It On The Run"	REO Speedwagon, 1980	Gary Richrath, 2
"Take It To The Limit"	The Eagles, 1975	Randy Meisner, Don Henley, and Glenn Frey, 1, 4
"Take Me Home, Country Roads"	John Denver, 1971	Bill Danoff, Taffy Nivert, and John Denver, 3

TITLE	PRIMARY RECORDING(S)	COMPOSER(S)
"Take On Me"	A-ha, 1985	Pal Waaktaar, Mags Furuholen, and Morten Harket, 4
"Take The Long Way Home"	Supertramp, 1979	Rick Davies and Roger Hodgson, 4
"Take The Money And Run"	Steve Miller, 1976	Steve Miller, 2
"Talking In Your Sleep"	The Romantics, 1983	Jimmy Marinos, George Canler, Wally Palmar, Mike Skill, and Peter Solley, 4
"Tapestry"	Carole King, 1971	Carole King, 5
"Tears In Heaven"	Eric Clapton, 1992	Eric Clapton and Will Jennings, 1
"Teen Angel"	Mark Dinning, 1959	Jean Surrey, 6
"Temptation Eyes"	The Grass Roots, 1971	H. Price and D. Walsh, 2
"Tenting To-night"	N/A	Walter Kittredge, 1
"That'll Be The Day"	Buddy Holly, 1957; Linda Ronstadt, 1976	Jerry Allison, Buddy Holly, and Norman Petty, 2, 3, 4
"That's The Way (I Like It)"	K. C. and the Sunshine Band, 1975	Harry "KC" Casey and Richard Finch, 4
"These Eyes"	The Guess Who, 1969	Randy Bachman and Burton Cummings, 2
"Think"	Aretha Franklin, 1968	Aretha Franklin and Ted White, 5
"Ticket To Ride"	The Beatles, 1965	John Lennon and Paul McCartney, 6
"('Til) I Kissed You"	The Everly Brothers, 1959	Don Everly, 5
"Time"	Pink Floyd, 1973	Nick Mason, Roger Waters, Richard Wright, and David Gilmour, 7
"Time After Time"	Cyndi Lauper, 1983	Cyndi Lauper and Rob Hyman, 6
"Tin Man"	America, 1974	Dewey Bunnell, 4
"To Love Somebody"	The Bee Gees, 1967	Barry Gibb and Robin Gibb, 3, 5
"Toys In The Attic"	Aerosmith, 1975	Steve Tyler and Joe Perry, 4
"Treat Me Right"	Pat Benatar, 1980	Pat Benatar and D. Lubahn, 2
"Try Not To Breathe"	REM, 1992	Bill Berry, Peter Buck, Mike Mills, and Michael Stipe, 2

TITLE	PRIMARY RECORDING(S)	COMPOSER(S)
"Turn The Beat Around"	Vicki Sue Robinson, 1976	Jackson and Jackson, 2
"Turn To Stone"	Electric Light Orchestra, 1977	Jeff Lynne, 1
"Turn! Turn! Turn! (To Everything There Is A Season)"	The Byrds, 1965	Pete Seeger (adapted from the book of Ecclesiastes), 1, 4
"25 or 6 to 4"	Chicago, 1970	Robert Lamm, 1, 2
"The Twist"	Hank Ballard, 1960; Chubby Checker, 1960	Hank Ballard, 3
"Twist And Shout"	The Isley Brothers, 1962; the Beatles, 1964	B. Russell and P. Medley, 1, 3, 5
"Under My Thumb"	The Rolling Stones, 1966	Mick Jagger and Keith Richards, 2
"Up Around The Bend"	Credence Clearwater Revival, 1970	John Fogerty, 1
"Up On The Roof"	The Drifters, 1963; James Taylor, 1979	Gerry Goffin and Carole King, 1
"Upside Down"	Diana Ross, 1980	Bernard Edwards and Nile Gregory Rodgers, 2
"Us And Them"	Pink Floyd, 1973	Roger Waters and Richard Wright, 7
"Venus"	Shocking Blue, 1970; Bananarama, 1986	Robert Leeuwen, 4
"Vision of Love"	Mariah Carey, 1990	Mariah Carey and Ben Margulies, 4
"Walk Like An Egyptian"	The Bangles, 1985	Liam Sternberg, 4
"Wannabe"	Spice Girls, 1997	Matthew Rowbottom, Richard Stannard, Emma Burton, Melanie Chisolm, Geraldine Halliwell, Melanie Brown, and Victoria Adams, 4
"Watching The Wheels"	John Lennon, 1980	John Lennon, 6
"We Built This City"	Starship, 1985	Bernie Taupin, Martin Page, Dennis Lambert, and Peter Wolf, 4
"We Got The Beat"	The Go-Gos, 1981	Charlotte Caffey, 4
"The Weight"	The Band, 1968	Robbie Robertson, 5
"We're An American Band"	Grand Funk, 1973	Don Brewer, 4
"Werewolves Of London"	Warren Zevon, 1978	LeRoy P. Marinell, Waddy Wachtel, and Warren Zevon, 2

TITLE	PRIMARY RECORDING(S)	COMPOSER(S)
"What A Fool Believes"	The Doobie Brothers, 1978	Michael McDonald and Kenny Loggins, 2, 7
"What Is Life?"	George Harrison, 1970	George Harrison, 6
"What's Love Got To Do With It?"	Tina Turner, 1984	Terry Britten and Graham Lyle, 3, 6
"What's The Buzz"	*Jesus Christ Superstar* cast, 1970	Andrew Lloyd-Webber and Tim Rice, 5
"Wheel In The Sky"	Journey, 1977	D. Valory, N. Schon, and R. Fleischman, 1
"While My Guitar Gently Weeps"	The Beatles, 1968	George Harrison, 6
"While You See A Chance"	Steve Winwood, 1980	Steve Winwood and W. Jennings, 2
"Whip It"	Devo, 1980	Mark Mothersbaugh and Gerald Casale, 4
"White Christmas"	N/A; pub. 1940	Irving Berlin, 6
"Who Can It Be Now?"	Men At Work, 1982	Colin Hay, 6
"Who'll Stop The Rain?"	Credence Clearwater Revival, 1970	John Fogerty, 5
"Who's Crying Now"	Journey, 1981	Steve Perry and Jonathan Cain, 4
"Wild Night"	Van Morrison, 1971	Van Morrison, 4
"Wild World"	Cat Stevens, 1970	Cat Stevens, 6
"Will You Love Me Tomorrow"	The Shirelles, 1960; Carole King, 1971	Gerry Goffin and Carole King, 2
"Without You"	Nilsson, 1971	Pete Ham and Tom Evans, 3, 4
"Woman"	John Lennon, 1980	John Lennon, 1, 5
"Won't Get Fooled Again"	The Who, 1971	Pete Townshend, 3
"Wonderful Tonight"	Eric Clapton, 1977	Eric Clapton, 2
"Words Get In The Way"	Gloria Estefan, 1986	Gloria Estefan, 4
"Words Of Love"	Buddy Holly, 1957	Buddy Holly, 1
"The World I Know"	Collective Soul, 1995	Ed Roland and Ross Childress, 2, 6
"Wrapped Around Your Finger"	The Police, 1983	Sting, 6
"Yesterday"	The Beatles, 1965	Paul McCartney and John Lennon, 3
"You Are The Sunshine of My Life"	Stevie Wonder, 1972	Stevie Wonder, 7
"You Can't Always Get What You Want"	The Rolling Stones, 1968	Mick Jagger and Keith Richards, 3, 4

TITLE	PRIMARY RECORDING(S)	COMPOSER(S)
"You Don't Have To Be A Star (To Be In My Show)"	Marilyn McCoo and Billy Davis, Jr., 1976	James Dean and John Glover, 3
"You Don't Know How It Feels"	Tom Petty, 1994	Tom Petty, 2
"You Don't Mess Around With Jim"	Jim Croce, 1972	Jim Croce, 4
"You Keep Me Hangin' On"	The Supremes, 1966	Eddie Holland, Lamont Dozier, and Brian Holland, 4
"You Learn"	Alanis Morissette, 1995	Alanis Morissette and Glen Ballard, 4, 6
"You Make Loving Fun"	Fleetwood Mac, 1976	Christine McVie, 5
"(You Make Me Feel Like) A Natural Woman"	Aretha Franklin, 1967; Carole King, 1971	Gerry Goffin, Carole King, and Jerry Wexler, 4
"You May Be Right"	Billy Joel, 1980	Billy Joel, 6
"You Might Think"	The Cars, 1984	Ric Ocasek, 4
"You're Gonna Lose That Girl"	The Beatles, 1965	John Lennon and Paul McCartney, 5, 6
"You're No Good"	Linda Ronstadt, 1974	C. Ballard, Jr., 4
"You're The Inspiration"	Chicago, 1984	Peter Cetera and David Foster, 4
"You've Got To Hide Your Love Away"	The Beatles, 1965	John Lennon and Paul McCartney, 4
"You've Lost That Lovin' Feelin'"	The Righteous Brothers, 1964	Phil Spector, Barry Mann, and Cynthia Weil, 5, 6
"You've Made Me So Very Happy"	Blood, Sweat & Tears, 1972	Berry Gordy Jr., Brenda Holloway, Patrice Holloway, and Frank Wilson, 4, 6
"Your Mama Don't Dance"	Loggins and Messina, 1972	Kenny Loggins and Jim Messina, 4
"Your Smiling Face"	James Taylor, 1977	James Taylor, 1
"Your Song"	Elton John, 1970	Elton John and Bernie Taupin, 3

notes

INTRODUCTION

1. Robert Pielke, *You Say You Want a Revolution: Rock Music in American Culture* (Chicago: Nelson-Hall, 1986), ix.
2. Andrew Chester, "For a Rock Aesthetic," *New Left Review* 59 (Jan.–Feb. 1970): 83.
3. *NASM [National Association of Schools of Music] Handbook*, 7, D, 2.
4. Christopher P. Gordon, *Form and Content in Commercial Music* (New York: Ardsley House, 1992), 1, 39–43.
5. Stefan Kostka, *Materials and Techniques of Twentieth-Century Music* (Englewood Cliffs, N.J.: Prentice Hall, 1990), 105.
6. Robert Walser, *Running with the Devil: Power, Gender, and Madness in Heavy Metal Music* (Hanover, N.H.: University Press, 1993), 31.
7. Charles M. H. Keil, "Motion and Feeling through Music," *Journal of Aesthetics and Art Criticism* 24 (Spring 1966): 338.
8. Richard Middleton, *Studying Popular Music* (Buckingham: Open University Press, 1990), 117. The order of the sentences quoted is the reverse of their order in the original.
9. Chester, "Rock Aesthetic," 83.
10. Roy Shuker, *Understanding Popular Music* (London: Routledge, 1994), 26, 143.
11. Ibid., 26.
12. Ibid., 144.
13. Ibid., 26, 143, 144.

14. Ibid., 136.
15. Paul McCartney, "The Beatles," television documentary, American Broadcasting Company, November 1995.
16. Jean-Jacques Nattiez, *Music and Discourse: Toward a Semiology of Music*, trans. Carolyn Abbate (Princeton, N.J.: Princeton University Press, 1990), 139.
17. Middleton, *Studying Popular Music*, 116–17.
18. Wilfred Mellers, *Twilight of the Gods: The Music of the Beatles* (New York: Viking Press, 1973); Philip Tagg, "Analysing Popular Music: Theory, Method and Practice," *Popular Music* 2 (1982): 37–67; Philip Tagg, *Kojak—Fifty Seconds of Television Music: Toward the Analysis of Affect in Popular Music* (Göteborg: Musikvetenskapliga Institutionen, 1979); Joe Steussy, *Rock and Roll: Its History and Stylistic Development* (Englewood Cliffs, N.J.: Prentice Hall, 1990); John Kovach and Graeme Boone, eds., *Understanding Rock: Essays in Musical Analysis* (New York: Oxford University Press, 1997).
19. Stefan Kostka and Dorothy Payne, *Tonal Harmony*, 3d ed. (New York, McGraw-Hill, 1995); Ralph Turek, *Elements of Music*, 2 vols., 2d ed. (New York: McGraw-Hill, 1996).
20. Edward Macan, *Rocking the Classics: English Progressive Rock and the Counterculture* (New York: Oxford University Press, 1977). See esp. p. 45.

CHAPTER 1: PHRASE RHYTHM

1. Fred Lerdahl and Ray Jackendoff, *A Generative Theory of Tonal Music* (Cambridge, Mass.: MIT Press, 1983), 30–33 (see esp. n. 10), 27.
2. William Rothstein, *Phrase Rhythm in Tonal Music* (New York: Schirmer, 1989), 28–29.
3. See Rothstein, *Phrase Rhythm*, 44–47.
4. The same, of course, may apply to instrumental lines.
5. See Rothstein, *Phrase Rhythm*, 52.
6. In some cases an argument from rhyme scheme could be made.
7. Joel Lester, *The Rhythms of Tonal Music* (Carbondale, Ill.: Southern Illinois University Press), 163–64.
8. J. B. Bury, *The Idea of Progress: An Inquiry into Its Origin and Growth* (n.p.: Macmillan, 1932; reprint, New York: Dover, 1955). See, e.g., pp. 35–36: "In this last stage of the Renaissance, which includes the first quarter of the seventeenth century, soil was being prepared in which the idea of Progress could germinate."
9. G. K. Chesterton, *Collected Works*, vol. 18, *Chaucer* (San Francisco: Ignatius Press, 1991), 268.
10. Jean-François Lyotard, "Defining the Postmodern," in *The Cultural Studies Reader*, ed. Simon During (London: Rutledge, 1993), 172.
11. Anthony Giddens, *The Consequences of Modernity* (Stanford, Calif.: Stanford University Press, 1990), p. 46.

12. Suzi Gablik, *Has Modernism Failed?* (New York: Thames and Hudson, 1984), 115–17.

CHAPTER 2: KEY AND MODE

1. H. C. Longuet-Higgins and M. J. Steedman, "On Interpreting Bach," *Machine Intelligence* 6 (1971): 221–41. See esp. pp. 223 and 237.
2. Carol L. Krumhansl, *Cognitive Foundations of Musical Pitch*, Oxford Psychology Series, no. 17 (New York: Oxford University Press, 1990), 17–31, 77–96 (emphasis in the original).
3. Errors are noted on pp. 83–85. The flaw noted on p. 93 is serious: the algorithm does not in fact "know" when it has determined the correct key. The algorithm makes a best guess with every new note, and Krumhansl, knowing the key, determines when the algorithm's best guess agrees with the correct answer.
4. David Butler, "Describing the Perception of Tonality in Music: A Critique of the Tonal Hierarchy Theory and a Proposal for a Theory of Intervallic Rivalry," *Music Perception* 6 (Spring 1989):225–26.
5. Ibid., 237–38.
6. See, e.g., Arnold Schoenberg, *Style and Idea*, ed. Leonard Stein, trans. Leo Black (New York: St. Martins Press, 1975), 219.
7. Paul Hindemith, *The Craft of Musical Composition*, vol. 1, *Theoretical Part*, 4th ed., trans. Arthur Mendel (Mainz: Schott, 1942), 134, 138.
8. *The New Grove Dictionary of Music and Musicians*, s.v. "Tonality," by Carl Dahlhaus.
9. Butler, "Perception of Tonality," 238.
10. In many pieces, each section employs a different initiating harmony. (See Chapter 6.) Usually only the initiating harmony of the first section proves to be the tonic.
11. The melodic pitch source of a piece in fact often differs from the harmonic pitch source. See Chapter 4 for further discussion of harmonic pitch sources.
12. In this discussion, I use set-theory terminology as a substitute for the traditional patterns of whole steps and half steps that usually accompany definitions of scales for two reasons. First, the nonhierarchical connotations of the terminology suit the introduction of a set of pitches whose hierarchy changes depending on the mode. Second, since one of the structures to be discussed is a pentatonic set, the terminology avoids the awkwardness of equating something called a "step and a-half" with something called a "scale step."

    The PC lists for pitch sources are given as sets in prime form. On the other hand, the PC list for a scale (a set interpreted in light of the identification of a tonic) should be read simply as an ascending order (not a prime form) with the note identified as tonic being designated as [0].

    Those unfamiliar with set theory will find a brief introduction in the glossary.

13. The melodies of heavy metal, a subcategory of rock, often employ other modal scales (including Locrian) in addition to these. For more information, see Robert Walser's *Running with the Devil* (Hanover, N.H.: University Press of New England, 1993), 46–48.

14. Note that the scalar basis can only be suggested, not precisely identified, because this hexachord does not include a tritone, an interval necessary for the identification of a particular diatonic set.

15. I am here, as elsewhere, including the listener in the category of analyst, even when he or she is unaware of that role. Many listeners lacking formal theoretical training know what note to start "Happy Birthday" on after hearing a V7 chord, though they may be unable to explain how they do it. At some level these people are analyzing—analyzing the sound of the chord and how it fits into the interpretive scheme of their musical memories.

16. In this book, a capital roman numeral VII refers to a major triad built on the note one whole step below tonic. See Chapter 4.

17. For information on sum tones, see *The New Grove Dictionary of Music and Musicians*, s.v. "Sound," by Charles Taylor, esp. sect. 9.

CHAPTER 3: CADENCES

1. See *Webster's New Twentieth Century Dictionary of the English Language*, 2d ed. (New York: Prentice Hall, 1983), s.v. "Cadence," def.

2. Heinrich Christoph Koch, *Introductory Essay on Composition: The Mechanical Rules of Melody, Sections 3 and 4*, trans. with an introduction by Nancy Kolaveff Baker (New Haven, Conn.: Yale University Press, 1983), 1. Words in brackets, which are given by Baker, indicate the wording from the original German publication (Leipzig: Adam Friedrich Böhme, 1787).

3. Ralph Turek, *Elements of Music*, vol. 1, 2d ed., (New York: McGraw-Hill, 1996), 296.

4. See Chapter 4 for an explanation of the major III in E major, as well as for the major VII in example 4.3.

5. This chapter deals with final chords only. Chapter 5 explores patterns of succession leading to these harmonies.

6. Concerning the similar practice in Latin, Wheelock refers to the placement of the verb at the end of a sentence as a "periodic style, which seeks to keep the reader or listener in suspense until the last word of a sentence has been reached." Note the similarity of the terms to those used in describing common-practice music: a "period" is a structure that "keeps the listener in suspense until the last" chord, i.e., the tonic chord, "has been reached." See Frederic M. Wheelock, *Latin: An Introductory Course Based on Ancient Authors*, 3d ed. (New York: Barnes and Noble, 1963), 15.

7. Shakespeare, *Richard II*, act II, scene i.

CHAPTER 4: CHORD TYPE
AND HARMONIC PALETTE

1. The next few examples all involve conflict between instrumental harmonies and pitches of a vocal melody. But the same kind of conflict occurs with instrumental melodies, as in solos and hook lines or fills.

2. A minor seventh above tonic is called the "lowered seventh," even in the context of an Aeolian or Mixolydian scale, where the minor seventh is intrinsic to the scale.

3. Paul Gambaccini, *Paul McCartney: In His Own Words* (New York: Flash, 1976), 19.

4. In sheet-music harmonic nomenclature, the symbols to the left of a slash indicate the upper notes of a harmony, and those to the right the bass note. The practice is the standard for indicating inversions and is useful in the notation of many harmonies not constructed from stacked thirds, such as the one discussed here.

5. The tradition of using roman numerals to indicate chords is approximately two hundred years old. The number represented corresponds to the position of the chord's root in the scale. Uppercase roman numerals indicate a major triad; those in lowercase indicate a minor triad. The reader will find further information in the glossary.

6. As with the lowered seventh scale degree (see note 2, this chap.), the chord built on that note is often called "♭VII," even though the root is an intrinsic part of the prevailing scale and even when the note is not literally a flat, as, for instance, D in the key of E.

7. The reader inexperienced in playing popular music must not assume that such musicians know nothing of theory simply because they have not been formally trained or are not precise with their terminology. These formally ignorant musicians are, in my experience, often better theorists with better ears than most college-trained musicians.

8. Eric Salzman and Michael Sahl, in *Making Changes: A Practical Guide to Vernacular Harmony* (New York: McGraw-Hill, 1977), present a slightly different solution to some of the problems of chord designation outlined in this chapter. They distinguish, for instance, between a Maj. III (E in C major) and a Flat III (E♭ in C major). They recognize both simply as various possibilities in the major mode without separating the possibilities into two basic palettes.

CHAPTER 5: HARMONIC SUCCESSION

1. As an example of the former, I offer a scene from a television drama whose name has been forgotten. In this scene, a young man takes his date to the local Inspiration Point, parks the car, tunes the radio to a rock station, puts his arm around the woman, and sighs, "Ahhh, rock 'n' roll. It still just uses the same three chords." His intention is apparently to try to relax the situation with a thought as comforting as a pair of well-worn slippers.

As an example of the latter, I offer the case of a colleague at the University of Oklahoma's School of Music who, upon hearing that I was to present some of these ideas on rock at a conference in Oakland, said, "You're going all the way to California to talk about rock music!? What's to talk about? It's just the same three chords over and over."

2. Bruce Benward and Gary White, *Music in Theory and Practice*, 4th ed., vol. 1 (Dubuque, Iowa: Wm. C. Brown, 1989), 210.

3. Richard Sorce, *Music Theory for the Music Professional: A Comparison of Common-Practice and Popular Genres* (New York: Ardsley House, 1995), xxi, 178–81.

4. Christopher P. Gordon, *Form and Content in Commercial Music* (New York: Ardsley House, 1992), 39–43, 1.

5. Benward and White are technically correct in saying that most popular music follows common-practice norms—if Broadway, country, most jazz up to about 1950, the Tin Pan Alley tradition, and the like are included in the genre "popular music." But these authors mislead by not enumerating the exceptions, especially given their 1989 date of publication.

6. Justin London, "'One Step Up': A Lesson from Pop Music," *Journal of Music Theory Pedagogy* 4 (Spring 1990): 112.

7. Ottman, for instance, divides harmonic succession into two main categories, the "commonly used" combinations and the "less common." See Robert W. Ottman, *Advanced Harmony*, 2d ed. (Englewood Cliffs, N.J.: Prentice Hall, 1972), 31, 35–36. Allen Irvine McHose in his statistical studies found that progression accounts for 76 percent of harmonic successions in Bach chorales: *The Contrapuntal Harmonic Technique of the Eighteenth Century* (Englewood Cliffs, N.J.: Prentice Hall, 1947), 10. I don't mean here to revert to the old error of defining tonal standards by the harmonic practice of Bach; I merely offer McHose's work as an example of using the word *progression* to refer to the statistically most common harmonic successions.

8. McHose, *Contrapuntal Technique*, 9; Ottman, *Advanced Harmony*, 31.

9. Walter Piston, *Harmony*, 5th ed., rev. and expanded by Mark DeVoto (New York: Norton, 1987), 178. See also William H. Reynolds, *Common-Practice Harmony* (New York: Longman, 1985), 78.

10. McHose, *Contrapuntal Technique*, 9; Ottmann, *advanced Harmony*, 31.

11. See, e.g., Stefan Kostka and Dorothy Payne, *Tonal Harmony*, 3d ed. (New York: McGraw-Hill, 1995), 112; and Paul O. Harder, *Harmonic Materials in Tonal Music*, pt. 1, 4th ed. (Boston: Allyn and Bacon, 1980), 202.

12. See, e.g., Kostka and Payne, *Tonal Harmony*, 118.

13. See Chapter 1 for a further discussion of overlap in rock.

14. See Chapter 3 for an explanation of how these V-I cadences often contradict the common practice in other ways.

15. I have worked with rock musicians who, without a history of formal education in theory, call a D major triad a "five of five" when found in the key of C, fully aware

that the term precisely describes the structure of the chord, though totally unaware of (or unconcerned with) the functional connotations of the term V chord when applied to music of other styles.

16. See Richard L. Crocker, *A History of Musical Style* (New York: Dover, 1986), 142.

17. See Reynolds, *Common-Practice Harmony*, 55; Harder, *Harmonic Materials*, 201; and Piston, *Harmony*, 24.

18. Reynolds, *Common-Practice Harmony*, 55.

CHAPTER 6: FORM

1. I am using "repetition" to refer to an immediate restatement of material and "return" when the restatement occurs only after intervening material.

2. That the theory of phrases and periods (or "sentences" as they used to be more logically called) comes from linguistic fields is undeniable. See, for instance, "Introduction to Part Six" in *Contemplating Music: Source Readings in the Aesthetics of Music*, selected and edited with introductions by Ruth Katz and Carl Dahlhaus (Stuyvesant, N.Y.: Pendragon Press, 1992), esp. p. 4. That the musical idea itself of periods comes from language is possible but unknown.

3. It is tempting to say that the anticipation evoked by the presence of these two dependent clauses simulates (and takes the place of) harmonic anticipation. But doing so would be to forget that we are dealing here with the type, not the copy— that musical anticipation, according to the theory, is modeled after sentence structure, not vice versa.

4. We have seen many ways in which IV performs a role traditionally taken by V. It often begins the second section of a piece, for instance, and it often serves as the penultimate chord in a cadence.

5. Saint Augustine, *On Music*, trans. Robert Catesby Taliaferro, in *The Fathers of the Church*, vol. 4 (New York: Fathers of the Church, Inc., 1947), 221, 237.

6. Much of the information in this paragraph and the next comes from Charles Hamm's fascinating *Yesterdays* (New York: Norton, 1979). The clearest overview of the issue is found on pp. 358–61. Other pertinent passages are listed in Hamm's index, under "chorus" and "verse-chorus form."

7. I.e., resolution or rest, in this case typically involving the tonic chord as the final harmony and the tonic pitch as the last note of the passage.

8. In traditional form theory, the passage labeled "B," what we are here calling the "bridge," is technically not considered a complete section in and of itself. Rather, in rounded-binary form, the combination of B and the return of A (in classical music usually a shortened or modified version of A) constitutes the second section. The reasoning is that the B passage leads into the return of A without having a closed cadence of its own. See, e.g., Ralph Turek, *The Elements of Music: Concepts and Applications*, 2d ed., vol. 1 (New York: McGraw-Hill, 1996), 460, 464. In rock, the frequent absence of tonal closure in *every* section makes this distinction much less important.

9. "V" standing for verse, "B" for bridge, and "C" for chorus.

10. See *The Penguin Book of American Folk Songs*, compiled and edited with notes by Alan Lomax (Baltimore: Penguin, 1964).

CHAPTER 7: ANALYZING A HIT

1. Leonard B. Meyer, *Explaining Music* (Chicago: University of Chicago Press, 1973), 6–7.

2. Ibid., 19.

3. The automobile is the preferred sociological setting for a performance of "Rhonda". It's difficult to imagine anyone having read this far without ever having sung this song in a car with friends. If you are in that minority, you must perform the experiment to verify the statement in the text.

4. Although the VII chord is not literally diatonic to the major scale (VII in G is built on F, while the G-major scale includes an F♯), it often appears with the diatonic subset of the major system. Its mixed character becomes more important later in this analysis.

5. Here we must certainly recognize the contributions of an arranger to the structure of the piece. One line in the album's liner notes reads: "All brass arrangements by [trombonist] James Pankow with some help from the rest of the boys." Incidentally, the instruments normally referred to as brass when speaking of pieces by Chicago usually include an alto saxophone, an instrument not typically classified among the brass.

6. The lyrics printed on the album cover read "time to *start* another one." The word as sung on the recording is clearly "dig."

7. Think C♯ and E. When comparing a flat key and a sharp key, key relationships are not always immediately apparent. Specifically, when the number of flats in the traditional key signature of the one key and the number of sharps in the key signature of the other add up to more than six, one of the keys must be enharmonically respelled for the key relationship to become clear. In the example given here, D♭ has five flats in its key signature, and E has four sharps. Five plus four equals nine, which is more than six, so we must think enharmonically. Thinking of D♭ as C♯ makes it clear that the relationship with E is a third. One may also simply play the tonic notes and note that they sound like a third (i.e., C♯ and E) rather than a second (i.e., D♭ and E).

8. Syncopation can be defined as a conflict between metrical accent and one other type of accent. Syncopation involving agogic accents (long notes) is the most common: longer, and thus more prominent notes, come on unaccented beats or parts of beats. while shorter notes (or no notes) come on accented beats. A note followed by a rest is considered to last until the beginning of the next note for purposes of analyzing syncopation. Thus, the chord on the second half of the fourth beat in example 7.7 is syncopated: because it functions virtually as a quarter note (due to the rest after it), it makes the second half of the fourth beat more

prominent than the metrically stronger fourth beat before it (which receives only an eighth note) and more than even the downbeat of the next measure (which begins no new note).

9. This analysis was greatly facilitated by means of a published transcription by Keith Emerson and John Curtin of portions of the piece. The transcription shown as example 7.10 is my own.

10. Edward Macan, *Rocking the Classics: English Progressive Rock and the Counterculture* (New York: Oxford University Press, 1977). The quotations from Gary Brooker, Tony Banks, and Keith Emerson are taken from pp. 38, 39, and 40, respectively.

Glossary

The terms, notations, and concepts introduced in this book are defined below. Numbers in parentheses indicate chapters offering a major discussion. Within entries, terms having their own entries are in boldface. Basic concepts of music theory are also included to assist the reader who has little formal training in the field but who wishes to learn more about the technical aspects of rock.

+ — The symbol for an **augmented triad.**

^ — The symbol for **scale degree.**

° — The symbol for a **diminished triad.**

1 + 1 model (1) — A model of **phrase rhythm** in which short vocal **phrases** come to their respective **cadences** on the second and fourth **downbeats,** i.e., **weak downbeats.** This model almost always represents a large-scale **dissonance** requiring as **resolution** the occurrence of one of the models of phrase rhythm that involve a cadence on a **strong downbeat.**

2 + 2 model (1) — A common model of **phrase rhythm** in which the vocal **cadence** comes on the third **downbeat** in a four-bar **hypermeasure,** creating a motion-to-rest ratio of 1:1.

added-note chord (4) — A **chord** that cannot be arranged in **stacked thirds** but that can be analyzed as a **triad** with an added second, fourth, or sixth above the **root;** the added second is sometimes called an added ninth (e.g.,

D can be found both a second and a ninth above any given C). C(add4) consists of C, E, G, and F. C(add6) (sometimes notated simply as C6) consists of C, E, G, and A. C(add2) (sometimes notated simply as C2) consists of C, E, G, and D. If an added second is called an added ninth, the word "add" is always used, as in "C(add9)." Any chord name with "9" and without the word "add" indicates that the chord has both a seventh and a ninth. C(add9) consists of C, E, G, and D. C9 consists of C, E, G, B♭, and D.

Aeolian scale (2) — A **natural-minor scale**.

agogic accent — The emphasis perceived on a note longer than the immediately preceding notes.

augmented triad (4) — A **triad** whose **stacked thirds,** from bottom to top, are major and major. C augmented (usually notated as C+) contains C, E, and G♯.

authentic cadence (3) — A name traditionally given to a harmonic **cadence** consisting of a V or vii° followed by a I or i.

bridge (6) — A passage, usually introduced after the second **chorus,** used to lead back to the **verse** or the final repetitions of the chorus.

cadence (1, 3) — The melodic, harmonic, or rhythmic pattern at the end of a **phrase**. The word may refer either to the end of a particular phrase or to a generic pattern typically found at the ends of phrases.

chord (4) — Any combination of tones sounding together. The most common chords in rock music are **triads, seventh chords, ninth chords, split-third chords, added-note chords, eleventh chords, open-fifth chords,** and **suspended chords**.

chord quality — The type of a given **chord,** as defined by the **intervals** making up the chord.

chord succession (5) — See **harmonic succession**.

chord symbol — A mostly alphanumeric representation of a **chord** indicating the **root** and **quality** of the chord, as well as its **inversion**. This book uses both a relative system of **roman numerals,** in which the root is numbered to show its relationship to a **tonic,** and an absolute system common to sheet music, in which the root is indicated by note name. In this second system, some common qualities are indicated as follows:

Symbol	Quality
E (note name alone)	*major triad*
E/B	*major triad* in second *inversion*
Em	*minor triad*
E+	*augmented triad*

Symbol	Quality
E°	*diminished triad*
E7	*dominant seventh*
EM7	*major seventh*
Em7	*minor seventh*
E°7	*diminished seventh*
Em7–5	*half-diminished seventh*
Esus	*suspended chord*

chorus (6) — (1) A musical section that recurs numerous times with a fixed text of several lines; (2) an entire song in **rounded-binary form**; (3) the A section of a song in rounded-binary form.

chromatic — (1) Having to do with notes outside a given **diatonic scale,** as F♯ with relation to the **key** of C; (2) having to do with any pattern involving two or more adjacent **half steps,** as in the notes C, C♯, and D; (3) having to do with two different notes with the same letter name, such as C and C♯.

chromatic-minor system (4) — I or i, N or II, III, IV, V, VI, and VII. In E, this **harmonic system** produces a **harmonic palette** consisting of the following **triads:** E, F or F♯, G, A, B, C, and D. In E minor, this system results in the same palette with only one difference: the **tonic chord** is E minor.

chromatic-second relationship (2) — The relationship between two **keys** whose **tonic harmonies** have the same quality and whose **tonic** pitches are a **half step** or **whole step** apart. C major and D major have a chromatic-second relationship, as do A major and B♭ major, and F minor and G minor.

chromatic-third relationship (2) — The relationship between two **chords** whose **roots** are a third apart and that have a **chromatic** relationship (in sense 3) between two of their pitches. C major and A major have a chromatic-third relationship; the roots C and A are a third apart (it is closer in this case to count from C down to A than from C up to A), and the C from the first chord and the C♯ from the second chord have a chromatic relationship. Two **keys** have a chromatic-third relationship if their **tonic chords** have a chromatic-third relationship.

closed cadence (3) — A **cadence** that carries a sense of tonal completion by means of ending with the **tonic** pitch and the **tonic harmony** on a **downbeat** at the end of a **phrase**.

common practice — A set of patterns forming the basis of normal harmonic style in Western music from around 1670 to around 1900 as well as in Western popular music up to the early 1950s.

compound-binary form (6) — A form consisting of two principal parts, the first part of which, itself as long as or longer than a normal song, usually divides into **strophes** or **verses** and **choruses,** and the second part of which is generally structured around several repetitions of a single melodic line or **chord succession,** or both.

consonance — (1) A **consonant** note, **interval,** or **chord**; (2) the property of being **consonant**.

consonant — (1) Harmonizing, belonging to a given **chord**. The note E is consonant with a C-major **triad** in that E is a member of the triad; (2) basic, standard, stable, or pleasant-sounding, when referring to a harmonic structure. Tastes and ideas concerning this issue change with time and culture. A **dominant seventh chord** was once considered a **dissonance,** but it is often used as a consonant **chord** in rock.

degree — See **scale degree**.

diatonic — Having to do with a set of pitches that can be defined exactly by a traditional key signature. See also **diatonic scale**.

diatonic scale (2) — Any **scale** whose pitches can be defined exactly by a traditional key signature. Such scales always have exactly five **whole steps** and two **half steps,** and the half steps always have at least two whole steps between them. C **major,** D **Dorian,** E **Phrygian,** F **Lydian,** G **Mixolydian,** and A **natural minor** (or Aeolian) are all diatonic scales; they all use the same set of pitches (although they each start on a different note from within that set)—the set of natural notes that is exactly denoted by the key signature of no sharps or flats.

diminished seventh chord (4) — A **seventh chord** whose **stacked thirds,** from bottom to top, are minor, minor, and minor; also typically described as a **diminished triad** with a diminished seventh above the **root**. E diminished seventh (usually notated as "E°7") contains E, G, B♭, and D♭.

diminished triad (4) — A **triad** whose **stacked thirds,** from bottom to top, are minor and minor. C diminished (usually notated as "C°") contains C, E♭, and G♭.

dissonance — (1) A **dissonant** note, **interval, chord,** or other musical structure. A pattern perceived as requiring **resolution**; (2) the property of being **dissonant**.

dissonant — (1) Harmonically clashing, not belonging to a given **chord**. The note C♯ is dissonant with respect to a C-major **triad** since it is not a member of the triad; (2) embellishing, secondary, unstable, or harsh-sounding, when referring to a harmonic structure. Tastes and ideas concerning this issue change with time and culture. A **dominant seventh chord** was once considered a **dissonance,** but it is often used as a **consonant chord** in rock.

dominant — The fifth note of a **scale**; also, a **chord** built on the fifth note of a scale. G is the dominant of C.

dominant seventh chord (4) — A **seventh chord** whose **stacked thirds,** from bottom to top, are major, minor, and minor; also typically described as a **major triad** with a minor seventh above the **root.** C dominant seventh (usually notated simply as C7) contains C, E, G, and B♭. The chord is called **dominant** because it is structured as if it were built on the fifth **degree** of a **scale:** C is the dominant of F, and the **key** of F contains all natural notes, with the exception of B♭.

Dorian scale (2) — A **scale** whose pattern of **whole steps** and **half steps** is 1 ¹/₂ 1 1 1 ¹/₂ 1. A C Dorian scale consists of C, D, E♭, F, G, A, B♭, and C.

downbeat (1) — The first beat of a measure.

eleventh chord (4) — A **chord** consisting of a fifth, seventh, ninth, and eleventh above the bass; the seventh is usually minor, the fifth and eleventh perfect, and the ninth major. C11, then, consists of C, G, B♭, D, and F.

elision model (1) — A model of **phrase rhythm** in which a **phrase** comes to a **cadence** on its fourth downbeat, which upon further listening proves to serve also as the first **downbeat** of the next **hypermeasure.** As a result, (1) what is at first perceived as a **weak downbeat** is later reinterpreted as a **strong downbeat,** and (2) a measure is "lost": two four-bar hypermeasures, for instance, end up having a duration of only seven measures.

enharmonic — Having the same sound but not the same spelling or name. F♯ and G♭ are enharmonic. Notes, **chords, scales,** and **keys** may all be enharmonic.

even-numbered downbeat (1) — The **downbeat** of either the second or the fourth measure of a four-bar **hypermeasure;** a **weak downbeat.**

extension-overlap model (1) — A model of **phrase rhythm** in which a **phrase** beginning near the first **downbeat** of a four-measure unit delays coming to a **cadence** until the fifth downbeat, i.e., the first downbeat of the next formal unit.

first-downbeat model (1) — A model of **phrase rhythm** in which a short vocal phrase ends on the first **downbeat** of a **hypermeasure.**

fugue (7) — A **polyphonic** piece in which the parts enter one at a time, each stating the main melodic theme (usually called the subject) of the piece.

half cadence (3) — A name traditionally given to a harmonic **cadence** ending with a V **chord.** It is so called because it appears halfway through a typical **period.**

half-diminished seventh chord (4) — A **seventh chord** whose **stacked thirds,** from bottom to top, are minor, minor, and major. It is called half-diminished because it can be thought of as a **diminished triad** with a minor seventh above the **root:** only one of the two elements of the chord is diminished. The chord is usually described in pop chord charts as a **minor-seventh chord** with a lowered fifth. E half-diminished seventh, usually notated as Em7−5 or Em7(b5), contains E, G, B♭, and D.

half step — The smallest **interval** in standard Western music (as opposed to Asian, for instance); e.g., from C to the C♯ just above it is a half step.

harmonic function (5) — The tendency of a **harmony** to be followed by some other particular harmony. In **common practice** music, harmonies generally follow tendencies and therefore have functions. In rock they generally do not.

harmonic inversion (4) — The placement in the bass of a member of a **chord** other than the **root.** When C major is played with E in the bass, the chord is said to be in inversion. A chord with its **root** in the bass is said to be in root position. A chord with its third in the bass is said to be in first inversion. A chord with its fifth in the bass is said to be in second inversion. A chord with its seventh in the bass is said to be in third inversion.

In sheet music, inversions are usually notated by means of a slash, with the chord name to the left of the slash and the bass note to the right. C/E indicates a C major **triad** with E in the bass. In **roman numerals,** inversions are indicated by arabic numerals corresponding to significant **intervals** above the bass note, as shown in the following chart:

Chord	Bass	Symbol
triad in root position	root	[none]
triad in first inversion	third	6
triad in second inversion	fifth	$\frac{6}{4}$
seventh chord in root position	root	7
seventh chord in first inversion	third	$\frac{6}{5}$
seventh chord in second inversion	fifth	$\frac{4}{3}$
seventh chord in third inversion	seventh	$\frac{4}{2}$ or 2

harmonic palette (4) — A standard set of **chords,** associated with a given **key** and a given **harmonic system,** from which composers choose the chords for a particular piece or part of a piece.

harmonic progression (5) — (1) A normal **harmonic succession** in a piece of **common-practice** music, i.e., one that functions to move forward toward ultimate **resolution** on the **tonic harmony;** (2) a series of at least two **chords** that follows **common-practice** norms.

harmonic succession, harmonic pattern (5) — A listing of **chords** in the order of their appearance in a particular piece or passage.

harmonic system (4) — One of three standard sets of **chord** relationships that, when applied to a particular **key,** produce a **harmonic palette**. The three standard systems are the **natural-minor system,** the **chromatic-minor system,** and the **major system**.

harmony (4) — A **chord**.

heterophony (4) — A **texture** involving two or more simultaneous variations of a melody.

hexachord (2) — Any group of six notes or pitch classes.

high hat — A device in a standard drum set consisting of two cymbals facing each other and a pedal that brings them into contact. In a standard rock beat, the high hat plays twice per beat.

homophonic (4) — Having a **texture** of **homophony**.

homophony (4) — A **texture** in which several parts are played at a time, most of which move in the same (or nearly the same) rhythm. Because of the lack of rhythmic independence, the parts often lose their distinction, and the notes are heard more as parts of **chords** than as melodies. Most rock uses **homophonic** texture.

hook — A distinctive melodic figure repeated several times during a piece and designed to provide quick familiarity and recognition. The opening guitar melody on the Beatles' "Day Tripper" is the classic example.

hypermeasure (1) — A metrical unit built of whole measures instead of beats. A typical hypermeasure is four measures long. Just as the first and third beats are considered strong beats in a four-beat measure, the first and third **downbeats** of a four-bar hypermeasure are considered **strong downbeats**.

hypermetrical unit (1) — A **hypermeasure**.

initiating harmony (6) — A **harmony** that occurs at the beginning of each **hypermeasure** of a piece or section of a piece. The initiating harmony of the first section of a piece will likely prove to be the **tonic harmony** of the piece.

interval — The distance between two notes; also the two notes themselves. Interval names have two parts: a number and a qualifier, as in "major third" (abbreviated M3). To determine the numerical part, count letter names starting with the first note as 1. C up to E is a third (C = 1, D = 2, E = 3). The system of assigning qualifying adjectives is somewhat complex. Explanations can be found in any beginning theory textbook.

inversion (4) — See **harmonic inversion**.

key (2) — A system of **tonality** as applied to a particular pitch. E.g., to say that a piece is in the key of C implies that the most stable **harmony** is a C major

235

triad, that the melody will be constructed from the notes of a particular **scale** (probably **major** or **Mixolydian**), and so on.

linear harmony (4) — A harmony that appears in a particular piece not because it holds a place in a standard **harmonic system** but because one or more of its notes form parts of lines moving by step. The **augmented triad** does not play a part in any standard **harmonic system;** but C+ may be used as a linear harmony when, for example, its G♯ is used between the G of a C major **triad** and the A of an A minor triad.

Lydian scale (2) — A **scale** whose pattern of **whole steps** and **half steps** is 1 1 1 ^{1}/$_2$1 1 ^{1}/$_2$. A C-Lydian scale consists of C, D, E, F♯, G, A, B, and C.

major scale (2) — A **scale** whose pattern of **whole steps** and **half steps** is 1 1 ^{1}/$_2$ 1 1 1 ^{1}/$_2$. A C-major scale consists of C, D, E, F, G, A, B, and C.

major seventh chord (4) — A **seventh chord** whose **stacked thirds,** from bottom to top, are major, minor, and major; also typically described as a **major triad** with a major seventh above the **root.** C major seventh (usually notated as CM7 or Cmaj7) contains C, E, G, and B.

major system (4) — I, ii, V/V, iii, V/vi, iv, IV, v, V, vi, V/ii, and VII. In E, this **harmonic system** produces a **harmonic palette** consisting of the following **triads:** E, F♯ minor, F♯ major, G♯ minor, G♯ major, A minor, A major, B minor, B major, C♯ minor, C♯ major, and D. The **diatonic** subset of the system includes only I, ii, iii, IV, V, vi, and sometimes VII.

major triad (4) — A **triad** whose **stacked thirds,** from bottom to top, are major and minor. C major (usually notated simply as C) contains C, E, and G.

melodic motion (1) — The period of rhythmic activity during a vocal **phrase;** everything in the phrase before the **cadence.**

melodic rest (1) — The period of rhythmic inactivity normally associated with **cadences;** it lasts from the attack time of the last note of one **phrase** to the beginning of the next **phrase.** A melodic rest therefore includes both the last note of the phrase and what is more commonly referred to as "the rest."

metrical accent — The emphasis perceived on strong beats in a measure (e.g., beats 1 and 3 in a four-beat measure).

minor seventh chord (4) — A **seventh chord** whose **stacked thirds,** from bottom to top, are minor, major, and minor; also typically described as a **minor triad** with a minor seventh above the **root.** C minor seventh (usually notated as Cm7) contains C, E♭, G, and B♭.

minor triad (4) — A **triad** whose **stacked thirds,** from bottom to top, are minor and major. C minor (usually notated as Cm) contains C, E♭, and G.

Mixolydian scale (2) — A **scale** whose pattern of **whole steps** and **half steps**

is 1 1 ½ 1 1½ 1. A C-Mixolydian scale consists of C, D, E, F, G, A, B♭, and C.

mode — (1) The quality of a key being major or minor. If a piece is in D minor, its mode is minor; (2) one of a number of scales from the pretonal era, e.g., Dorian, Phrygian, Lydian, or Mixolydian.

modulation (2) — A change of **key** within a piece.

monophonic (4) — Having a **texture** of **monophony**.

monophony (4) — A **texture** involving a single, unaccompanied melody.

motion-to-rest ratio (1) — The ratio between the duration of **melodic motion** and the duration of **melodic rest** in a formal unit.

natural-minor scale (2) — A **scale** whose pattern of **whole steps** and **half steps** is 1 ½ 1 1 ½ 1 1. A C natural-minor scale consists of C, D, E♭, F, G, A♭, B♭, and C.

natural-minor system (4) — i, III, iv, v, VI, and VII. In E minor, this **harmonic system** produces a **harmonic palette** consisting of the following **triads:** E minor, G, A minor, B minor, C, and D.

Neapolitan — A **major triad** built on the lowered second **scale degree**. For example, D♭ in the **key** of C, or F in the key of E; written as ♭II or N.

ninth chord (4) — A **chord** of five note names whose notes can be arranged into **stacked** (or overlapping) **thirds**. C, E, G, B♭, and D form a ninth chord.

odd-numbered downbeat (1) — The **downbeat** of either the first or the third measure of a four-bar **hypermeasure; a strong downbeat**.

open cadence (3) — A **cadence** that carries a sense of being tonally incomplete, usually by means of not ending on the **tonic** pitch, not ending on the **tonic harmony,** not coming on a **downbeat,** or some combination of the above.

open-fifth chord (4) — A **chord** of two note names whose notes are a fifth apart. C5, sometimes notated as C(no 3), consists of C and G.

P — Perfect. A perfect fourth (P4) is an **interval** of a fourth in the most common form (e.g., C to F).

palette (4) — See **harmonic palette**.

parallel keys (2) — **Keys** having the same **tonic**. D major and D minor are parallel keys.

PC (2) — A **pitch class**.

pedal (or pedal tone) — A note held through several changes of harmony; the effect is most striking when some of the accompanying harmonies do not contain the held note. Although the name comes from the practice of holding a bass note by means of a pedal on an organ, pedal tones can be found in any register.

pentachord (2) — Any group of five notes or pitch classes.

pentatonic scale (2) — A **scale** made up of the following intervals: **whole step,** whole step, step and a half, whole step, step and a half. A C-pentatonic scale consists of C, D, E, G, A, and C.

perfect authentic cadence (3) — A **common-practice cadence** involving V-I motion in the **harmonies** with $\hat{2}$-$\hat{1}$ or $\hat{7}$-$\hat{1}$ in the melody at the same time. The term "perfect" is used in an archaic sense, meaning "thorough" or "complete." "Authentic" stems from medieval terminology concerning methods of dividing an octave scale into two parts. An octave conceived of as a fifth plus a fourth was said to be authentic. Thus, G represents the authentic division of an octave starting on C. The fifth relationship between the roots of the harmonies in the V-I cadence (G and C in the key of C, for instance) recalls the earlier theory.

period — A traditional form consisting of one **phrase** with an **open cadence** followed by a phrase ending with a **closed cadence**.

persistently initiating harmony (6) — An **initiating harmony**.

persona — A fictitious, usually unnamed character who is imagined to sing a song with a lyric text. When Paul McCartney sings about a band on the run, we understand that he is not singing about personal experiences: Paul McCartney never escaped prison after being given a life sentence. Instead, we understand that he is assuming a character, or persona.

phrase (1) — A unified melodic or harmonic motion; also a group of measures held together by such a motion. A phrase typically lasts no longer than five measures.

phrase rhythm (1) — The metrical structure of the formal units of a piece and of its vocal **phrases** ; also the rhythmic relationship between the formal units and the vocal phrases.

Phrygian scale (2) — A **scale** whose pattern of **whole steps** and **half steps** is $1/2$ 1 1 1 $1/2$ 1 1. A C-Phrygian scale consists of C, D♭, E♭, F, G, A♭, B♭, and C.

pickup — one or more notes felt to lead into the next downbeat.

pitch centricity — The property of a piece whereby one of its pitches is considered to be the most important, or foundational, pitch of the piece.

pitch class (2) — The idea of a pitch without regard to octave placement. When we say that the **root** of a certain **chord** is B♭, we aren't referring to any particular B♭ (the B♭ just below middle C, for instance). We are referring to the pitch class B♭, not to a specific pitch. In some contexts the term refers to the idea of a pitch without regard to octave placement or **enharmonic** spelling.

pitch content (of a **harmony,** of a melody, of a passage) (2) — The pitches included in the structure or structures in question. The pitch content of a C major **triad** is C, E, and G. The pitch content of "Mary Had a Little Lamb" (in C) is C, D, E, and G. The term is closely related to, but not identical to, **pitch source**.

pitch source (2) — The (usually supposed) set of pitches from which a composer chooses the notes of a melody or passage. It is possible that the passage not use all the notes of the pitch source and that it occasionally use notes outside the pitch source. In the case of a melody whose **pitch content** is F, G, A, B♭, C, and D, one might suppose that the notes of the melody were drawn from the F major **scale,** the E just never happening to appear in this particular tune. In this case, one would say the pitch source of the melody is the F major scale. The F major scale could also be seen as the pitch source for the first half of "Hey Jude," whose **pitch content** is F, G, A, B♭, C, D, E♭, and E, if the occasional E♭s are viewed as embellishments.

plagal cadence (3) — A name traditionally given to a harmonic **cadence** consisting of IV or iv followed by I or i.

polyphonic (4) — Having a **texture** of **polyphony**.

polyphony (4) — A **texture** involving two or more simultaneous melodies kept distinct by rhythmic independence.

refrain (6) — One or two textual lines that recur fairly periodically in a given song.

relative keys (2) — **Keys** having the same traditional key signature. G major and E minor are relative keys since they each have a key signature of one sharp.

resolution — (1) Any structure perceived, because of either conditioning or acoustics, to complete a pattern, to provide stability, or to relieve the tension inherent in preceding structures. If only the first seven notes of a **major scale** are played, one experiences a desire or expectation to hear the final note of the scale. The eighth note of the scale is the resolution of the pattern; (2) the emotional effect of any such structure. This effect, actually within the listener, is often felt to reside in the music: "This **chord** wants to go to that chord, which would bring resolution to the piece."

riff — A short melodic figure, usually played on an instrument.

roman numeral (4) — A **chord symbol** showing the relationship of a given **chord** to a **tonic harmony**. The roman numeral corresponds to the placement of the harmony's **root** within the **scale:** F is the fourth **scale degree** in a C scale (C = 1, D = 2, E = 3, F = 4), so the F major **triad** is called IV in the **key** of C. The same chord is I in the key of F and III in the key of D or D minor. In this book, roman numerals also indicate the quality of a chord: upper case means major and lower case means minor. Thus, iii in the key of C is E minor (a chord from the **major system**), whereas III is E♭ major (a chord from the **chromatic-minor system**). Upper case with a plus sign (+) indicates an **augmented triad;** lower case with a raised degree symbol (°) indicates a **diminished triad.** Additions such as a seventh are noted by the use of arabic numerals, e.g., V7. **Inversions** are indicated as shown under the entry for inversion.

root — The lowest note of a **chord** when stacked in thirds. In the **chord** C/E (see **harmonic inversion**), E is the lowest note. But when the notes of the chord are arranged in **stacked thirds** (C, E, G), C is the lowest note; C is therefore the root of the chord. A chord is named after its root.

root movement (root motion) (5) — The direction and distance between the **roots** of two successive **chords**. In the **harmonic succession** C-D, the root movement is an ascending second (or "up by second").

root position — The state of a **chord** whose **root** is in the bass.

rounded-binary form (6) — A form consisting of two sections in which the second section, a **bridge,** leads back to a statement of the first.

scale (2) — A group of notes (usually thought of as a **pitch source**) arranged in ascending order, starting and ending with the **tonic** pitch if such a pitch has been identified.

scale degree — A note of a **scale**. The fifth scale degree means the fifth note of a scale. G is the fifth scale degree of C (C = $\hat{1}$, D = $\hat{2}$, E = $\hat{3}$, F = $\hat{4}$, G = $\hat{5}$).

secondary dominant (4, 5) — A **chromatic chord** thought of as having been built on the **dominant** of some note other than the **tonic**. In the context of the **key** of C, an A major **triad** contains one **chromatic** note: C♯. Nevertheless, the chord can be found in a piece in C. In such a situation, this chord was traditionally explained as the dominant, not of C but of another note of the **scale** — D—and usually moved to a chord built on that note (i.e., in a piece in the key of C, A major was usually followed by D minor). No such tendencies exist in rock, although the terminology has survived. In **roman-numeral** analysis, a secondary dominant is indicated by means of a slash: V/ii means the dominant chord of the second note of the scale. In the key of C, A major is analyzed as V/ii.

set theory (2) — A theory that, among other things, provides a method for naming any group of notes according to the **intervals** between the notes. This name, called a "prime form," is given as a list of numbers in brackets, which are easily translated into more familiar musical terminology. In a prime form, each number stands for a **pitch class**. [0] stands for the starting pitch class. Other numbers indicate **half steps** above the starting pitch; for

240

instance, if [0] stands for G, then [1] stands for G♯, [2] for A, and so on. With G still as the reference pitch, [02479] stands for G, A, B, D, and E, the standard **pentatonic** set. In this book, the number 10 is represented by a T, and the number 11 by an E.

seventh chord (4) — A **chord** of four note names whose notes can be arranged into **stacked** (or overlapping) **thirds**. In the standard voicing for the guitar, an E **dominant seventh chord** is played with two Es, two Bs, one D, and one G♯; but these six notes have only four note names, and the notes can be arranged in stacked thirds: E, G♯, B, D.

split-third chord (4) — Any **triad** or **seventh chord** with both a major third and a minor third, as in C, E♭, E, and G. A **dominant seventh chord** with a split third is usually notated as a dominant seventh with a raised ninth, as in C, E, G, B♭, and D♯.

stacked thirds — A combination of notes in which the **interval** between notes 1 and 2 is a third, the interval between notes 2 and 3 is also a third, etc. C, E, and G are arranged in stacked thirds. From C to E is a third, and from E to G is a third.

stop time (6) — A technique in which all instruments play the same rhythm, usually consisting of short notes widely and unevenly separated.

strong downbeat (1) — The **downbeat** of either the first or the third measure of a four-bar **hypermeasure**.

strophe (6) — One statement of the repeated passage forming the basis of a **strophic form**.

strophic form (6) — A form consisting of two or more exact (or essentially exact) repetitions of the same musical material.

subdominant — The fourth note of a **scale;** also, a **chord** built on the fourth note of a scale. F is the subdominant of C.

suspended chord (4) — Any **chord** that contains a fourth above the **root** in place of a third above the root. The name comes from the traditional practice of holding over the fourth from the previous chord and then resolving it; in rock, suspended chords require neither preparation nor **resolution,** so the name implies neither. Csus, sometimes notated as C(sus4), consists of C, F, and G.

syncopation — A conflict between **metrical accent** and any other type of accent. The most common type of syncopation involves metrical and **agogic accents:** a relatively weak metrical position carries the beginning of a longer note than that on a nearby metrically strong position.

tessitura — A segment of a musical range. A voice in the upper end of its range is in a high tessitura.

textual accent — The emphasis perceived on a note carrying an accented syllable.

texture (4) — The number of parts in a piece and their rhythmic relationship. The three main textures of Western music history are **monophony, polyphony,** and **homophony**. A fourth texture, found, for instance, in Indonesian music, is **heterophony,** a texture in which the various parts play versions of the same melody at different speeds or levels of embellishment. Given any texture but monophony, the texture may be said to be thick or thin, depending on the number of parts active.

title lyric (title line)(6) — The phrase in the lyrics of a song that is the same as the title of the song, such as "stairway to heaven" found at the end of several **verses** of the Led Zeppelin classic. Not every song has a title lyric.

tonality (2) — A system of normal musical structures and normal sequences of structures that, when used in a piece, enables a listener who is familiar with the system to make projections during the piece about the time and pitch of **resolutions** of currently heard events. Such projections are not made as predictions of what will happen, but standards by which what does in fact happen are judged. Such a system involves a complex hierarchy of structures. The most stable pitch in any **key,** for instance, is the **tonic** pitch—one of the least stable, the leading tone (the seventh **scale degree**). When the current harmony is V, however, the tonic pitch may be treated as an embellishment (in C major, for instance, the pitch C in relation to a G major **triad**) while the leading tone is a member of the **chord**. The V chord as a whole, however, is less stable than the tonic harmony. Rock borrows some aspects of its particular complex tonal hierarchy, such as the relative stability of scale degrees, from previous tonal styles. Other aspects, such as placement of the tonic harmony within a **hypermeasure** and the normal order of harmonies, are peculiar to rock music.

tonic (2) — The first note of a **scale;** the main note of a **key;** the note after which a **scale** or key is named. Also, a **chord** built on the first note of a scale.

triad (4) — A **chord** of three note names in which the notes can be arranged into **stacked** (or overlapping) **thirds**. An E major chord is a triad. In standard voicing for the guitar, the chord is played with three Es, two Bs, and one G♯, though these six notes have only three note names, and the notes can be arranged in stacked thirds: E, G♯, B.

tritone — An **interval** of six **half steps;** exactly half an octave. The name results from the interval's equivalence in size to three **whole steps** (or tones).

verse (6) — A section of a song that recurs a number of times with a different text every (or nearly every) time.

verse-chorus-bridge form (6) — A form in which at least two repetitions of a verse-chorus pair are followed by a **bridge,** which leads back to repetitions of earlier passages. The two basic forms are VCVCBC and VCVCBVC.

weak downbeat (1) — The **downbeat** of either the second or the fourth measure of a four-bar **hypermeasure**.

whole step — Two **half steps**. From any C to the D just above it is a whole step.

whole-tone scale (7) — A **scale** made up entirely of **whole steps**. Each whole-tone scale has six notes, although the bottom note usually reappears an octave higher as the seventh and last note. The notes C, D, E, F♯, G♯, B♭, C make up a whole-tone scale. Note: one letter name is always skipped in any whole-tone scale.

index